Mixed Methods Research
in Language Teaching and Learning

Mixed Methods Research in Language Teaching and Learning

A. Mehdi Riazi
Macquarie University

SHEFFIELD UK   BRISTOL CT

Published by Equinox Publishing Ltd.

UK: Office 415, The Workstation, 15 Paternoster Row, Sheffield, South Yorkshire
        S1 2BX
USA: ISD, 70 Enterprise Drive, Bristol, CT 06010

www.equinoxpub.com

First published 2017

British Library Cataloguing-in-Publication Data

A catalogue record for this book is available from the British Library.

ISBN-13   978 1 78179 137 0   (hardback)
          978 1 78179 138 7   (paperback)

Library of Congress Cataloging-in-Publication Data

Names: Riazi, A. Mehdi, author.
Title: Mixed methods research in language teaching and learning / A. Mehdi Riazi.
Description: Sheffield, UK ; Bristol, CT : Equinox Publishing Ltd, [2017] |
    Includes bibliographical references and index.
Identifiers: LCCN 2016030274| ISBN 9781781791370 (hb) | ISBN 9781781791387 (pb)
Subjects: LCSH: Language and languages--Study and teaching--Research--
Methodology. | Second language acquisition--Research--Methodology.
    | Applied linguistics--Research--Methodology.
Classification: LCC P53.755 .R49 2017 | DDC 418.0071--dc23
LC record available at https://lccn.loc.gov/2016030274

Typeset by Sparks – www.sparkspublishing.com

Printed and bound by Lightning Source UK Ltd, Milton Keynes and
Lightning Source Inc., La Vergne, TN

To my sisters and brothers, from whom I learned a lot and whom I respect a lot.

Contents

List of Figures

List of Tables

Preface

Writing a book is similar to hiking in several ways: it is exciting, challenging and rewarding. It is exciting because you will conquer a summit, a target you have defined for yourself in advance. The whole writing gives you a sense of excitement because it gives you an opportunity for discovery and achievement. When hiking for the first time you are excited to see and appreciate the newness of nature and the route all along the path to the top, marching up and down with the parade of hikers. You have the same feeling when writing a new book – discovering a field and its nuances in the book brings you a lot of excitement. The excitement covers both the discovery and the achievement attached to it.

The excitement of achieving the goal may, however, obscure the challenges you will face when writing a book. As with hiking, there are many challenges in writing a book you will need to manage. Among these is the challenge of the book's structure – how a single chapter and whole chapters should be organized to produce a coherent book; the challenge of the audience, the readership of the book; the challenge of using plain language to make complex topics simple and understandable; and so on.

Despite the challenges, writing a book is rewarding. The sense of satisfaction is with you from the beginning, all along the route and especially when you are there, at the top, where you can feel that you have achieved your goal. The sense of reward is greater than when hiking because not only have you achieved a personal goal, as is the case in hiking, but you also have a good feeling that you have been able to contribute to your field and hopefully presented others with a useful source for their studies.

I wrote this book when I was on sabbatical leave during the first half of 2016. The majority of the chapters were written while I was in Sydney; the remaining chapters were completed when I was in Vancouver and at the University of British Columbia working on another project with a colleague in the Language and Literacy Education Department (LLED). While in Vancouver, I had the opportunity to hike up Grouse Mountain several times with a couple of good friends. The coincidence of writing the book chapters and hiking Grouse Mountain was very revealing for me.

This book could not have been completed without the support of others, however. I would like to remember and thank several people who were helpful in making this project a reality. Chris Candlin was supposed to co-author this book with me. We co-authored an article on mixed methods research (MMR) that was published in the journal *Language Teaching* in 2014. Unfortunately, he passed away before this project was started. Chris was a key figure and very insightful in Applied Linguistics and research methodology. It was a shame not having Chris beside me when writing these chapters, but he is with me in spirit and is someone I will always remember.

When writing the initial chapters, the challenge of the audience was a crucial one. I was hoping to find a buddy who could read the chapters as an authentic reader, and I was lucky enough to know Wanda Snitch, who at the time was a doctoral student in the Department of Education at Macquarie University, Sydney. In many respects Wanda was the best person to act as a reader; she was the kind of real audience I was searching for. Wanda was passionate about mixed methods research and was using MMR as her own methodology in her doctoral thesis. Wanda kindly accepted my invitation and read each draft of the chapters carefully and provided me with useful feedback and comments that helped me with my revisions. She was also an advocate of plain language. She usually brought to my attention when and where the language became dense. I am therefore very thankful to Wanda. Her timely response was another helpful organizing mechanism for me. She helped me to make sure I had a chapter ready for her immediately after I had received her feedback on an earlier chapter, which led to me completing my writing on time. Thank you, Wanda, for your effective role.

I am also thankful to several people at Equinox. I am grateful to Janet Joyce for welcoming the idea and approving the proposal for the book. I am also thankful to Valerie Hall, who did all the administrative work, as well as the copyeditor, Vivienne Church.

Finally, my gratitude goes to Macquarie University for accepting my proposal for the six-month sabbatical leave during which I completed the book.

Introduction

Mixed methods research is now an established research paradigm in social sciences and education, with a recognized journal, *Journal of Mixed Methods Research*, and a plethora of published books and research articles. It is widely discussed and used in health, social sciences and education broadly. However, it has received relatively less attention in Applied Linguistics in general, and language teaching and learning in particular, with only a few books and a handful of analytical papers on the subject. There have been some attempts to make this new research approach better recognized and understood in our field. This book thus aims to corroborate the initiated attempts. The book is unique in several respects. It is the first of its kind to bring all the current and sometimes diversified, if not confusing, topics related to MMR into one volume using plain and understandable language. Second, it has postgraduate students as well as novice researchers as its main audience, and therefore aims to provide them with the necessary theoretical and practical guides for understanding and designing MMR projects. Third, the book covers both the theoretical and the practical aspects of MMR, starting with a theoretical discussion of the subject before moving on to more practical aspects of designing and implementing MMR studies.

To achieve its goals, the book is organized into three parts. The first part, consisting of two chapters, addresses the theoretical aspects of MMR. The first chapter provides an overview of the three methodological approaches – quantitative, qualitative and mixed methods – and establishes a context for the whole book. Chapter 2, building on the first chapter, introduces and discusses the underlying worldviews or philosophical underpinnings of MMR. Four conceivable worldviews are presented and discussed in this chapter – pragmatism, transformative, dialectical pluralism and critical realism. I have attempted to make these philosophical underpinnings as simple and comprehensible as possible despite the nature and complexity of philosophical discussions. Those who are not interested in worldviews may, therefore, skip this chapter, though the discussion offers a useful insight into the conceptualization of MMR.

The second part of the book, covering five chapters, discusses practical aspects of MMR. Chapter 3 introduces and discusses purposes for mixing methods. It particularly looks at triangulation, complementarity, initiation, development and expansion for mixing quantitative and qualitative methods. Chapter 4 expands the topic and discusses other MMR research designs. Chapter 5 elaborates on formulating research questions, instruments of data collection and data collection procedures in MMR. Chapter 6 addresses another important issue in MMR, analysis of the data and making inferences from the findings. The chapter discusses three types of inferences common in MMR: inductive, deductive and abductive or retroductive. Chapter 7 brings together the theoretical and practical discussion of MMR and describes and explains how to write MMR proposals. The chapter is especially useful for postgraduate students and novice researchers who would like to embark on MMR studies and prepare thesis and research proposals with an MMR orientation.

The third and final part of the book reviews and discusses published MMR articles using FRAMMR (Framework for Analyzing Mixed Methods Research). Chapter 8 introduces and explains different parts of the FRAMMR framework. The framework is then used to review and analyze MMR articles related to different topics of language teaching and learning. Each of the subsequent chapters reviews and analyzes two MMR articles in the field. Chapter 9 considers articles related to teaching and learning grammar and vocabulary. Chapter 10 analyzes two articles related to an investigation of oral and written proficiency of second language learners. Chapter 11 looks at two articles related to language learners' attitudes and motivation. Finally, Chapter 12 analyzes two articles related to language testing and assessment. At the end of each of these four chapters there is a summary of two further articles to help readers to use the FRAMMR framework and analyze the articles to enhance their understanding of MMR.

Chapter 13 provides a synopsis of the book, the major steps in planning and conducting MMR, and the challenges confronting mixed methods researchers.

The book can be used as a main or complementary text in research methodology courses in postgraduate courses. Those interested in MMR may also use the book independently. As such, readers may concentrate on chapters that are of particular interest to them.

I hope readers find the book interesting and useful in their studies. No single book is complete and capable of addressing all the needs of interested readers in a particular field, and this book is no exception. I would therefore appreciate and welcome any suggestions and/or comments readers may have for the improvement of the volume and that I can consider in subsequent editions of the book.

Mehdi Riazi
June 2016

Part One

Theoretical and Philosophical Aspects of Mixed Methods Research

- Chapter 1 Researching Language Teaching and Learning: Three Research Approaches
- Chapter 2 Underlying Worldviews (Philosophies) for Mixing Methods

1 Researching Language Teaching and Learning: Three Research Approaches

This chapter will:
- define research and explain research processes;
- discuss research trends in language teaching and learning;
- explain and discuss three research approaches or paradigms: quantitative, qualitative and mixed methods;
- provide a brief comparative summary of the three research approaches.

Introduction

This introductory chapter gives the reader a brief explanation and discussion of three research approaches: quantitative, qualitative and mixed methods research (MMR). The aim is to create a context for the subsequent chapters of the book. The purpose of the chapter is to help readers understand the scope of knowledge production in the field of language teaching and learning through different research approaches or paradigms and research methodologies.

There is a plethora of textbooks on conducting research in applied linguistics in general, and language teaching and learning in particular. Some of these textbooks have a pure quantitative orientation (e.g. Brown, 1988; Hatch & Lazaraton, 1991; Woods *et al.*, 1986), some have a pure qualitative orientation (e.g. Duff, 2008; Richards, 2003) and still others have tried to cover both quantitative and qualitative approaches (Brown & Rodgers, 2002; Dornyei, 2007; Mackey & Gass, 2016; Paltridge & Phaketi, 2015) and even cover some aspects of MMR such as that of Dornyei. Some have produced useful texts having exclusively teachers in mind for doing action research (e.g. Burns, 2010; Griffee, 2012; Wallace, 1998) and are therefore practical. This book is thus intended to have its main focus on mixed methods research by explaining and discussing all aspects of this approach to language teaching and learning research. The aim is to unfold both the theoretical and the practical aspects of this new research approach and to bring to the foreground the main features so that readers can come to grips with it more easily.

Before the three research approaches are explained and discussed, an overview of the research process and the key stages and procedures involved in this process will be discussed. This will help readers to develop the necessary background for a better understanding of the three approaches.

Research definition, purpose and process

Research 'simply means trying to find answers to questions' (Dornyei, 2007, p. 15), but more specifically, research is 'the organized, systematic search for answers to the questions we ask' (Hatch & Lazaraton, 1991, p. 1). Research is usually divided into primary, also called empirical, and secondary or library research. In some texts, empirical is exclusively used with scientific method and quantitative research. However, in this book this term is used as an alternative for primary research including both quantitative and qualitative approaches in which first-hand data are collected and analyzed.

Brown (1988) defined primary research as an investigation in which researchers collect primary or first-hand data from participants, analyze the data and then draw some conclusions based on the results of their analysis. He defined secondary or library research as where researchers look at what other researchers have already said about a particular issue. While some researchers may conduct secondary research simply to synthesize and produce reports from research-based results on a particular topic, this type of research is considered an essential part of the primary research. Conducting library research and critically reviewing the related literature on a topic will allow researchers to (a) contextualize their research problem and (b) narrow down their question so that their research will fill a gap in the current literature on the topic. A broad classification of research is presented in Figure 1.1.

The main feature of research based on the above definitions is its systematic approach to finding answers to questions. Good research is systematic at all stages in the research process, so that some researchers, such as Shulman (1981), prefer to call it 'disciplined inquiry'. Shulman explained that an important feature of 'disciplined inquiry is that its data, arguments and reasoning be capable of withstanding careful scrutiny by another

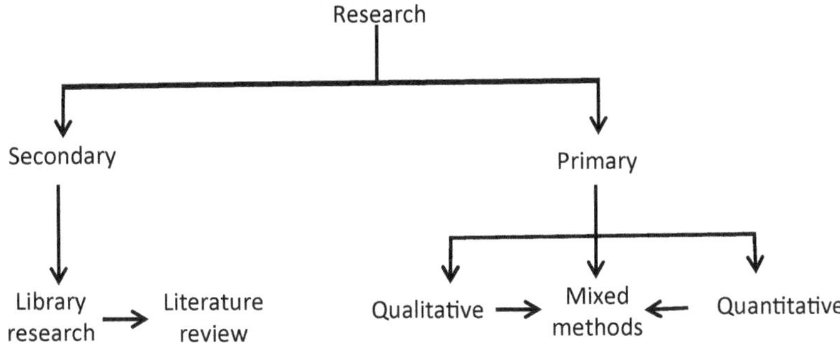

Figure 1.1 A broad classification of research in language teaching and learning

member of the scientific community' (p. 6). To differentiate research or disciplined inquiry from other sources of opinion, Shulman drew on the relevant literature and contended that 'disciplined inquiry has a quality that distinguishes it from other sources of opinion and belief. The disciplined inquiry is conducted and reported in such a way that the argument can be painstakingly examined' (p. 5). Brown (2004, p. 478) added: 'Research must not only be principled, but also orderly, methodical, precise, and well organized, all of which are listed as synonyms for systematic in my computer's dictionary.'

For research to be considered systematic and disciplined, researchers need to pay careful attention to different stages in the research process. Figure 1.2 presents three key stages in the research process along with their corresponding procedures. The figure shows the main stages and procedures and their relationships in the research process, although actual research tends to be recursive. That is, researchers may move back and forth through the three stages or make changes in the procedures as they progress in their research.

The three main stages shown in Figure 1.2 and the corresponding procedures are common among different approaches to research. However, the nature of each stage and procedure is absolutely different in quantitative, qualitative and mixed methods approaches. Each of the three research approaches includes different methods, that is, particular procedures for collecting and analyzing data. As such, alternative approaches and their methods not only approach the conducting of research differently but typically ask different questions and, hence, generate quite different answers. The following section will discuss different research trends, including the

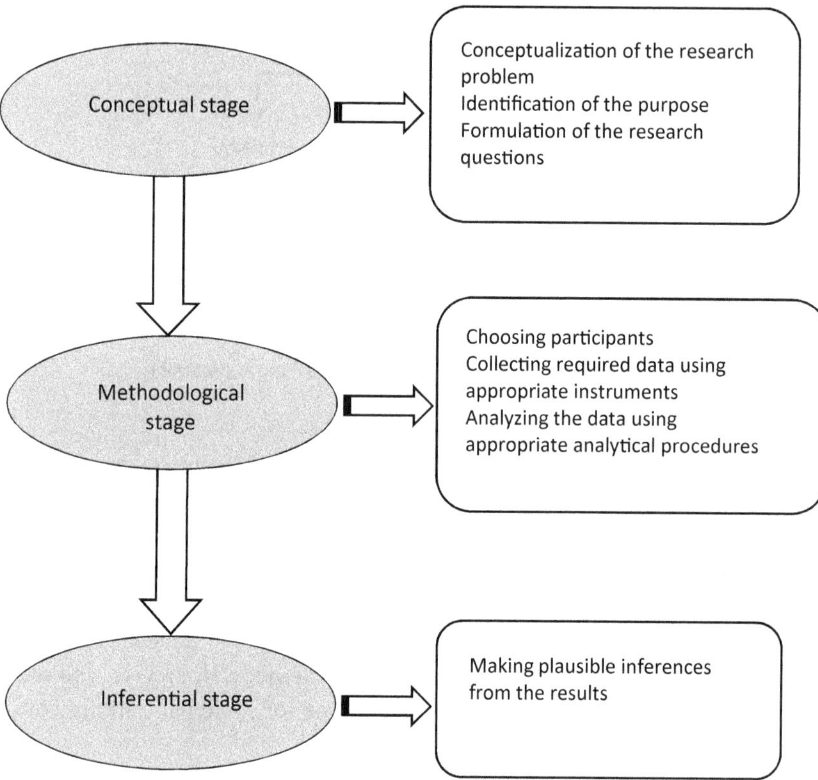

Figure 1.2 Stages in the research process and corresponding procedures

three research approaches – quantitative, qualitative and mixed methods – used by language teaching and learning researchers.

Trends in language-related research: reviews of published articles

Lazaraton (2000) analyzed all primary data-based research articles in four applied linguistics journals over a seven-year period (1991–1997). The four journals were *Language Learning*, *The Modern Language Journal* (*MLJ*), *Studies in Second Language Acquisition* (*SSLA*) and *TESOL Quarterly* (*TQ*). Broadly, these four journals publish research on issues related to the acquisition, teaching and learning of second languages (L2). Lazaraton included in her analysis only primary research, that is, those articles that reported firsthand results of empirical research with the goal of exploring what kind of research articles are published in these journals. Overall, 332 empirical articles were included in the analysis.

Published articles were classified into quantitative and qualitative using the criterion of whether the researchers presented statistical analysis of the quantitative data or reported qualitative analysis of field notes and narrative data from participants. Table 1.1 presents the results of Lazaraton's analysis.

The following observations can be made from the data presented in Table 1.1.

Table 1.1 Number and percentages of empirical articles published in four journals over seven years (1991–1997)

Research orientation	*Journals*				
	Language Learning	*The MLJ*	*SSLA*	*TESOL Quarterly*	Total
Quantitative	96 (97%)	100 (93%)	57 (92%)	39 (62%)	292 (88%)
Qualitative	3 (3%)	8 (7%)	5 (8%)	24 (38%)	33* (10%)
Partially qualitative	?	?	?	?	7 (2%)
Total	99	108	62	63	332 (100%)

* Although the numbers in this row add up to 40, in the original paper the total number of qualitative articles was reported to be 33.

1. The empirical research articles published in the four leading journals in applied linguistics predominantly followed a quantitative orientation (88% compared with 10% qualitative).
2. Less than 10% of the empirical research articles published in three out of the four journals followed qualitative approaches.
3. Only *TESOL Quarterly* among the four journals published a relatively sizable number (24%) of qualitative research articles.
4. Lazaraton was not able to classify seven articles as either quantitative or qualitative because while these articles used statistical analysis, the majority of the articles also included quotes from participants. However, Lazaraton did not provide a breakdown of these articles in the four journals.

The predominant trend of quantitatively oriented research in applied linguistics including the field of language teaching and learning represents the dominant positivist research paradigm in this field that has traditionally sought linear or cause-and-effect relationships between variables. The high prevalence of quantitative methods is even more visible in some fields of applied linguistics such as language testing and assessment. Chalhoub-Deville and Deville (2008), for example, reviewed articles in the two major language assessment journals, *Language Testing* and *Language Assessment Quarterly*, from their commencement (in 1984 and 2004, respectively) up to 2005. Based on their analysis of the methodology section of the articles published in these two journals, they concluded that the predominant research methodology used in the studies reported was quantitative.

These findings were corroborated by Turner (2013), who also examined the methodological trends in published articles in the three major journals of the field, *Assessing Writing, Language Testing* and *Language Assessment Quarterly*. Turner's analysis of the methodology section of the published articles showed that up to approximately 2003, language assessment researchers used predominantly quantitative methods in their investigation of issues related to language assessment. This trend of heavy reliance on quantitative methods seems to be gradually changing, however, and is being complemented by qualitative and mixed methods research.

Subsequently, Lazaraton (2005) extended the survey of the contents of the four journals up to 2001. She found that the overall percentage of data-based qualitative articles had risen to 14%, a 4% increase from 1997 to 2001. This percentage had reached 40% in *TESOL Quarterly* compared with 24% in 1997.

Benson and his colleagues published another useful survey of the published articles in 2009. Their article focused on qualitative empirical data-based articles published in ten major journals between 1997 and 2006. Chronologically, it follows Lazaraton's (2000) analysis of published articles, which covered the period 1991–1997, and in terms of scope they included more journals and articles. Benson *et al.* (2009) surveyed 2,202 articles published in *Applied Linguistics* (*AL*), *Canadian Modern Language Review* (*CMLR*), *Foreign Language Annals* (*FLA*), *International Review of Applied Linguistics* (*IRAL*), *Language Learning, Language Teaching, The Modern Language Journal, Studies in Second Language Acquisition, System* and *TESOL Quarterly*. Table 1.2 presents a breakdown of the number and percentage of qualitative articles in the ten journals over a nine-year period (1997–2006). Benson and his colleagues relied initially on the research article authors' use of the term 'qualitative' to include the articles

Table 1.2 Number and percentages of data-based qualitative articles in ten major journals over nine years (1997–2006)

	No. of qualitative articles	*Other (quantitative, non-empirical)*	*Total*
Applied Linguistics	62 (32%)	132 (68%)	194
CMLR	66 (37%)	112 (63%)	178
FLA	74 (19%)	316 (81%)	390
IRAL	23 (15%)	133 (85%)	156
Language Learning	17 (8%)	198 (92%)	215
Language Teaching	17 (13%)	111 (87%)	128
The MLJ	55 (23%)	182 (77%)	237
SSLA	9 (5%)	190 (95%)	199
System	76 (23%)	248 (77%)	324
TESOL Quarterly	78 (43%)	103 (57%)	181
Total	477 (21.7%)	1,725 (78.3%)	2,202

in their qualitative category. However, if the authors did not use the term 'qualitative' but used comparable approaches, the articles were still included in the category.

The following observations can be made from the data presented in Table 1.2.

1. Of the total number of 2,202 articles in the ten journals, only 477 (about 22%) had a qualitative orientation. Benson *et al.* included 24 articles using both qualitative and quantitative methods in their qualitative category. About 78% either had a quantitative orientation or were not primary research.
2. Six out of ten journals – *AL, CMLR, FLA, The MLJ, System* and *TQ* – accounted for 86% of the qualitative articles.
3. *TESOL Quarterly* included both the highest number (78) and the highest percentage (43%) of qualitative articles among the ten journals, followed by *CMLR* (37%) and *AL* (32%).

Benson and his colleagues explained that they did not focus on the relative contributions of quantitative and non-empirical articles and so their results could not be directly compared with those of Lazaraton (2000, 2005). However, the percentage of qualitative articles (22%) reported in Benson *et al.*

(2009) was higher than Lazaraton's percentages of 10% in 2002 and 14% in 2005. It can therefore be implied that the number of qualitative articles is growing in leading journals where papers related to language teaching and learning are published.

Interestingly, neither Lazaraton (2000, 2005) nor Benson *et al.* (2009) included MMR in their survey of the published articles in the field. There may have been two reasons for this. Either the number of MMR articles was negligible and so did not attract researchers' attention, or MMR was not their focus at all. Indeed, Benson *et al.* make a brief comment that some articles used both quantitative and qualitative data. They further explain: 'The number of articles in this category was initially quite large; most quantitative studies we surveyed appeared to make use of at least some qualitative data' (p. 86). However, they were able to separate 24 quantitative–qualitative studies that were sharply distinguishable from the large number of those articles with an MMR orientation and include them in their qualitative category. They justified their decision that in the rest of the articles with an MMR orientation 'combining quantitative and qualitative methods was typically a deliberate strategy used in order to weigh the two types of evidence against each other' (p. 87).

Fortunately, Hashemi (2012) and Hashemi and Babaii (2013) conducted a content analysis of research articles published in seven journals in applied linguistics focusing on MMR articles in those journals. The journals were *Applied Linguistics, English for Specific Purposes (ESP), Language Learning, Language Teaching Research (LTR), Language Testing (LT), The Modern Language Journal* and *TESOL Quarterly* and the survey covered a period of 14 years from 1995 to 2008. Using key terms or phrases such as mixed methods, multimethod, qualitative, quantitative, triangulation, integrating methods, and combining methods, the researchers were able to identify 273 articles in the seven journals over the search period. Through rigorous and iterative content analysis, the researchers ended up with 205 articles with an MMR orientation. The other 68 articles were not actually combining qualitative and quantitative methods by any means; rather, either some statistics or verbal descriptions were used only as part of a mainly qualitative or quantitative study (Hashemi, 2012).

As Table 1.3 shows, *The Modern Language Journal* had the highest percentage (22.44%) of MMR articles over the 14 years, followed by *Language Testing* (16%), *English for Specific Purposes* (15.12%) and *TESOL Quarterly* (14.7%). The percentages appear to demonstrate researchers' growing interest in using MMR to address language-related issues. Cheng and Fox (2013) also reviewed recent doctoral dissertations in the field of language assessment and concluded that the use of multiple methods derived from

Table 1.3 Frequency and percentages of the MMR articles published in seven journals over 14 years (1995–2008)

	No. of articles	*Percentage in the whole data set*
Applied Linguistics	29	14.15%
English for Specific Purposes	31	15.12%
Language Learning	27	13.18%
Language Teaching Research	9	4.4%
Language Testing	33	16.0%
The MLJ	46	22.44%
TESOL Quarterly	30	14.7%
Total	205	100

different methodological approaches is increasing in doctoral dissertations compared with those using single research methods.

Hashemi and Babaii (2013), however, explained that 'although a considerable number of articles used both qualitative and quantitative methods, only a small number achieved high degrees of integration at various stages of the study as a quality standard for mixed research' (p. 828). Indeed, this is one of the main concerns and motivations behind the current book, which intends to explain and discuss different aspects of MMR in researching language-related research problems, to help researchers use the methodology in more principled and innovative ways.

Having presented a synopsis of the research trends in published articles in the main and leading journals in the field of applied linguistics including language teaching and learning, the focus will now shift to the explanation and discussion of the three research approaches or paradigms used to investigate language-related problems. Understanding these three approaches will help readers to better make sense of the research reports they read as well as to better design their own research projects.

Three research approaches or paradigms

The stance taken in this book is that of a post-paradigm debate (Gage, 1989; Guba & Lincoln, 1994) era using 'compatibility thesis' (Howe, 1988) as the dominant discourse. Informed by the compatibility thesis, researchers (see, e.g. King, 2010) argue that division and polarization between quantitative and qualitative researchers are now much less prominent than in the 1990s. There is a growing recognition of the need to draw on and integrate both quantitative and qualitative methods in a single study in order to gain a more complete understanding of some research problems (Melzi & Caspe, 2010). Fishman (2010) also advocates an inclusive research approach that is supportive and provides room and recognition for both explanatory and exploratory approaches in second language education.

Rather than holding a dualistic perspective on qualitative and quantitative approaches to research, as was developed during the paradigm debate era, the trend is now to represent research methodology as a continuum and a matter of degrees. Conceiving research as a continuum makes it possible to think in degrees of quantitative and qualitative components in research projects rather than perceiving them in a dichotomous way.

Figure 1.3, adapted from Johnson, Onwuegbuzie and Turner (2007) and Teddlie and Tashakkori (2009), presents the continuum of research methodology with potential areas for mixing quantitative and qualitative methods with different levels of integration.

Figure 1.3 Research methodology continuum

Based on Figure 1.3, rather than conceiving quantitative and qualitative approaches to research as mutually exclusive paradigms, they can be positioned on a continuum allowing for mixing at different levels across the continuum. Accordingly, it is possible to think of three main research paradigms – quantitative, qualitative and mixed methods – as well as quantitative- or qualitative-dominant mixed methods. Each of the three research paradigms is explained and discussed below.

Quantitative approach

The quantitative approach to research has a longer history compared with qualitative and mixed methods approaches in social sciences in general, and in applied linguistics in particular. As discussed above, a quantitative approach still seems to be the dominant approach for researching language-related problems. In the context of language teaching and learning research, a quantitative approach to research seeks to explain the observed variation and variability in language learning and teaching by seeking relationships among variables.

Quantitative methods

The quantitative approach to research typically includes questionnaire surveys and experiments. Through surveys it is possible to investigate the relationship between a variety of variables such as language learners' demographic variables (age, gender, level of education, nationality, etc.) and learners' learning preference styles, language learning strategies, language learning attitudes and motivation, and so on. Similar survey and correlational studies can be done with language teachers to seek the relationship between teachers' demographic variables and their teaching styles and strategies. There is a significant amount of survey and correlational research conducted by researchers in the field of language teaching and learning. Readers can access these studies by simply searching 'survey research' and 'language teaching and learning' in Google or other search engines and databases.

Through experimental research, researchers can investigate cause-and-effect relationships between variables, which is not possible in correlational studies such as those carried out by survey researchers. In experimental designs, one or two variables (independent variables) are changed so that their effect could be studied on another variable, called a dependent variable, such as test scores. Experimental designs are also common in the field of language teaching and learning. Experimental researchers are usually interested in investigating whether particular variations in teaching methods, instructional materials, use of technology or other classroom dynamics would affect students' learning. As can be implied, experimental methods require high levels of intervention and control on the part of the researcher so that they can make cause-and-effect inferences.

Logic underlying quantitative research

The logic underlying quantitative methods is a deductive one. Researchers start with general theoretical propositions and seek specific evidence from their data to support or refute those theoretical propositions. The term 'hypothetico-deductive' is usually used to define a quantitative approach to research since it involves 'a priori deduction of hypotheses from a theory or conceptual framework and the testing of those hypotheses using numerical data and statistical analyses' (Teddlie & Tashakkori, 2009, p. 23). Figure

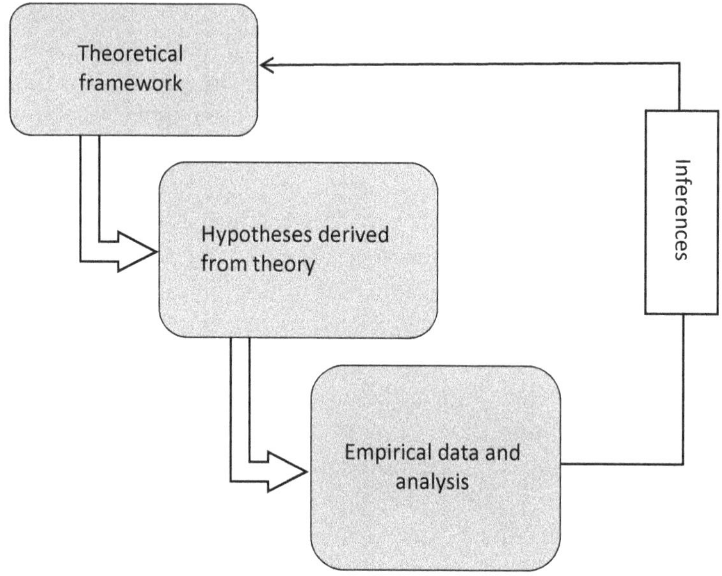

Figure 1.4 A quantitative approach to research

1.4 presents a graphical representation of this quantitative approach to research. Depending on whether the hypotheses are proved or rejected by the evidence obtained from the quantitative data analysis, the researcher makes inferences about the viability of the theoretical framework used in the research.

Representation of quantitative research

Other terms used to describe quantitative research include theory-driven, top-down, hypothesis testing and etic approach. Since in quantitative research researchers basically test hypotheses related to the theoretical framework that informs the study, it has been referred to as theory-driven. Yet since in a quantitative approach researchers start with a general theory and test specific hypotheses related to that theory, it is also referred to as top-down and hypothesis testing. Hypotheses may be explicitly stated in quantitative studies, or they may be implied from the research questions and checked against the outcomes of the statistical analyses. Finally, the term 'etic' is used to describe quantitative research to imply an outsider's (the researcher's) construction and interpretation of the research problem. It is believed that in quantitative research, researchers develop an objective and value-free position in the process of investigating the object of the study.

The foundations of quantitative research include the presumption that 'verifiable patterns' (Patton, 2002, p. 91) are inherent in research phenomena that could be explored (through investigating relationships) and/or explained (through examining causal relationships). The quantitative methods are, therefore, supposed to address objective realities and represent 'a reality-oriented perspective' (Patton, 2002, p. 93), which is known as a positivistic perspective. This perspective requires researchers to play a value-free or objective role in the whole process of research as if the researcher is able to fully detach themselves from the object of study.

Quantitative data and analysis

Quantitative research relies on numerical data and statistical analyses. Two types of statistics are used in quantitative research: descriptive and inferential. Descriptive statistics are used to describe the sample of the study and include measures of central tendency such as mean, median and mode, and measures of variability or dispersion such as range, variance and standard deviation. Each of these measures is called a 'statistic' and so together they form descriptive statistics that are used to describe the characteristics of the sample of the study.

Inferential statistics, meanwhile, are used to make inferences about the population from which the sample of study is derived. In quantitative research, it is the population that is ultimately the researcher's concern and not the sample, because researchers measure defined variables in order to explain relationships and to advance generalizable inferences about the target population. This process is done through selecting a representative sample from a target population (for example, university undergraduate students), collecting data from the sample and calculating descriptive statistics related to different variables, then running inferential statistics to make inferences about the characteristics of the target population based on sample statistics. Figure 1.5 depicts the process.

Quality standards in quantitative research

Traditionally, quantitative research has been judged against standards such as reliability and validity. Reliability basically means consistency and is used in quantitative research to evaluate both the instruments of data collection and the procedures of research. Since any conclusions and inferences are made based on the data collected from certain instruments, researchers need to show that their instruments were consistent and that

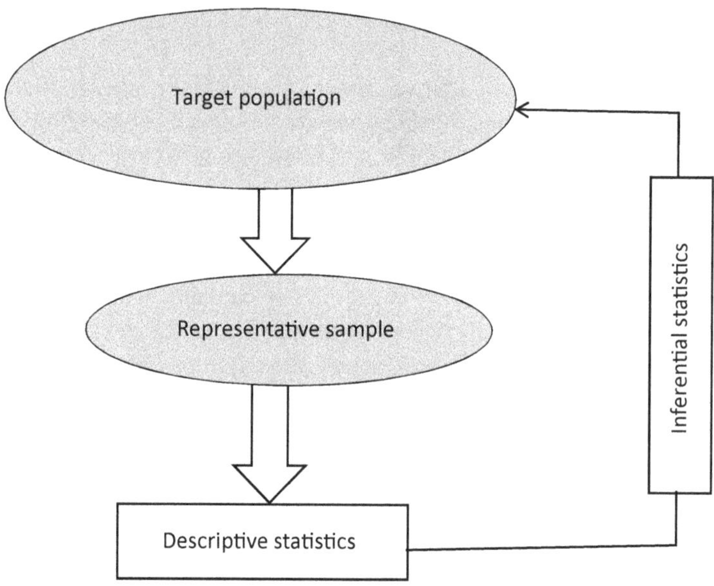

Figure 1.5 Making inferences about the target population based on sample characteristics

the resulting data are reliable. There are different ways to check the reliability of quantitative instruments of data collection, such as test-retest and internal consistency. The reliability of the quantitative data collection instruments is mainly calculated through statistical procedures and is reported using an index of 0–1. The closer the index is to one (1.0), the higher the reliability of the instrument will be. At the data collection procedure level, reliability means consistent and detailed explanation of the procedures used to collect data from participants. The criterion here would be replicability of the study – that is, other researchers must be able to replicate the study based on the description of the data collection procedures.

Validity means meaningfulness of the results and is of two types in quantitative research: internal and external. Internal validity means that the research outcomes could be attributed to the relationship between variables included in the study and not other variables. In doing so, researchers need to show how they defined and operationalized variables of the study and how they controlled other extraneous variables that could have affected the results. External validity means the extent to which the findings of the sample could be generalized to the target population. To claim for generalizability, researchers need to show that (a) their sample is representative of the target population, and (b) their statistical analysis warranted the type of generalizations they made.

Qualitative approach

Notwithstanding the contribution of quantitative research to understanding language-related problems, some scholars and researchers have raised concerns about its relevance and applicability to some language-related problems. Fishman (2010), for example, suggests that human beings and their behaviours are so complex and manifold that neutral and precise measurement of related variables is essentially impossible. Rather than seeking generalizations through statistical analyses, alternative researchers suggest that social and educational problems require more in-depth understandings, even though this might prove more limited in its scope. Cultural understanding, with culture conceived at all possible levels, is thus considered the primary goal of social and educational research represented by qualitative research.

Qualitative methods

Richards (2003) discussed seven 'core traditions' (p. 13) in qualitative research that are relevant to language teaching and learning:

- ethnography;
- grounded theory;
- phenomenology;
- case study;
- life history;
- action research;
- conversation analysis.

Benson *et al.*'s alternative classification (2009) distinguished between two groups of qualitative methods based on whether qualitative researchers investigated 'people, situations, and social processes involved in language teaching and learning (column A), or they investigated spoken or written texts (column B)' (p. 85). Table 1.4 presents the two groups of qualitative methods suggested by Benson *et al.* (2009) along with the number of articles they were able to attribute to these methods in their survey of the ten journals discussed earlier.

Table 1.4 Qualitative methods identified by Benson *et al.* (2009)

Group A: Addressing people, situations and social processes		*Group B: Investigating spoken and written texts*	
Method	*No. of articles that used the method*	*Method*	*No. of articles that used the method*
Case study	225	Discourse analysis	53
Ethnography	49	Classroom interaction	49
Longitudinal	19	Conversation analysis	20
Think-aloud	16	Corpus study	6
Narrative	12	Genre analysis	4
Self-study	6	Systemic functional	1
Stimulated recall	7		
Action research	4		
Diary study	4		
Phenomenology	2		
Total	344		133

Benson *et al.* explained that while researchers used spoken and written data in methods in Group A, they were generally focusing more on people, situations and processes involved in language teaching and learning. As Table 1.4 shows, 'case studies' outnumbered other qualitative methods accounting for about half (225) of the total number (477) of articles in which qualitative methods were used by researchers.

Logic underlying qualitative research

The logic underlying qualitative research is an inductive logic. Qualitative researchers start with the data and through systematic analysis of the qualitative data they strive to generate hypothetical explanations about the research phenomenon. In more rigorous qualitative research approaches such as a grounded theory (Riazi, 2016), researchers can even develop a theoretical explanation about the research phenomenon. Figure 1.6 presents a schematic diagram for qualitative research.

Representation of qualitative research

Other terms used to describe qualitative research include data-driven, bottom-up and an 'emic' approach to research. Researchers basically start with

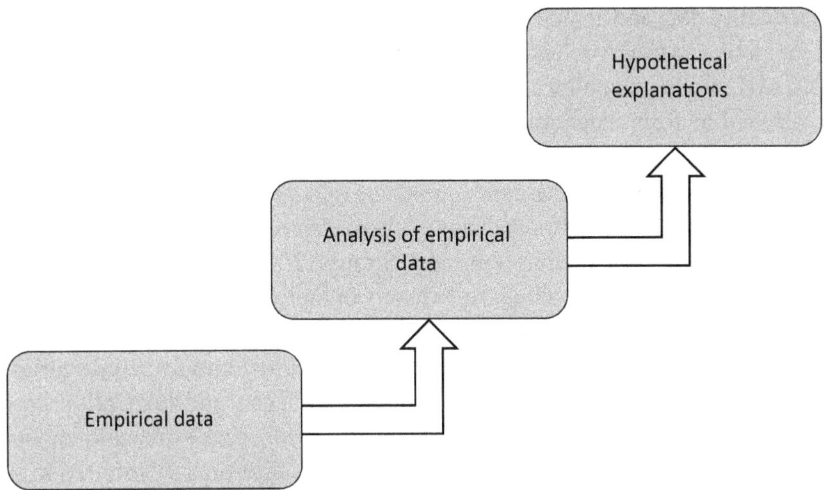

Figure 1.6 An inductive qualitatively oriented approach to research

data to develop theoretical explanations about the research issue. In other words, researchers start with specific observations (data) and develop more general explanations (theory). As such, research questions may be revised in the qualitative research process as the design and methods develop and given the emergent nature of the qualitative research. The term 'emic' is used to describe qualitative research to denote an insider's (the participant's) construction and interpretation of the reality. It is believed that researchers are not able to detach themselves from the object of study if they are going to present a meaningful understanding of the research problem (nor is it desirable).

The foundations of qualitative research include the presumption that there are 'multiple realities' (Patton, 2002, p. 98) of the same research phenomenon constructed by different people. These realities could be explored from the perspective of people involved in situations and processes related to the phenomenon. The qualitative methods are, therefore, supposed to explore subjective realities represented by a constructivist and interpretive perspective. This perspective requires researchers to be part of the social or educational phenomenon to be able to see, reconstruct, interpret and report the phenomenon from the perspective and experiences of those participants who are involved in the situations and processes. Rather than generating certainties through generalizations as in quantitative research, qualitative researchers generate possible theoretical insights about research phenomena.

Qualitative data and analysis

Qualitative research relies on narrative data and thematic analysis (Riazi, 2016). Usually, the collected data are coded inductively. The codes are then classified to form categories. Themes are then developed based on the relationship between the categories so that more general explanations could be developed about the research problem. In a grounded theory approach, these levels of qualitative data analysis are referred to as open coding, axial coding and selective coding (Glaser & Strauss, 2009; Richards, 2003).

At the level of open coding, researchers immerse themselves into the collected data and try to code segments of the data using idea units. At the second level, the coded data are reviewed and classified into some categories. Finally, at the third level, certain categories are selected and the relationships (themes) between them are used to develop a theoretical explanation about the research phenomenon. Qualitative research is thus broadly referred to as an exploratory and theory generation approach compared with the explanatory theory verification approach of quantitative research. Some researchers (see, for example, Punch, 1998) do not agree with this dichotomization on the grounds that either approach could be used for both theory generation and theory verification purposes.

Quality standards in qualitative research

Qualitative researchers have developed similar criteria to those of reliability and validity to evaluate the quality of this type of research. Lincoln and Guba (1985) introduced four criteria to check the trustworthiness of qualitative research.

1. Dependability.
2. Credibility.
3. Transferability.
4. Confirmability.

Based on their definition of the above terms, dependability is similar to reliability in quantitative research since it refers to the consistency of the procedures and findings. Credibility is similar to internal validity in quantitative research and indicates the meaningfulness of findings as related to the described procedures. Transferability is similar to external validity or generalizability and refers to the extent to which findings of a qualitative research could be applied to other similar contexts. Finally, confirmability can be considered as an equivalent to objectivity in quantitative research. Although qualitative research is known to be subjective, researchers seek, through confirmability, the degree to which the results of their study could be confirmed by other investigators. Procedures such as inter-coder reliability or investigator triangulation can contribute to the confirmability of qualitative research.

In addition to the above criteria, and to enhance the persuasive evidence in qualitative research, Denzin (1978) introduced four types of triangulation qualitative researchers could aim to achieve. These four types of triangulation are as follows.

1. Data triangulation.
2. Methodological triangulation.
3. Investigator triangulation.
4. Theory triangulation.

Data triangulation refers to the use of different data sources for convergence purposes. For example, researchers may seek to cross-validate (triangulate) findings from classroom observation data and findings from student and/or teacher interview data. In that case, and if findings corroborate each other, this can be taken as evidence for data and methodological triangulation. Investigator triangulation means involving more than one investigator in a single study. For the above example, more than one investigator may observe classrooms to provide evidence for investigator triangulation if findings across different observers (investigators) could be cross-validated. From another perspective, inter-observer or inter-rater or inter-coder reliability that researchers conduct and report to show consistency of observations, ratings and coding may be used to argue for investigator triangulation. Finally, theory triangulation refers to the use of different theoretical perspectives to interpret a set of data.

Quantitative and qualitative research

There is significant literature on how quantitative and qualitative research might be compared. It is beyond the scope of this chapter to present a detailed discussion of this literature, especially because of the orientation of the book, which promotes mixing the two approaches. However, Table 1.6 at the end of this chapter summarizes the key features of the three methodological approaches: quantitative, qualitative and mixed methods.

The terms etic, from 'phonetic' (language general), and emic, from 'phonemic' (language specific), used to address rules of language (Pedersen, 1999) have been used to differentiate between quantitative and qualitative approaches to research. An etic approach denotes universal laws and behaviours that apply to all humans and are not restricted to a particular group or culture. In contrast, an emic approach refers to constructs or behaviours that are unique to some individuals within particular social and cultural contexts and thus are not generalizable (Ponterotto, 2005).

More specifically, McKay (2006), for example, lists contrasts between qualitative and quantitative approaches to research. The contrastive areas include:

- assumptions about the nature of reality;
- the roles of researchers;
- the purposes of research;
- research questions;
- a variety of issues concerned with research design and methods.

As discussed above, a quantitative approach to research seeks to explain different phenomena by making generalizations about the object of study. This is done by posing questions and testing hypotheses related to the theories about the research phenomenon. The assumption is that there is an objective reality that could be investigated by researchers who are detached from that reality and hold a value-free position. The researchers then use structured research designs and methods through which numerical data are collected and analyzed using statistical procedures to make generalizable inferences about the target population.

In contrast, qualitative researchers believe that there are multiple subjective realities about a research phenomenon as constructed by different people who are involved in the situations and processes related to the phenomenon. The purpose of qualitative research is then to explore an understanding of how different people construct and interpret the realities they are involved with. For the researcher to be able to unfold the participants' construction and interpretation of their experiences, the researcher needs to be part of the reality. Research questions in qualitative research may develop throughout the research process and as the design and methods emerge as a result of the researcher's involvement in the process.

Quality standards and criteria

To compare quantitative and qualitative research in terms of relevant quality standards or criteria, Brown (2004, p. 496) used the concepts of 'consistency', 'verifiability', 'fidelity' and 'meaningfulness' underlying the standards in the two research approaches. Table 1.5 presents Brown's juxtaposition of the two research approaches in terms of quality standards.

Table 1.5 Corresponding quality standards in the two research approaches

Quantitative research	*Key concept*	*Qualitative research*
Reliability	*Consistency*	Dependability
Objectivity	*Verifiability*	Confirmability
Internal validity	*Fidelity*	Credibility
External validity (generalizability)	*Meaningfulness*	Transferability

Overall, however, it can be said that qualitative researchers tend to describe their procedures in more detail in light of the fact that procedures are not as straightforward as they are in quantitative research.

Mixed methods research approach

Tashakkori and Teddlie (2003) were among those researchers who initially promoted mixed methods research by calling it 'the third methodological movement' (p. 4). They referred to three methodological research practices.

1. Quantitatively oriented research practices rooted in the (post)-positivist paradigm.
2. Qualitatively oriented research practices rooted in the constructivist and interpretivist paradigm.
3. Mixed methods research practices rooted in the pragmatist paradigm and embracing both quantitative and qualitative orientations.

Tashakkori and Teddlie contended that a major advantage of MMR is that it enables the researcher to simultaneously include the two methodological approaches in a single study. This would allow researchers to ask both explanatory/confirmatory (quantitatively oriented) and exploratory (qualitatively oriented) research questions. The MMR will, therefore, enable researchers to aim at both verifying and generating theoretical explanations in the same study.

Tashakkori and Teddlie are among those MMR researchers who consider pragmatism as the underlying worldview for mixing methods. There are, however, other worldviews or underlying philosophical perspectives that MMR researchers may draw on. These include transformative, dialectical pluralism and critical realism worldviews. These underlying worldviews that can potentially inform mixing methods are explained and discussed in Chapter 2. Depending on which of these worldviews inform MMR researchers, they may approach the conceptualization, methodological and inferential stages differently in their research process.

MMR researchers have attempted to identify certain purposes for mixing methods. Greene, Caracelli and Graham (1989) were among the first researchers to identify five main purposes for mixing methods by examining 57 published MMR articles. These five purposes – triangulation, complementarity, initiation, development and expansion – are explained and discussed in detail in Chapter 3.

As an alternative to MMR purposes, some researchers have suggested different mixed designs. These design typologies are based on the chronological order and dependency of the two strands (concurrent vs. sequential) and the level of emphasis applied to either of the two strands in the research process. Morse (1991), Teddlie and Tashakkori (2006) and Creswell and Plano Clark (2011) are among those researchers who have suggested a variety of mixed designs, which are explained and discussed in Chapter 4.

The underlying logic for MMR is an abductive one. Johnson and Onwuegbuzie (2004, p. 17) explain that the underlying logic for the three methodological approaches includes 'the use of induction (or discovery of patterns), deduction (testing of theories and hypotheses), and abduction (uncovering and relying on the best of a set of explanations for understanding one's results)'. Figure 1.7, adapted from Johnson and Christensen (2012), can therefore depict the underlying logic for MMR.

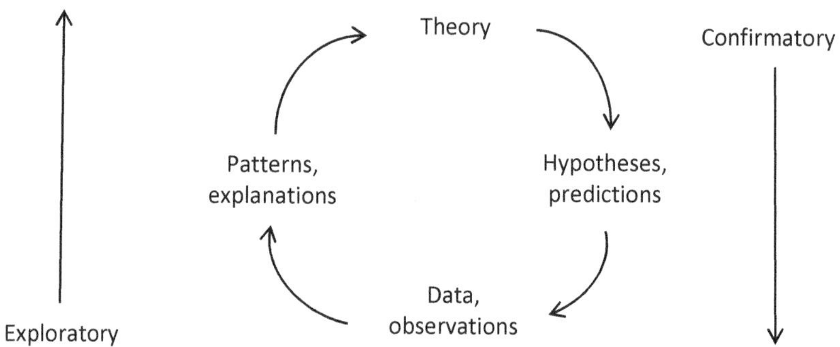

Figure 1.7 Underlying logic for MMR

MMR relies on both numerical and narrative data and thus employs both statistical and thematic analysis to achieve and present a fuller explanation and understanding of the research problem. Depending on whether MMR studies use concurrent or sequential designs, quantitative and qualitative data may be gathered and analyzed independently, or one data set and analysis may inform the other. In either case, MMR researchers make use of both statistical and thematic analysis in their studies to produce quantitative, qualitative and mixed meta-inferences about the research problem. Formulation of research questions and data collection instruments and procedures, and data analysis and making inferences are explained and discussed in Chapters 5 and 6.

With regard to the role of values in research, MMR researchers hold multiple stances, for example, 'researchers include both biased and unbiased perspectives' (Creswell & Plano Clark, 2011). Teddlie and Tashakkori (2009, p. 90) also clarified that 'pragmatists decide what they want to study based on what is important within their personal value systems. They then study that topic in a way that is congruent with their value systems, including units of analysis and variables that they feel are most likely to yield interesting responses'. They further clarified the contrast between pragmatists and transformative scholars as regards values. While transformativists consider values as a function to enhance social justice, pragmatists postulate that research is influenced by the values of investigators.

Synopsis of the three research approaches

The three research methodological approaches are usually compared in terms of their underlying worldviews or philosophy of knowledge. There are four fundamental concepts that constitute a philosophy of knowledge:

- ontology (the nature of reality or object of study);
- epistemology (the relationship between the knower and the known; how we know what it is);
- methodology (the rationale for choosing methods that correspond to a definite ontology and epistemology);
- axiology (the role of values in research) (Denzin & Lincoln, 2011).

Table 1.6 presents a summary of the three research approaches in terms of their features and characteristics. The table provides a useful comparison of the three approaches, although there might be some levels of generalization. In reality, there is usually some flexibility, especially in MMR.

Table 1.6 A comparison of the three research approaches

Area of comparison	*Quantitative*	*Mixed methods*	*Qualitative*
Worldview (philosophy)	(Post)positivist (single reality)	Pragmatist Transformativist Critical realist	Constructivist, Interpretivist (multiple realities)
Nature of reality (object of study)	An objective reality	Both objective and subjective	A subjective reality
Researcher–researched relationship	Detached	Dual relationship depending on the research strand	Mingled
Role of values	Value-free	Depends on the underlying worldview	Value-laden
Logic of inquiry	Deductive (theory-driven)	Adductive (a fuller explanation)	Inductive (data-driven)
Type of investigation	Interventionist (explanatory)	Both explanatory and exploratory	Interpretivist (exploratory)
Purpose	Generalization	A variety of purposes by mixing the two methodologies	In-depth understanding
Type of data and analysis	Numerical, statistical analysis	Both numerical and narrative analyzed through statistical and thematic analyses	Narrative, thematic or content analysis
Sampling procedure	Probability random sampling	Identical Parallel Nested Multilevel	Non-probability purposive sampling
Quality criteria	Reliability Replicability Internal validity External validity	Combination of the two sets of criteria	Dependability Confirmability Credibility Transferability + four triangulation methods

In the next chapters, all aspects of MMR will be explained and discussed. In Chapter 2 the underlying worldviews or philosophies of mixing methods will be explained and discussed. Then, in the chapters in Part Two, the purposes for mixing methods (Chapter 3), design typologies (Chapter 4), research questions, sampling procedures and data collection (Chapter 5), data analysis and inferences (Chapter 6) and writing MMR proposals (Chapter 7) will be elaborated.

Once these various aspects and characteristics of MMR have been outlined in Part Two, sample MMR studies will be reviewed and analyzed in Part Three. The intention has been to cover the theoretical aspects of MMR as well as to illustrate how researchers employ MMR in their language-related investigations. In Part Three, and after each chapter in that section, a learning task is provided for readers to engage in a hands-on activity and analyze sample MMR studies. Reading the analysis of MMR studies and conducting further analysis of sample studies will help readers to design their own studies in more principled and careful ways.

References

Benson, P., Chik, A., Gao, X., Huang, J. & Wang, W. (2009). Qualitative research in language teaching and learning journals, 1997–2006. *The Modern Language Journal, 93*, 79–90.

Brown, J.D. (1988). *Understanding research in second language learning.* Cambridge: Cambridge University Press.

Brown, J.D. (2004). Research methods for applied linguistics: Scope, characteristics, and standards. In A. Davies & C. Elder (Eds.), *The handbook of applied linguistics* (pp. 476–500). Oxford: Blackwell.

Brown, J.D. & Rodgers, T. (2002). *Doing applied linguistics research.* Oxford: Oxford University Press.

Burns, A. (2010). *Doing action research in English language teaching. A guide for practitioners.* New York: Routledge.

Chalhoub-Deville, M. & Deville, C. (2008). Utilizing psychometric methods in assessment. In E. Shohamy & N. H. Hornberger (Eds.), *Encyclopedia of language and education* (2nd ed., Vol. 7, pp. 211–224). New York: Springer Science + Business Media LLC.

Cheng, L. & Fox, J. (2013). Review of doctoral research in language assessment in Canada (2006–2011). *Language Teaching, 46*, 518–544.

Creswell, J.W. & Plano Clark, V. (2011). *Designing and conducting mixed methods research* (2nd ed.). Thousand Oaks, CA: Sage.

Denzin, N.K. (1978). *Sociological methods.* New York: McGraw-Hill.

Denzin, N.K. & Lincoln, Y.S. (Eds.) (2011). *Handbook of qualitative research* (4th ed.). Thousand Oaks, CA: Sage.

Dornyei, Z. (2007). *Research methods in applied linguistics.* Oxford: Oxford University Press.

Duff, P. (2008). *Case study in applied linguistics.* New York: Routledge.

Fishman, J.A. (2010). Theoretical and historical perspectives on researching the sociology of language and education. In K.A. King & N.H. Hornberger (Eds.), *Research methods in language and education: Encyclopedia of language and education* (Vol. 10, pp. 3–15). New York: Springer.

Gage, N. (1989). The paradigm wars and their aftermath: A 'historical' sketch of research and teaching since 1989. *Educational Researcher, 18*, 4–10.

Glaser, B.G., & Strauss, A.L. (2009). *The discovery of grounded theory: Strategies for qualitative research.* New York: Transaction Publishers.

Greene, J.C., Caracelli, V.J. & Graham, W.F. (1989). Toward a conceptual framework for mixed-method evaluation designs. *Educational Evaluation and Policy Analysis, 11*(3), 255–274.

Griffee, D.T. (2012). *An introduction to second language research methods: Design and data* (4th ed.). Berkeley, CA: TESL-EJ Publications.

Guba, E.G. & Lincoln, Y.S. (1994). Compel paradigms in qualitative research. In N.K. Denzin & Y.S. Lincoln (Eds.), *Handbook of qualitative research* (pp. 105–117). Thousand Oaks, CA: Sage.

Hashemi, M.R. (2012). Reflections on mixing methods in applied linguistics research. *Applied Linguistics, 33*, 206–212.

Hashemi, M.R. & Babaii, E. (2013). Mixed methods research: Toward new research designs in applied linguistics. *The Modern Language Journal, 97*(4), 828–852.

Hatch, E. & Lazaraton, A. (1991). *The research manual: Design and statistics for applied linguistics.* Boston, MA: Heinle & Heinle.

Howe, K.R. (1988). Against the quantitative-qualitative incompatibility thesis (or dogmas die hard). *Educational Researcher, 17*, 10–16.

Johnson, R.B. & Christensen, L. (2012). *Educational research: Quantitative, qualitative, and mixed approaches* (4th ed.). Thousand Oaks, CA: Sage.

Johnson, R.B. & Onwuegbuzie, A.J. (2004). Mixed methods research: A research paradigm whose time has come. *Educational Researcher, 33*(7), 14–26.

Johnson, R.B., Onwuegbuzie, A.J. & Turner, L.A. (2007). Toward a definition of mixed methods research. *Journal of Mixed Methods Research, 1*(2), 112–133.

King, K.A. (2010). Introduction to Volume 10: Research methods in language and education. In K.A. King & N.H. Hornberger (Eds.), *Research methods in language and education: Encyclopedia of language and education* (Vol. 10, pp. xiii–xviii). New York: Springer.

Lazaraton, A. (2000). Current trends in research methodology and statistics in applied linguistics. *TESOL Quarterly, 34*(1), 175–181.

Lazaraton, A. (2005). Quantitative research methods. In E. Hinkel (Ed.), *Handbook of research in second language learning* (pp. 209–224). Mahwah, NJ: Lawrence Erlbaum.

Lincoln, Y.S. & Guba, E.G. (1985). *Naturalistic enquiry*. London: Sage.

Mackey, A. & Gass, S.M. (2016). *Second language research: Methodology and design* (2nd ed.). London: Routledge.

McKay, S.L. (2006). *Researching second language classrooms*. Mahwah, NJ: Lawrence Erlbaum Associates.

Melzi, G. & Caspe, M. (2010). Research approaches to narrative, literacy, and education. In K.A. King & N.H. Hornberger (Eds.), *Research methods in language and education: Encyclopedia of language and education* (Vol. 10, pp. 151–163). New York: Springer.

Morse, J.M. (1991). Approaches to qualitative-quantitative methodological triangulation. *Nursing Research, 40*, 120–123.

Paltridge, B. & Phaketi, A. (Eds.) (2015). *Research methods in applied linguistics*. London: Bloomsbury.

Patton, M.Q. (2002). *Qualitative research and evaluation methods* (3rd ed.). Thousand Oaks, CA: Sage.

Pedersen, P. (1999). Culture-centered interventions as a fourth dimension of psychology. In P. Pedersen (Ed.), *Multiculturalism as a fourth force* (pp. 3–18). Philadelphia, PA: Brunner/Mazel.

Ponterotto, J.G. (2005). Qualitative research in counseling psychology: A primer on research paradigms and philosophy of science. *Journal of Counseling Psychology, 52*(2), 126–136.

Punch, K. (1998). Introduction to social research: Quantitative and qualitative approaches. London: Sage.

Riazi, A.M. (2016). *The Routledge Encyclopedia of Research Methods in Applied Linguistics: Quantitative, qualitative, and mixed-methods research*. London: Routledge.

Riazi, A.M. & Candlin, C.N. (2014). Mixed-methods research in language teaching and learning: Opportunities, issues and challenges. *Language Teaching, 47,* 135–173.

Richards, K. (2003). *Qualitative inquiry in TESOL*. London: Palgrave Macmillan.

Shulman, L.S. (1981). Disciplines of inquiry in education: An overview. *Educational Researcher, 10*(6), 5–23.

Tashakkori, A. & Teddlie, C. (Eds.) (2003). *Handbook of mixed methods in social and behavioural research*. London: Sage.

Teddlie, C. & Tashakkori, A. (2006). A general typology of research designs featuring mixed methods. *Research in the Schools, 13*(1), 12–28.

Teddlie, C., & Tashakkori, A. (2009). *Foundations of mixed methods research: Integrating quantitative and qualitative approaches in the social and behavioural sciences*. Thousand Oaks, CA: Sage.

TESOL Quarterly (2003). Some guidelines for conducting quantitative and qualitative research in TESOL. *TESOL Quarterly, 37*, 147–178.

Turner, C.E. (2013). Mixed methods research. In A.J. Kunnan (Ed.), *The companion to language assessment* (pp. 1403–1417). Hoboken, NJ: Wiley-Blackwell.

Wallace, M.J. (1998). *Action research for language teachers*. Cambridge: Cambridge University Press.

Woods, A., Fletcher, P. & Hughes, A. (1986). *Statistics in language studies*. Cambridge: Cambridge University Press.

2 Underlying Worldviews (Philosophies) for Mixing Methods

This chapter will:
- discuss four underlying worldviews (philosophies) for mixing methods:
  - pragmatist
  - transformative
  - dialectical pluralist
  - critical realist;
- elaborate on worldviews in terms of:
  - ontology (nature of reality)
  - epistemology (knowledge acquisition)
  - methodology (systematic procedures of data collection and analysis)
  - axiology (the place and role of values in research);
- distinguish between MMR as method and MMR as methodology.

Introduction

This chapter builds on the discussion of approaches to research presented in Chapter 1 by focusing on philosophical underpinnings or worldviews for mixing methods.

One of the main issues, and perhaps the main challenge, confronting mixed methods researchers regards the justification for mixing methods from the two methodological approaches. To address this issue, MMR researchers have drawn from four worldviews – pragmatism, transformative, dialectical pluralism and critical realism – to rationalize mixing methods from quantitative and qualitative approaches. Understanding these four worldviews and how they might affect different stages in the research process would help readers not only to better understand discourses around MMR, but also to decide how they might approach designing and implementing their own research projects. As Plano Clark *et al.* (2008) rightly state, a challenge facing MMR researchers is to be familiar with ongoing questions about underlying worldviews and how they might be able to defend their MMR design choice in terms of the informing worldviews. Mixed methods researchers' familiarity with different underlying worldviews, on the one hand, and their own stances as researchers, on the other, could enable them to better articulate their theoretical position when investigating more complex problems. Mertens (2010, p. 9) even considers this to be a responsibility of teachers to nurture students' 'abilities to think through their choices in terms of mixed methods research based on a critically examined understanding of their philosophical assumptions'.

Underlying worldviews

A worldview or philosophy for doing research 'refers to the conceptual roots undergirding the quest for knowledge' (Ponterotto, 2005, p. 127). Worldviews have also been referred to as paradigms. Morgan (2007, p. 49) defines paradigms as 'systems of beliefs and practices that influence how researchers select both the questions they study and methods that they use to study them'. Given some ambiguities related to the word 'paradigm', Shannon-Baker (2015) uses perspectives instead and argues that paradigms or perspectives can help researchers frame their approach to a research problem and how to address it given certain beliefs about the world. In this book, worldviews and philosophical underpinnings are used as alternatives for paradigms and perspectives.

As discussed in Chapter 1, included in worldviews or research paradigms are implied assumptions about the nature of reality and the research problem (ontology), and the relationship between the researcher and the researched or beliefs about the nature of knowledge (epistemology), the systematic procedures of data collection and analysis (methodology), and the role and place of values in the research process (axiology) (Denzin & Lincoln, 2000; Guba & Lincoln, 1994). Proponents of quantitative and qualitative methodologies base their arguments on positivist and constructivist worldviews and developed convictions about how the object of study (the being researched) must be investigated to produce plausible knowledge. This debate, conventionally referred to as the paradigm war, divides researchers into two camps, positivists vs. constructivists (Guba & Lincoln, 1994), represented by quantitative and qualitative researchers in different fields, including applied linguistics and language teaching and learning.

From a paradigmatic perspective, the specific methods identified and used in each of the two research approaches are linked to the particular

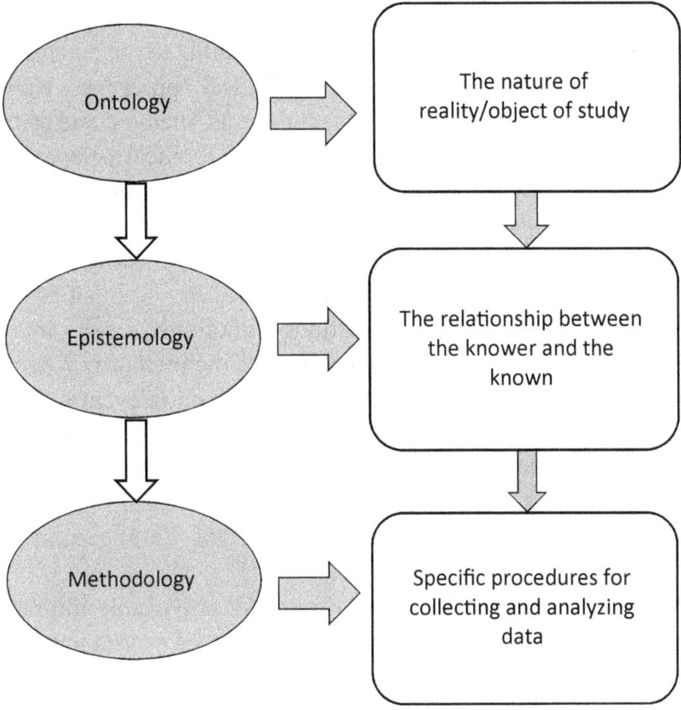

Figure 2.1 The relationship between ontology, epistemology and methodology in research

ontological and epistemological stances of each approach, as presented in Figure 2.1.

Quantitative methods, for example, are linked to an objective epistemology in which reality or object of study is perceived to be 'out there', amenable to investigation by researchers in a value-free way. The researcher (knower) is thus detached from the researched (would-be known) from this perspective, allowing the researcher to investigate and explain relationships, patterns and regularities in the research phenomenon in an objective way using well-defined and accepted methods.

Qualitative methods, meanwhile, are linked to a subjective epistemology that considers reality to be a construction of human minds, and as such multiple constructed realities might constitute the object of the study. From this perspective, researchers are part of the research phenomenon, and so they attempt to reconstruct the perceived realities represented by participants in light of the participants' and researcher's value systems.

MMR as method vs. MMR as methodology

Mixed methods is presented as a methodology parallel to but emerged from mixing quantitative and qualitative methodological approaches. However, there are two representations of mixed methods: as 'method' and as 'methodology'. When positioned as a 'method', the theoretical perspectives of the nature of the reality (object of study) and the relationship between the researcher (knower) and the researched (would-be known) are considered irrelevant. Rather, the main concern would be with selecting and mixing methods from the two methodological approaches in ways that enable researchers to answer their research questions without necessarily involving a discussion of the theoretical underpinnings of the methods. When positioned as a 'methodology', mixing methods draws on relevant ontological (the nature of reality/object of study) and epistemological (the relationship between the researcher and the researched) perspectives (Riazi, 2016). Pragmatist researchers (e.g. Creswell & Plano Clark, 2007; Feilzer, 2010; Plano Clark *et al.*, 2008; Tashakkori & Teddlie, 1998, 2003) generally use a methods-based definition of MMR.

The conceptualization of MMR as a 'method' is typically informed by a pragmatist worldview, a predominantly recognized worldview or philosophical underpinning for mixing methods. According to Onwuegbuzie, Collins and Frels (2013), pragmatism is, by most counts, one of the most commonly used philosophical frameworks for mixed methods. Pragmatist MMR researchers have been motivated to avoid 'either–or' methodological debates and justify mixing methods more practically by shifting their main focus from theoretical discussions to practical research questions they could answer using both quantitative and qualitative data and analysis procedures.

Other MMR researchers using other worldviews for mixing methods typically approach mixing methods as a methodology derived from certain ontological, epistemological and axiological perspectives. Although Tashakkori and Teddlie (1998) originally considered pragmatism as the only framework for mixing methods, in their latest textbook on mixed methods research (Teddlie & Tashakkori, 2009) they include another framework, the transformative perspective (Mertens, 2007, 2009, 2010), as another potential underlying worldview for mixing methods. Mertens (2012, p. 256) also observed:

> In the mixed methods world, three paradigmatic stances that are rooted in contrasting philosophical assumptions have been developed: dialectical pluralism that stands at the nexus of the constructivist

and postpositivist paradigms (Greene & Hall, 2010), the pragmatic paradigm (Biesta, 2010), and the transformative paradigm (Mertens, 2009; Mertens *et al.*, 2010).

According to Mertens (2012), the incompatibility arguments are responded to by these three paradigmatic stances and through 'their characterization of mixed methods as a methodological approach that is compatible with different sets of philosophical assumptions'.

In addition to the three worldviews proffered by Mertens, critical realism has been nominated by other researchers (Christ, 2011, 2013; Danermark *et al.*, 2002; Lipscomb, 2011; Maxwell, 2011; Riazi & Candlin, 2014; Zachariadis *et al.*, 2013) as yet another legitimate underlying worldview for mixing methods. There has been a tendency to consider overlaps between critical realism and postpositivism on the one hand, and critical realism and a transformative worldview on the other. However, the position advocated and promoted in this book is to consider critical realism as an independent worldview (especially from transformative). The goal of this chapter is thus to explain and discuss the four underlying worldviews – pragmatist, transformativist, dialectical pluralist and critical realist – that are conceived as worldviews informing mixing methods from quantitative and qualitative methodological approaches. The discussion of the philosophical foundations of mixing methods provides a context for following chapters.

Pragmatist worldview

The paradigm debate and the aftermaths created an unsatisfactory situation and motivated some researchers to look for and develop a counterargument. The movement of the MMR was, therefore, to disrupt the link between ontology, epistemology and methodology and to consider research questions as the driving force in making decisions about the use of methods. Researchers such as Creswell (1995, 2003), Tashakkori and Teddlie (1998, 2003) and Johnson and Onwuegbuzie (2004), for example, found pragmatism an underlying worldview that could inform mixing methods from apparently opposing research paradigms to answer research questions without necessarily being involved in paradigmatic debates. The credibility of MMR from a pragmatist perspective relied on its capacity to enable researchers to develop a better understanding of research phenomena by drawing on complementary methods from the two research approaches without getting involved in theoretical discussions.

Pragmatist rationalization

Pragmatists argue for the rejection of the 'either–or' methodological position and recognize mixing methods from apparently opposing paradigms. Pragmatically oriented MMR researchers thus subscribe to a 'compatibility thesis' (Howe, 1988) and argue that combining methods from the two research approaches is not only possible but desirable as far as the research questions demand mixing. This position is in sharp contrast to the 'incompatibility thesis' that motivated the paradigm debate and considered the two methodological approaches (quantitative and qualitative) to be mutually exclusive and even opposing.

Many researchers have advocated and promoted a pragmatist MMR. Johnson and Onwuegbuzie (2004, p. 18), for example, argue: 'The project of pragmatism has been to find a middle ground between philosophical dogmatism and skepticism and to find workable solutions to many long-standing philosophical problems.' Teddlie and Tashakkori (2009) also contend that researchers' disappointment with the paradigms debate in the mid- and late 1990s resulted in a reconciliation of the research communities and thus methodologies. In that context, mixing methods is seen as a catalyst for promoting feasibility and answering practical research questions. By rejecting either a top-down deductive quantitative or a bottom-up inductive qualitative approach to research, pragmatically oriented mixed methods researchers take the position 'that research on any given question at any point in time falls somewhere within the *inductive-deductive research cycle*' (Teddlie & Tashakkori, 2009, p. 87, italics original). This theoretical position allows investigators to not only traverse between the two research approaches, but also use methods from the two approaches simultaneously and in a single study.

In addition, and by rejecting the objective/subjective dichotomy, pragmatically oriented mixed methods researchers perceive knowledge construction across a continuum, and not categorically as either objective or subjective. This perspective recognizes both objective (confirmatory/explanatory) and subjective (descriptive/exploratory) knowledge outcomes when researchers engage in different types of data collection and analysis related to different research questions. This also leads pragmatically oriented mixed methods researchers to discard the value-free vis-à-vis value-laden perspectives in research assigned to quantitative and qualitative approaches. They argue that there is no need to be particularly obsessed about the role of values in research and maintain that mixed methods researchers use their value system to make decisions about what they want to study, and that their values are accounted for by the choices they make (Teddlie & Tashakkori, 2009).

Principles of pragmatist MMR

In unfolding how a pragmatist worldview informs MMR, researchers have attempted to discuss and unfold the principles. Johnson and Onwuegbuzie (2004) suggest that the following principles characterize a pragmatist approach to MMR.

- rejection of binary (either–or) choices suggested in research paradigms;
- recognition of knowledge derived from and based on the reality of the world and constructed by those who live in and experience that world;
- preference for action and answering practical research questions rather than involving theoretical/philosophical debates.

Similarly, Tashakkori and Teddlie (2009) also draw on the following assumptions in developing their pragmatic conceptualization of MMR:

1. That research is a continuum, and studies differ in their degree of using deductive–inductive logic at different stages in the research process.
2. Research questions must drive the methods of a study, and the utility of qualitative and quantitative methods must be based on their potential for answering research questions.
3. There should at least be an overarching research question that drives every mixed methods study and that involves the integration of quantitative and qualitative questions.
4. Data collection and analysis techniques are distinct from the methods and design, and most data collection techniques can potentially yield qualitative and quantitative data that may be analyzed qualitatively or quantitatively.
5. Mixed methods should be differentiated from mixed methodology, which is considered a scholarly field of developing, studying and discussing the issues and procedures for integrating the qualitative and quantitative approaches to research.

From their perspective, 'pragmatism offers a third choice that embraces superordinate ideas gleaned through consideration of perspectives from both sides of the paradigms debate in interaction with research question and real-world circumstances' (Teddlie & Tashakkori, 2009, p. 73). For pragmatist

MMR researchers, then, research questions are the prime springboard for determining the choice of research methods and mixing them to investigate and answer important questions in ways that could not be done adequately using a single approach.

Highlights of pragmatist MMR

- recognition of the 'compatibility thesis';
- rejection of either–or position (either quantitative or qualitative);
- refusing objective vs. subjective dichotomy of knowledge;
- discarding value-free vs. value-laden perspectives as they relate to researchers' value system;
- considering research as a continuum rather than a polar dichotomy, with the possibility of mixing methods from the two approaches at different levels across the continuum;
- giving a primary role to research questions when selecting methods and mixing them.

Both transformative and critical realists have been critical of building MMR on a pragmatist paradigm.

Transformativist worldview

Researchers such as Mertens (2007, 2009, 2010) have advocated and advanced the transformative perspective as the underlying worldview for mixing methods. Transformative MMR researchers define their research mandate as collaborative participatory action research to serve political action, individual and community empowerment, and any other changes in society that might benefit marginalized groups. As Creswell and Plano Clark (2011) contend, the purpose of transformativist research is to identify power imbalances in society and advance social justice causes through change-oriented research projects. Hence, from a transformative perspective, mixing quantitative and qualitative methods is not only possible but also desirable if such mixing could lead to the achievement of the transformative goals in society.

In her justification of the transformative worldview underpinning MMR, Mertens (2007) cites House and Howe's (1999) criticism of practicality (pragmatism) as the basis for conducting MMR by questioning 'Practical for what?' Mertens argues that research should not only be grounded in social contexts, but should also seek higher social goals (justice) than simply being useful to those in power. By investigating issues related to marginalized groups, Mertens contends that transformative researchers would find it valuable to use quantitative or qualitative methods, or a mixture of both. In other words, transformative researchers welcome MMR in so far as it can produce more comprehensive results that guarantee and promote greater social justice. However, it seems a transformative perspective advocates a narrower use of MMR in a broader sense of research.

Transformativist rationalization

Mertens (2007) rationalizes transformative as a legitimate worldview for mixing methods by arguing that there are multiple realities constructed by different social institutions, and that 'power and privilege are important determinants of which reality will be privileged in a research context' (p.212). She contends that to address inequality and injustice in society resulting from the practices of the dominant power, the transformative worldview, with its associated philosophical assumptions, provides a suitable framework by using culturally competent, mixed methods strategies. Mertens suggests that the qualitative strand can be used to gather community perspectives, while the quantitative strand is useful for demonstrating outcomes that have credibility for different stakeholders. Transformative mixed methodologies, as perceived by Mertens (2007, p.212), 'provide a mechanism for addressing the complexities of research in culturally complex settings that can provide a basis for social change'.

A transformative perspective accounts for the dilemma of objective and subjective knowledge by recommending the involvement of the participants and their collaboration with researchers in addressing higher-order transformative causes. The involvement and collaboration of researchers and participants is seen to eliminate discrepancies between researcher and participant perspectives, leading to a more balanced view regarding the social issue under investigation. Mertens (2003) interprets objectivity in transformative research as providing a balanced view such that 'bias is not interjected because of a lack of understanding of key viewpoints' (p. 141). Mertens also emphasizes the significance of researchers being present in research sites and communities so that they can appreciate participants' subjective experiences by developing an insider understanding.

From an axiological (role of values) perspective, transformative researchers not only appreciate value-laden research but also consider attention to values as best suited for advancing their transformative goals. This transformative perspective on the role of values in research is different from the one held by pragmatists, as discussed above and in Chapter 1. According to Teddlie and Tashakkori (2009): '(A) major contrast between pragmatists and transformative scholars concerns values. From the transformative perspective, the values that guide research function to enhance social justice rather than individual researcher interests' (pp. 91–92). The main focus of transformative research on values has represented the transformative approach to mixed methods as an 'axiological framework' (Biddle & Schafft, 2015) that determines other components such as the nature of reality (ontology), the relationship between the researcher and the researched (epistemology) and the procedures for data collection and analysis (methodology). This strong axiological position derives from 'the recognition of power differences and the ethical implications that derive from those differences in terms of discrimination, oppression, misrepresentation, and being made to feel and be invisible (marginalized)' (Mertens *et al.*, 2010, p. 195).

Principles of transformativist MMR

The following principles are derived from Mertens and her colleagues' discussion of transformative mixed methods.

1. Knowledge, as the outcome of research, reflects the power relationships within society. The purpose of research and thus knowledge construction is to aid people to improve society.
2. Power is an issue that must be addressed at each stage of the research process, and researchers might make use of a variety of quantitative and qualitative methods to determine the focus of research, with a specific concern for power issues.
3. There are multiple realities that are socially constructed, but it is necessary to be explicit about the social, political, cultural, economic, ethnic, racial, gender, age and disability values that define realities.
4. Transformative researchers need to be aware of societal values and privileges in determining the reality that holds potential for social transformation and increased social justice (Mertens, 2007, p. 216).
5. Transformative MMR places central importance on the lives and experiences of those who suffer oppression and discrimination, regardless of its basis.
6. Researchers working within this paradigm are consciously aware of power differentials in the research context and they search for ways to ameliorate the effects of oppression and discrimination by linking their research activities to social action and wider questions of social inequality and social injustice (Mertens, 2003, p. 159).

7. Three basic principles underlie regulatory ethics in research: respect, beneficence and justice. The transformative axiological assumption promotes these principles on several fronts.

8. The philosophical assumptions associated with the transformative paradigm emanate from an ethical stance that emphasizes the pursuit of social justice and the furtherance of human rights. Based on this axiological assumption, the researcher is able to derive implications for the nature of reality, knowledge and systematic inquiry that are commensurate with this ethical stance (Mertens, 2012, p. 256).

Highlights of transformative MMR

- Mainly concerned with social justice and transforming the lives of the unprivileged in the society.
- Knowledge reflects social and power relations in the society and the purpose of knowledge construction is to improve the relationships.
- Considers a balanced view in knowledge construction, including key viewpoints from community members and researchers.
- Values are essential in advancing transformative goals and MMR researchers need to be aware of societal values and privileges.

Dialectical pluralist worldview

An explanation of dialectical pluralism requires, first, a brief description of two other worldviews, postpositivism and constructivism. According to Lincoln and Guba (2000), postpositivists moderated positivists' naive concept of reality as objectively and fully knowable. Although, like positivists, postpositivists believe in a reality out there, they argue that the objective reality is only imperfectly knowable given the limited intellectual abilities of human beings. This leads then, as Lincoln and Guba contend, to a key distinction between the positivist and postpositivist views, that of 'theory verification' versus 'theory falsification' (Lincoln & Guba, 2000, p. 107). Rather than trying to verify theories, as positivists intended to do, postpositivists attempt to find counter evidence for a stated explanation (hypothesis) if it is to be false. This is done through hypothesis-testing procedures in quantitative research and nullifying a proposed explanation using statistical procedures. Both positivist and postpositivist worldviews are considered to be the informing paradigms for quantitative research.

Constructivism, as a counter worldview to (post)positivism, adheres to the assumption that reality is constructed in the minds of individuals (both researchers and researched). As such, (a) researchers are part of the reality and cannot be detached from the object of study (participants), and (b) there are multiple and equally valid realities to be investigated and reported (Guba & Lincoln, 1994; Lincoln & Guba, 2000). Constructivists, therefore, take an interpretive or hermeneutic approach to research and maintain that researchers need to unfold meaning through deep reflection and systematic interaction between researchers and participants (Schwandt, 2000). Accordingly, understanding of what constitutes reality is co-constructed by the researcher and their participants through an interactive dialogue. Rather than following an etic approach, as is the case in (post)positivism, constructivists follow an emic approach. Constructivism is the underlying worldview for qualitative research broadly.

Based on the brief elaboration on (post)positivism and constructivism:

- quantitative researchers (attributed to (post)positivism) aim for explanation and prediction by seeking generalizable statements about research phenomena,

while

- qualitative researchers (attributed to constructivism) direct their attention to the understanding of lived experiences (Schwandt, 2000).

The dialectical pluralism (DP) worldview is mainly promoted by Greene (2007), Greene and Hall (2010) and Johnson (2011, 2012, 2015). The term 'dialectic' indicates the unique and divergent perspectives, and the term 'pluralism' is used to show that the two divergent perspectives could be brought together. The core argument in DP is that the two main paradigms, (post)positivism and constructivism, can be used together in a 'respectful dialogue' (Greene & Hall, 2010, p. 124) to inform, design and conduct MMR. Greene and Hall further explain that DP seeks to 'surface, engage and legitimize difference in the social world, toward greater understanding and acceptance of difference' (p. 140). By implication, therefore, the main emphasis is on the recognition of divergence in data and result and how such divergence might help researchers to develop a better understanding of the research phenomenon.

Principles of dialectical pluralist MMR (Greene & Hall, 2010)
The following principles can be extracted from Greene and Hall (2010) in regard to DP MMR.

1. DP as a worldview for mixed methods offers a research opportunity that not only recognizes difference and diversity between worldviews but also emphasizes such diversity in making decisions about research and reporting outputs.
2. Seen as above, DP provides an opportunity for mixed methods researchers to combine two or more research paradigms that might be of relevance to their project.
3. The methods used should depend on the study at hand, and researchers should collect and analyze data, and report the study in ways that promote dialogue, particularly between the quantitative and qualitative data sets.
4. Inferences are based on dialogues between quantitative and qualitative findings, including addressing those aspects that raise tensions, contradictions and paradoxes.

Johnson (2015, p. 3) has, however, suggested a version of DP which 'is distinct from but also complementary to Greene's work'. She considers DP as a 'metaparadigm' that attempts to find a way to interact with both differences and similarities of the two paradigms in terms of goals, values, methodologies and perspectives. From Johnson's perspective, DP recognizes a pluralistic ontology by recognizing both objective and subjective realities, and a dialectical epistemology by relying on a dialogical or hermeneutic approach to understanding differences represented by different realities.

Johnson considers DP as a change theory that requires listening, understanding, learning and acting on the part of researchers. 'Dialectically, DP uses back-and-forth disputation and examination and can include the dynamic logic of thesis, antithesis, and synthesis – synthesis/integration is a key requirement of successful equal-status MMR' (Johnson, 2015, p. 2).

Principles of dialectical pluralist MMR (Johnson, 2012, 2015)
The following principles are implied from Johnson (2012, 2015, pp. 5, 6) when DP is used as the underlying worldview for MMR.

1. Dialectically listen, carefully and thoughtfully, to different paradigms, disciplines, theories, and stakeholder and citizen perspectives.

2. Combine important ideas from competing paradigms and values into a new workable whole for each research study or programme evaluation.
3. Explicitly state and 'pack' the approach with stakeholders' and researchers' epistemological and social–political values to guide the research (including the valued ends one hopes for and the valued means for getting there).
4. Use respectful dialogue with multiple perspectives and mental models.
5. Rely on multiple methods.
6. Attempt to produce negotiated, thoughtful positional adjustment and a win–win solution.
7. Produce dynamic balance, respecting stability and change.
8. Respect pluralism ontologically and epistemologically.

The MMR studies informed by dialectical pluralism may be conducted either by individual researchers using and dialoguing between different values, concepts and paradigmatic differences, or by research teams with different paradigmatic affiliations conversing with each other at different stages in the research process for complementary purposes. Accordingly, DP 'offers a framework regarding the handling and analysis of data, relationships among researchers and with participants, and dialogue across paradigmatic perspectives' (Shannon-Baker, 2015, p. 10). Seen from this perspective, Shannon-Baker regards DP as 'an ideal paradigm to consider when placing equal priority among strands in a mixed methods study' (p. 10).

Critical realist worldview

Another worldview that has emerged from the positivist and constructivist 'paradigm wars' of the 1980s (Denzin & Lincoln, 2011) is critical realism (CR), which has gained popularity in social sciences over the last few decades (Fletcher, 2016). In fact, CR emerged as an alternative to both positivism and constructivism (Denzin & Lincoln, 2011). However, it draws elements from both worldviews in its account of the nature of reality (ontology) and knowledge acquisition (epistemology).

Critical realists oppose a pragmatist approach to MMR on the grounds that 'the practical and the empirical take precedence over the ontological and the epistemological' aspects of research (Danermark *et al.*, 2002, p. 152). In contrast, they advocate positioning MMR within critical realism not only because such a perspective allows for mixing methods from quantitative and qualitative approaches in one study, but also because this can be accomplished by locating the research question(s) within a coherent ontological perspective. Danermark *et al.* (2002) highlight the differences between pragmatism and critical realism as underlying paradigms for MMR, by emphasizing that the 'mix must be governed not only by the research question but, more fundamentally, also by the ontological perspective from which you [the researcher] proceed' (p. 153).

Critical realist rationalization

Drawing on Bhaskar (1998), Fletcher (2016) explains that from a CR perspective, both positivism and constructivism have promoted a reductionist conceptualization of reality – that is, reducing the nature of reality (ontology) to our knowledge of reality (epistemology). Positivists assert that reality is what can be empirically known, for example through experiments. Constructivists, meanwhile, consider reality as entirely constructed through and within human knowledge or discourse. Fletcher claims that despite the apparent opposition between the constructivist (relying on inductive logic and emic approach) and positivist (relying on deductive logic and etic approach) worldviews, each reduces reality to human knowledge, whether that knowledge is attributed to the researcher or to participants.

From a critical realist perspective, reality is stratified into three layers, empirical, actual and real, as presented in Figure 2.2. The foundational level of the real is associated with mechanisms that generate the outcomes or the

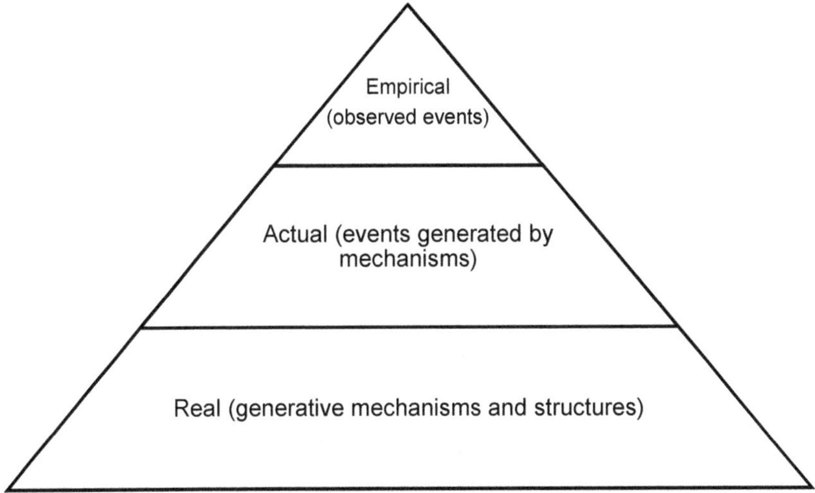

Figure 2.2 Three layers or domains of reality from a critical realist perspective

actual layer. The actual level of reality is thus where events occur whether or not we experience them. However, not all the generated events or outcomes might be observed by researchers and so the third layer of reality, the empirical, thus constitutes those events that are observed and reported.

It should be made clear, however, that the three layers of 'empirical', 'actual' and 'real' are not mutually exclusive. Rather, these three layers need to be conceptualized as three overlapping sets or domains. The actual domain, for example, includes not only the events but also the experiences of the events. Similarly, the domain of real includes both the actual events and the experiences of those events. The point, though, is that more often than not the researcher's focus is based only on the empirical domain by investigating merely the felt experiences and not necessarily attending to the domain of real where generative mechanisms for the event to emerge are located. As such, explanations about the observed realities are approximations and thus transitive.

Danermark *et al.* (2002) argue for five fundamental ontological assumptions: (1) the stratification of reality, (2) the transitive and intransitive dimension of reality, (3) causation in terms of underlying generative mechanisms, (4) the importance of context in the conceptualization of the phenomenon, and (5) the fact that outcomes from the empirical level most often have to be expressed in terms of tendencies, not as regularities expected at deeper levels. This is because true occurrence of events and their underlying regularities is often different from what is observed at the empirical level. Researchers' observations and interpretation of reality are predominantly related to the empirical level and thus transitive and fallible. A deeper understanding of the reality will therefore require an attempt at unfolding the generative mechanisms at the real layer that have led to actual and, in turn, empirical phenomena. In other words, critical realism distinguishes between the real (cause), the actual (event) and the empirical (experience) as they relate to particular events. Accordingly, any attempt at causal explanation must explain the causal forces that are referred to as generative mechanisms. The goal of critical realists (including CR MM researchers) is thus to explain social phenomena through understanding and explaining generative mechanisms in addition to their observation and explanation of the phenomena at the empirical level.

The logic for making inferences in critical realism is abductive (theoretical re-description) or retroductive. It is a process of working backwards from the observable empirical events to the underlying mechanisms that could logically have produced those events (Danermark *et al.*, 2002). This is usually done through an iterative process so that researchers can improve their understanding of those mechanisms. Fletcher (2016) explains that the open social world and its conditions can prevent or facilitate the actualization of a structure's causal power. This would mean that it may or may not result in an observable empirical phenomenon. For this reason, the process of abduction or retroduction helps investigators to examine particular social conditions under which a causal mechanism takes effect in the world.

Traditionally, quantitative and qualitative researchers have used deductive and inductive logic to justify the relationship between data and theory. Using abductive or retroductive logic, as it is used in CR, will 'break out of the very limited confines of a context of justification constituted by an inductive or deductive relationship between data and theory' (Wuisman, 2005, p. 376). This will allow researchers to apply deductive and inductive logic of making inferences in an iterative cycle of providing theoretical explanations between data and theory.

Abductive and retroductive logic leads to another important feature of critical realism, that of the role of theory in research. Bhaskar (1979, cited in Fletcher, 2016) recognized the use of existing theory as a starting point for developing hypotheses about generative mechanisms to be addressed in empirical research. According to Bhaskar (1979, p. 62): 'Once a hypothesis about a generative structure has been produced in social science it can be tested quite empirically, although not necessarily quantitatively.' The point to consider would be that existing theories may not necessarily reflect reality as it happened at the actual layer. Some theories may be more accurate than others in this respect. Researchers must, therefore, according to Bhaskar (1979, p. 6), 'avoid any commitment to the content of specific theories and recognize the conditional nature of all its results'. Once the data are collected and analyzed, the results 'can support, elaborate, or deny that theory to help build a new and more accurate explanation of reality' (Fletcher, 2016, p. 4).

The term 'critical' in critical realism has been interpreted differently by commentators. Some (see, for example, Hammersley, 2009) have taken it to refer to critical theory or the transformative paradigm – that is, attributing 'critical' to the position of the researcher in regard to social injustice. However, Cruickshank (2002) clarifies this point in the following way: '(C)ritical philosophy is therefore critical because it accepts neither the view that there are fixed philosophical first principles that guarantee epistemic certainty, nor the idea that first-order activities are self-justifying' (p. 54). The critical realist perspective discussed in this book is thus in line with the latter position. That is, critical of both a naive realism (that absolute knowledge of reality is possible) and an extreme constructivism (that there is no reality independent of our knowledge).

Principles of CR MMR

The following principles could be implied from the literature (Bhaskar, 1979; Danermark *et al.*, 2002; Fletcher, 2016) on critical realism.

1. The nature of reality (ontology) should not be reduced to our knowledge of reality (epistemology).
2. Both positivists and constructivists are reductionist in their envisioning of reality, thus the term 'critical' in critical realism.
3. Explaining social phenomena using methods solely from the natural sciences could be flawed because reality will be reduced to an empirical realization and what could be explained by the researcher.
4. Seeking an understanding of the social phenomena based on purely subjectivist assumptions (i.e. social reality is nothing but a social construction by participants) is flawed.
5. Gaining knowledge in terms of theoretical explanations of why certain phenomena occur can help us get closer to reality, that is, identifying generative mechanisms underlying social events.
6. Both induction and deduction logics are useful research tools and of equal importance to abduction or retroduction logic for making inferences about social phenomena.
7. Once hypotheses are derived from existing theories about generative mechanisms, they can be checked empirically using both quantitative and qualitative data and analysis and through abductive or retroductive logic.

Conducting CR MMR starts with a conceptualization of the research phenomenon based on existing theories that account for the empirical (the what) and the real (the how and why) of reality. Certain hypotheses may be developed at this stage and based on the conceptual framework to be then checked against the empirical data. Observation of the events at the empirical level will then require the collection of both 'extensive (i.e. data on widespread trends, such as statistical data) and intensive (i.e. in-depth interpretive data, as obtained through interviews or focus groups for example' (Fletcher, 2016, p. 5). The two methodological approaches of quantitative and qualitative are thus used in tandem to provide evidence for accepting or refuting hypotheses and thus retaining, refuting or modifying existing theories in order to provide a better understanding and closer-to-reality explanation about the social phenomena.

The inferencing process includes both abductive and retroductive approaches. Through abduction, the empirical data and results are re-described in light of theoretical concepts. Danermark *et al.* (2002, p. 205) explain that abduction is the 'inference or thought operation, implying that a particular phenomenon or event is interpreted from a set of general ideas or concepts' with an acknowledgement that the chosen theories are fallible. Through retroduction, researchers focus on causal mechanisms and conditions by moving from concrete (observations) to abstract (theoretical explanation) and back again.

From a CR perspective, the choice of methodology and specific methods and the logic for making inferences depend on the integral part of each in the research process. This process, as Wuisman (2005) explains, starts with the researcher's observation of an unexplained event – unexplained in the sense that the researcher finds a gap in the existing theories and his or her observation. This leads the researcher to develop some hypotheses using abduction logic, that is, working backwards from the observable events to some theoretical explanations about the underlying mechanisms that could logically have produced those events. The second stage in the process would be to determine whether the proposed theoretical explanation, based on the hypothesis, is valid or not. This will require an examination of the cases to represent the proposed explanation. In the third stage, by way of induction the researcher should use the carefully gathered, detailed information about the cases to determine whether the proposed explanation does, in fact, match the observed case. If not, the perceived gap is not closed and a new hypothesis (tentative explanation) needs to be conjectured based on abduction.

In sum, from a CR perspective, rather than focusing on the design technicalities of sequencing and implementing methods in service of research questions (see, for example, Creswell, 2003; Tashakkori and Teddlie, 1998), mixed methods researchers need to be more creative in designing their studies following abductive and retroductive logics. As such, the following phases are suggested in designing an MMR project.

1. Conceptualizing the research problem against two backdrops of (a) the situatedness of the problem, thus considering contextual factors, and (b) considering relevant and existing theories and how these might help the conceptualization of the problem.
2. Hypothesizing about possible underlying generative mechanisms and structures that are capable of generating the phenomenon. This phase includes the identification of conditions and properties necessary to generate the phenomenon.

3. Searching for the cases and making several deductions relevant to the patterns and regularities in the cases if the hypothesized explanation is to be operative as a general rule.
4. Collecting appropriate data using suitable instruments of data collection that could produce rich data related to the deeper levels of reality to determine, through induction, whether the underlying generative mechanisms and the deduced regularities really obtain, and to what extent.
5. Using the back-and-forth movement between the observed events and the theoretical explanations to close the gap observed. This will help analytical and theoretical stabilization of the activated and unactivated generative mechanisms yielding the outcomes or events under study.
6. The final phase in a CR MMR would be to critically examine and eliminate alternative explanations. This is the stage of developing and using meta-inferences in MMR through which findings produced through different methods are integrated in favour of a fuller understanding of the observed phenomenon. It usually entails a complementary theoretical explanation of how different mechanisms and structures interact under particular conditions to yield observed social phenomena.

According to Mingers (2001, p. 246), the above phases correspond to the questions of 'What is happening? Why is it happening? How could the explanation be different? And, so what?' Danermark *et al.* (2002) contend that the abductive and retroductive processes should not only inform the design of the studies, but also be used at different stages in the research process to guide research activities as the study progresses.

Concluding remarks

This chapter provides an overview of four underlying worldviews for MMR. The rationale for presenting and discussing these worldviews was to inform the reader that there are alternative ways of theorizing and designing MMR projects. This is particularly important because, by far, pragmatism has come to be known as the predominant underlying worldview for mixing methods from different research paradigms. Knowing about other worldviews will hopefully help readers to not only understand published MMR studies in a broader theoretical context, but also to think about their own projects in light of these worldviews and how they might want to adopt and adapt them at a conceptual level.

In the next chapter, the rationale for mixing methods will be discussed from another perspective, the goals for which MMR researchers have mixed methods in practice. Chapter 3 will, therefore, discuss the five purposes – triangulation, complementarity, initiation, development and expansion – that have been identified by MMR scholars as the main purposes for mixing methods by researchers. The link between these five purposes and the worldviews discussed in this chapter will be elaborated on when it is deemed to be relevant.

References

Bhaskar, R. (1979). *The possibility of naturalism: A philosophical critique of the contemporary human sciences*. Atlantic Highlands, NJ: Humanities Press.

Bhaskar, R. (1998). Philosophy and scientific realism. In M. Archer, R. Bhaskar, A. Collier, T. Lawson, & A. Norrie (Eds.), *Critical realism: Essential readings* (pp. 16–47). London: Routledge.

Biddle, C. & Schafft, K.A. (2015). Axiology and anomaly in the practice of mixed methods work: Pragmatism, valuation, and the transformative paradigm. *Journal of Mixed Methods Research, 9*(4), 320–334.

Biesta, G. (2010). Pragmatism and the philosophical foundations of mixed methods research. In A. Tashakkori & C. Teddlie (Eds.), *Sage handbook of mixed methods in social and behavioral research* (2nd ed., pp. 95–117). Thousand Oaks, CA: Sage.

Christ, T. (2011, April). Critical realism and pragmatism: A lens for mixed, action and qualitative research. Professors of Education Research Symposium: Evolving Paradigms in Mixed Methods Research, American Education Research Association, New Orleans, LA.

Christ, T. (2013). The worldview matrix as a strategy when designing mixed methods research. *International Journal of Multiple Research Approaches, 7*(1), 110–118.

Creswell, J.W. (1995). *Research design: Qualitative, quantitative, and mixed methods approaches*. Thousand Oaks, CA: Sage.

Creswell, J.W. (2003). *Research design: Qualitative, quantitative, and mixed methods approaches*. London: Sage Publications.

Creswell, J.W. & Plano Clark, V.L.P. (2007). *Designing and conducting mixed methods research*. Thousand Oaks, CA: Sage Publications.

Creswell, J.W. & Plano Clark, V. (2011). *Designing and conducting mixed methods research* (2nd ed.). Thousand Oaks, CA: Sage.

Cruickshank, J. (2002). Critical realism and critical philosophy. *Journal of Critical Realism, 1*(1), 49–66.

Danermark, B., Ekstrom, M., Jakobsen, L. & Karlsson, J.C. (2002). *Explaining society: Critical realism in the social sciences*. London: Routledge.

Denzin, N.K. & Lincoln, Y.S. (2000). Introduction: The discipline and practice of qualitative research. In N.K. Denzin & Y.S. Lincoln (Eds.), *Handbook of qualitative research* (2nd ed., pp. 1–28). Thousand Oaks, CA: Sage.

Denzin, N.K. & Lincoln, Y.S. (Eds.) (2011). *Handbook of qualitative research* (4th ed.). Thousand Oaks, CA: Sage.

Feilzer, M.Y. (2010). Doing mixed methods research pragmatically: Implications for the rediscovery of pragmatism as a research paradigm. *Journal of Mixed Methods Research, 4*, 6–16.

Fletcher, A.J. (2016). Applying critical realism in qualitative research: Methodology meets method. *International Journal of Social Research Methodology*. DOI: 10.1080/13645579.2016.1144401

Greene, J. (2007). *Mixed methods in social inquiry*. San Francisco, CA: Jossey-Bass.

Greene, J.C. & Hall, J.N. (2010). Dialectics and pragmatism: Being of consequence. In A. Tashakkori & C. Teddlie (Eds.), *Sage handbook of mixed methods in social and behavioral research* (pp. 119–144). Thousand Oaks, CA: Sage.

Guba, E.G. & Lincoln, Y.S. (1994). Competing paradigms in qualitative research. In N.K. Denzin & Y.S. Lincoln (Eds.), *Handbook of qualitative research* (pp. 105–117). Thousand Oaks, CA: Sage.

Hammersley, M. (2009). Why critical realism fails to justify critical social research. *Methodological Innovations Online, 4*(2), 1–11.

House, E. & Howe, K. (1999). *Values in evaluation and social research*. Thousand Oaks, CA: Sage.

Howe, K.R. (1988). Against the quantitative-qualitative incompatibility thesis (or dogmas die hard). *Educational Researcher, 17*, 10–16.

Johnson, R.B. (2011, May). Dialectical pluralism: A metaparadigm to help us hear and 'combine' our valued differences. Paper presented in plenary session at the Seventh International Congress of Qualitative Inquiry, Urbana-Champaign, IL.

Johnson, R.B. (2012). Dialectical pluralism and mixed methods. *American Behavioral Scientist, 56*(6), 751–754.

Johnson, R.B. (2015). Dialectical pluralism: A metaparadigm whose time has come. *Journal of Mixed Methods Research*. Published online before print October 12, 2015, DOI: 10.1177/1558689815607692

Johnson, R.B. & Onwuegbuzie, A.J. (2004). Mixed methods research: A research paradigm whose time has come. *Educational Researcher, 33*(7), 14–26.

Lincoln, Y.S. & Guba, E.G. (2000). Paradigmatic controversies, contradictions, and emerging confluences. In N.K. Denzin & Y.S. Lincoln (Eds.), *The handbook of qualitative research* (2nd ed., pp. 163–188). London: Sage.

Lipscomb, M. (2011, April). Critical realism and realist pragmatism in mixed methods: Problematics of event identity and abductive inference. Professors of Education Research Symposium: Evolving Paradigms in Mixed Methods Research, American Education Research Association, New Orleans, LA.

Maxwell, J. (2011, April). Paradigms or toolkits? Philosophical positions as heuristics for mixed methods research. Professors of Education Research Symposium: Evolving Paradigms in Mixed Methods Research, American Education Research Association, New Orleans, LA.

Maxwell, J.A. & Mittapali, K. (2010). Realism as a stance for mixed methods work. In A. Tashakkori & C. Teddlie (Eds.), *Handbook of mixed methods in social and behavioral research* (pp. 193–215). Thousand Oaks, CA: Sage.

Mertens, D.M. (2003). Mixed methods and the politics of human research: The transformative-emancipatory perspective. In A. Tashakkori & C. Teddlie (Eds.), *Handbook of mixed methods in social and behavioral research* (pp. 135–164). Thousand Oaks, CA: Sage.

Mertens, D.M. (2007). Transformative paradigm: Mixed methods and social justice. *Journal of Mixed Methods Research, 1*, 212–225.

Mertens, D.M. (2009). *Transformative research and evaluation.* New York: Guilford Press.

Mertens, D.M. (2010). Philosophy in mixed methods teaching: The transformative paradigm as illustration. *International Journal of Multiple Research Approaches, 4*, 9–18.

Mertens, D.M. (2012). What comes first? The paradigm or the approach? *Journal of Mixed Methods Research, 6*(4), 255–257.

Mertens, D.M., Bledsoe, K.L., Sullivan, M. & Wilson, A. (2010). Utilization of mixed methods for transformative purposes. In A. Tashakkori & C. Teddlie (Eds.), *Handbook of mixed methods in social and behavioral research* (pp. 193–215). Thousand Oaks, CA: Sage.

Mingers, J. (2001). Combining IS research methods: Towards a pluralist methodology. *Information Systems Research, 12*(3), 240–259.

Morgan, D. (2007). Paradigms lost and pragmatism regained: Methodological implications of combining qualitative and quantitative methods. *Journal of Mixed Methods Research, 1*(1), 48–76.

Onwuegbuzie, A.J., Collins, K.M.T. & Frels, R.K. (2013). Towards a new research philosophy for addressing social justice issues: Critical dialectical pluralism 1.0. *International Journal of Multiple Research Approaches, 7*(1), 9–26.

Plano Clark, V.L., Creswell, J.W., O'Neil Green, D. & Shope, R.J. (2008). Mixing quantitative and qualitative approaches: An introduction to emergent mixed methods research. In S.N. Hesse-Biber & P. Leavy (Eds.), *Handbook of emergent methods* (pp. 363–387). New York: Guilford Press.

Ponterotto, J.G. (2005). Qualitative research in counseling psychology: A primer on research paradigms and philosophy of science. *Journal of Counseling Psychology, 52*(2), 126–136.

Riazi, A.M. (2016). Innovative mixed-methods research (IMMR): Moving beyond design technicalities to epistemological and methodological realisations. *Applied Linguistics, 37*(1), 33–49.

Riazi, A.M. & Candlin, C.N. (2014). Mixed-methods research in language teaching and learning: Opportunities, issues and challenges. *Language Teaching, 47*, 135–173.

Sayer, A. (1992). *Method in social science: A realist approach.* London: Routledge.

Schwandt, T.A. (2000). Three epistemological stances for qualitative inquiry: Interpretivism, hermeneutics, and social constructionism. In N.K. Denzin & Y.S. Lincoln (Eds.), *Handbook of qualitative research* (2nd ed., pp. 189–213). Thousand Oaks, CA: Sage.

Shannon-Baker, P. (2015). Making paradigms meaningful in mixed methods research. *Journal of Mixed Methods Research.* Published online before print March 20, 2015, DOI: 10.1177/1558689815575861

Tashakkori, A. & Teddlie, C. (Eds.) (1998). *Mixed methodology: Combining qualitative and quantitative approaches.* Thousand Oaks, CA: Sage.

Tashakkori, A. & Teddlie, C. (Eds.) (2003). *Handbook of mixed methods in social and behavioural research.* London: Sage.

Tashakkori, A. & Teddlie, C. (2009). Integrating qualitative and quantitative approaches to research. In L. Bickman & D.J. Rog (Eds.), *The SAGE handbook of applied social research methods integrating qualitative and quantitative approaches to research* (pp. 283–318). Thousand Oaks, CA: Sage.

Teddlie, C. & Tashakkori, A. (2009). *Foundations of Mixed Methods Research: Integrating quantitative and qualitative approaches in the social and behavioral sciences.* Thousand Oaks, CA: Sage.

Wuisman, J.J.M. (2005). The logic of scientific discovery in critical realist social scientific research. *Journal of Critical Realism, 4*(2), 366–394.

Zachariadis, M., Scott, S. & Barrett, M. (2013). Methodological implications of critical realism for mixed methods research. *MIS Quarterly, 37*, 855–879.

Part Two

Practical Aspects of Mixed Methods Research

3 Following a Purpose and Achieving Goals in MMR

This chapter will:

- discuss the purposes for which researchers mix methods;
- explain and review the five identified MMR purposes:
  - triangulation
  - complementarity
  - initiation
  - development
  - expansion;
- discuss challenges facing MMR researchers.

Introduction

This chapter explains and reviews the five main purposes which have been proposed for mixing methods from quantitative and qualitative approaches. The theoretical justification for mixing methods was discussed in Chapter 2. Following that discussion, this chapter elaborates on the purposes for which MMR researchers mix methods. Researchers have strived to answer the question of 'why mixing?' by reviewing and analyzing the published MMR studies. This approach to the identification of purposes for mixing methods can thus be called a data-driven approach because it relies on the information derived from research reports.

Drawing on a review and analysis of published MMR studies, Greene *et al.* (1989) identified five main purposes for mixing methods: triangulation, complementarity, initiation, development and expansion. These purposes will be explained and discussed in this chapter.

The data-driven approach to finding reasons for mixing methods complements the theoretical discussion presented in Chapter 2. Alternative frameworks, including three MMR design typologies, are also reviewed and discussed in the next chapter. The theoretical discussions in Chapter 2, the explanation of the purposes for mixing methods in this chapter and the discussion of design typologies in the next chapter will provide a rich and useful context for readers. In addition, readers should find these discussions helpful for planning and designing their own MMR studies in more principled and innovative ways.

Purposes for mixing methods: a data-driven approach

Greene *et al.* (1989) were among the first researchers to follow a data-driven approach to identify the purposes for which researchers mixed methods. Using a purposeful or purposive sampling procedure (Riazi, 2016), they examined 57 published MMR articles related to evaluation research to discover the underlying purposes for which investigators had mixed methods from the two methodological approaches. They used the purposive sampling procedure because they intended to choose only those studies that had an MMR orientation.

Drawing on both the extant theoretical discussions on MMR and the procedures through which investigators had mixed methods from the two methodological approaches, Greene *et al.* were able to develop a conceptual explanatory framework for describing mixed method purposes. The framework included their five different MMR purposes of triangulation, complementarity, initiation, development and expansion. Each of these five purposes is reviewed and discussed below.

Triangulation in quantitative research

Triangulation has been used in all the three research paradigms, quantitative, qualitative and mixed methods.

According to Webb *et al.* (1966), triangulation was originally used in quantitative research in which researchers used different measurement procedures to reduce measurement errors and improve validity of the reported observations. Campbell and Fiske (1959), for example, used this concept of triangulation and developed the multitrait–multimethod (MTMM) approach (Riazi, 2016) for test validation. In brief, through this approach, testing researchers could choose some target traits such as language proficiency, intelligence and critical thinking and measure them using different methods, including multiple choice, fill in the blanks and matching, to check the construct validity of each trait. In other words, to explore whether these are different or the same constructs. If correlations were found between different measures (that is, different methods) of the same trait, this would be regarded as evidence for the validity of the construct or trait. Campbell and Fiske named this convergent validity. Yet the expectation was to find no or very low correlations between different measures of different traits if they were to represent different constructs. Campbell and Fiske called this type of evidence discriminant validity. MTMM has been an appealing approach in test validation and has been used by many test specialists.

Triangulation in qualitative research

Denzin (1978, 1988) was among the first researchers to promote and discuss the concept of triangulation to enhance credibility in qualitative research. He suggested four types or methods of triangulation: triangulation through different data sources, different methods, different investigators and different theories or theoretical orientations.

Qualitative researchers have been using all or some of Denzin's suggested triangulation methods to enhance the credibility of their interpretation of data and analysis. For example, congruence between different observers of a classroom would provide evidence for investigator triangulation. Similar results from classroom observations and interviews with teachers and students would provide evidence for triangulation through data and methods.

Triangulation in MMR

Greene *et al.* (1989) popularized triangulation in MMR as one of the five purposes for which researchers may mix methods from the two methodological approaches. It has been one of the predominant goals for mixing methods in many disciplines, including language teaching and learning (Riazi & Candlin, 2014). This use of triangulation in MMR is based on Denzin's framework. The very nature of MMR studies requires researchers to mix quantitative and qualitative methods in a single study to answer appropriate research questions. Greene *et al.* found, from their analysis of MMR studies, that researchers attempted to corroborate or cross-validate findings achieved from one or more methods in one strand with those obtained from one or more methods in another strand. Greene *et al.*'s interpretation of triangulation as represented in MMR studies was considered to correspond to both data and method triangulation in Denzin's framework.

Figure 3.1 presents a schematic diagram of this concept of triangulation purpose in MMR studies, indicating that quantitative and qualitative data are collected and analyzed independently through different strands, and then the findings from one or more methods in each strand are used for corroboration or cross-validation purposes. Most often, the two strands in MMR studies receive the same level of emphasis and thus their design can be generally represented as QUAL + QUAN. Other potential variations of MMR designs with triangulation purpose are presented and discussed in the next chapter.

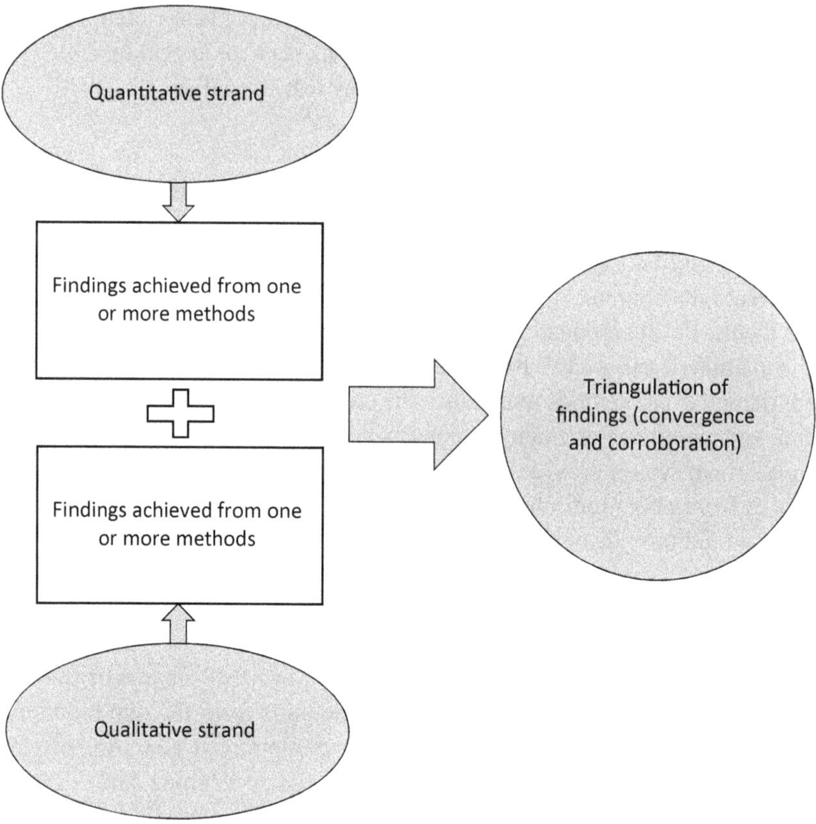

Figure 3.1 Triangulation purpose in MMR

In addition to data and method triangulation, it can be argued that MMR accounts for investigator triangulation in Denzin's framework, since in MMR studies two or more research strands are involved, requiring two investigators with different perspectives to collaborate with each other at all stages in the research process. MMR studies are either conducted by one researcher in two roles (a quantitative and a qualitative investigator), or by independent but collaborating quantitative and qualitative investigators, each drawing on their own research orientation to data collection and interpretation. If a researcher with two different roles or two independent researchers are able to interpret data and cross-validate their findings and provide converging evidence for their results, this would thus correspond to the investigator triangulation in Denzin's classification.

Reflection

MMR researchers can argue for three types of triangulation to enhance the credibility of their research. They can support their argument by referring to:

- triangulation through quantitative and qualitative data sources;
- triangulation through methods;
- triangulation through quantitative and qualitative investigators.

Examples of MMR studies with triangulation purpose

In its simplest form, data and method triangulation is used when, for example, a researcher checks the validity of the participants' responses to quantitative questionnaire items using qualitative interviews provided by a small number of the participants. This is indeed a less common use of triangulation (Knafl & Breitmayer, 1989) that is used to ensure the validity of the instruments used.

In other situations, a researcher may collect structured classroom observations using a classroom observation scheme (e.g. Allen *et al.*, 1984) and produce quantitative data regarding teaching and learning activities in particular classrooms. In addition, the researcher may collect qualitative data through interviews with teachers and students about their perspectives on the teaching and learning activities they were involved with in the classrooms. Results from the two data collection methods (structured classroom observations and open interviews) and the two data sources (quantitative data from observations and qualitative data from interviews) could be used for triangulation and corroboration purposes and thus enhance the credibility of the reported findings.

As noted above, the quantitative and qualitative strands in MMR studies with a triangulation purpose usually receive equal status and the two data sources are collected concurrently or independently. Such MMR studies can lead to data and method triangulation, and as discussed above, even investigator triangulation. As a result, MMR researchers can provide more valid and credible explanations about the research phenomenon. However, the triangulation purpose in MMR has faced some criticism and so researchers face some challenges when using it as their purpose in MMR.

Challenges facing researchers

The main challenge facing MMR researchers when mixing methods for a triangulation purpose is how the object or construct of the study is defined. In order to be able to cross-validate findings from one data source and method with those of another, researchers need to ensure they are dealing with the same construct definition operationalized in different instruments of data collection. Otherwise, they may be criticized for comparing oranges with apples. In other words, the requirement for cross-validating findings from two data sources obtained through two methods is that the same construct definition informs the two data collection and analysis procedures.

The question then, and thus the challenge, is the extent to which researchers can provide evidence, and make a claim, for the same construct definition in the quantitative and qualitative strands of their MMR study. Gorard and Taylor (2004) and Kelle (2001) believe that the mutual validation goal in MMR studies as represented in the triangulation purpose is problematic. These researchers base their argument on the fact that different research approaches define and conceptualize research constructs differently. In line with this argument, Denzin (2012) asserts that in his original formulation of the concept of triangulation, he 'referred only to the use of multiple forms of qualitative research methods, not the combination of quantitative and qualitative methods' (p. 82). Drawing on Flick (2007), Denzin argues that rather than conceiving triangulation as a tool or a strategy for validation of findings, it must be considered as an alternative to validation, 'an attempt to secure an in-depth understanding of the phenomenon in question' (Denzin, 2012, p. 82). Accordingly, Denzin challenges MMR researchers in the way they have interpreted and applied triangulation in their studies.

Challenges of using triangulation in MMR

- The requirement for corroborating findings from one data source and method with those of the other is that the same construct definition informs data collection and analysis procedures.
- Different methodological approaches define research constructs in different ways, which may not necessarily converge.
- Denzin warns that his use of triangulation encompasses multiple methods from the qualitative approach, and not methods from quantitative and qualitative approaches.

A second challenge facing MMR researchers in this regard is the situation where findings from the two data sources and methods do not converge. This may happen quite frequently when, despite the researcher's initial expectation, findings from the quantitative strand do not converge with the findings from the qualitative strand. This divergence in the findings would lead to puzzlement on the part of MMR researchers, especially novice researchers, making it difficult for them to produce plausible interpretations and make appropriate inferences.

Expanding the scope of triangulation

To find a solution to the above two challenges and criticisms facing MMR researchers pursuing a triangulation purpose, Howe (2012), drawing on Mathison (1988), suggests an alternative and a more 'holistic' conception of triangulation – a conception that allows researchers to provide a more comprehensive understanding of the research problem regardless of whether the research construct is operationalized in similar or different ways and regardless of whether findings from one data source and method converge or diverge with those of the other. Howe argues that triangulation must be used as an umbrella term, with an explanatory power, using different data sources and methods to provide a more comprehensive understanding about the research problem.

A classic example Howe provided in this regard was when physicians interview their patients and use results from this qualitative strand with results obtained from a quantitative strand such as medical tests. While the results obtained and the inferences made on the basis of the two data sources and methods may converge or diverge, they complete a part in the whole puzzle and help physicians to make reasonable inferences as to how to explain and deal with the situation.

Howe's perspective on triangulation opened some room for a broader definition of the term, 'methodological triangulation' (Morse, 1991, 2003), which could overlap with other purposes in Greene *et al.*'s framework. Mertens and Hesse-Biber (2012), in their editorial to the special issue of the *Journal of Mixed Methods Research* in which Howe's paper was published, also recognized that 'there are alternative perspectives on the use of triangulation that argue for its usefulness as a 'dialectical' process whose goals seek a more in-depth nuanced understanding of research findings and clarifying disparate results by placing them in dialogue with one another' (p. 75).

The methodological triangulation perspective and how it applies to MMR will be further discussed in the next chapter, where alternatives to Greene *et al.*'s framework are presented and discussed.

Triangulation purpose as used in this book

In this book a distinction is made between a narrower definition of 'triangulation' as suggested and used in Greene *et al.*'s (1989) framework and that of Morse (1991) and Howe's (2012) broader definition of triangulation, 'methodological triangulation'. Greene *et al.*'s definition of triangulation is the popular one and commonly used by MMR researchers when reporting their studies. This conception of triangulation considers the object of the study as fully knowable through different methods and data sources. Hence, different methods are used to collect data in unproblematic ways and to represent information about the construct of the study. According to Mason (2006), the logic underlying this perspective on triangulation is convergence and corroboration. This conception of triangulation is, therefore, distinguished from 'methodological triangulation', which can potentially cover all the individual purposes identified and suggested by Greene *et al.*

Complementarity purpose

Greene *et al.* (1989) contended that complementarity 'seeks elaboration, enhancement, illustration, clarification of the results from one method with the results from another' (p. 259). To seek elaboration and enhancement, MMR researchers need to conceptualize the research problem as multi-layered or multi-dimensional, each layer or dimension in need of one data source and analysis. Figure 3.2 presents a graphical representation of the complementarity purpose.

In MMR studies with complementarity purpose, two or more strands might be involved depending on how the research problem is conceptualized. In each strand different methods of data collection and analysis could then be used, and depending on the level of emphasis each strand receives in the overall design, a variety of designs might be used to represent MMR studies with complementarity purpose.

The conceptualization of the research phenomenon as multi-dimensional allows for the consideration of co-existing and interrelated dimensions in the research phenomenon. This would represent a dynamic perception of the research phenomenon, including the processes involved as well as the outcomes expected in an interrelated and reciprocal way.

When MMR studies with complementarity purpose are well designed and properly conducted, the integration of the quantitative and qualitative strands is genuinely done at all levels in the research process, from the conceptualization of the research problem to interpreting findings and making inferences. In contrast to triangulation purpose, in which results from

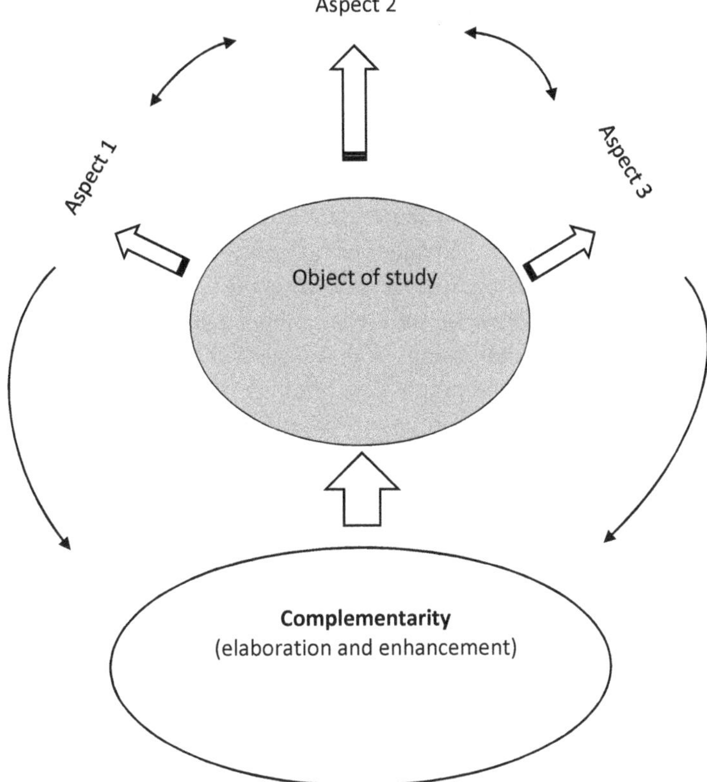

Figure 3.2 The complementarity purpose

one strand of the study are used to support results from the other strand for validation purposes, in MMR studies with complementarity purpose, researchers seek evidence from each method to explain different layers or dimensions of the research problem and together provide a more holistic understanding of the research phenomenon.

One of the challenges confronting MMR studies with triangulation purpose, as discussed above, is when despite initial expectations, the findings of the two strands do not converge. This can happen when, in fact, the researcher is investigating different layers or dimensions of the construct under investigation, each lending itself to different types of data and analysis. In such cases, researchers need to reconceptualize the construct to account for and elaborate on different aspects involved. Inferences made from different data sources and methods are then integrated to provide a more comprehensive explanation about the research phenomenon and enhance its understanding.

MMR studies with complementarity purpose are therefore robust because they are able to investigate and explain more complex social and educational phenomena. As Bryman (1988, 1992) states, in MMR studies with complementarity purpose, researchers use quantitative and qualitative approaches to address different aspects of the same research problem so that they can present a fuller picture of the phenomenon. In such cases, both quantitative and qualitative approaches are used to address the what and the how or why questions, seeking elaboration on the structures and processes involved as well as establishing relationships and reasons behind those relationships. As a result, among the five purposes for mixing methods, complementarity purpose stands out because through it researchers are able to conceptualize more complex research problems and use different research approaches to interrogate different processes, structures, interactions and outcomes.

Highlights

Complementarity purpose allows MMR researchers to:

- conceptualize more complex research phenomena with different layers and dimensions;
- seek elaboration and enhancement of different dimensions using different data sources and analyses;
- provide a more comprehensive understanding of the research phenomenon.

According to Woolley (2009): 'The quantitative approach is characteristically indirect and reductive; the qualitative approach is characteristically direct and holistic. These are the strengths of each; these are the different levels of inquiry at which they are directed' (p. 8). When used in complementary ways, the two data sources and methods provide multi-perspectives corresponding to different aspects of the research problem.

Examples of MMR studies with complementarity purpose

An example of an MMR study with complementarity purpose, which is also reviewed in Part Three of this book, is Lee and Greene (2007). Lee and Greene investigated the predictive validity of an institutional English as a Second Language (ESL) placement test in a large public university in the United States. The researchers were concerned about the extent to which scores on an institutional placement test could predict international graduate students' academic performance and their language difficulties in content courses during the first semester of their graduate education. The researchers conceptualized the construct of 'academic performance' and 'language proficiency' as multi-dimensional. They used students' academic performance represented by their grade point average (GPA) as merely one of the aspects of the construct of 'academic performance and success'. They extended their conceptualization of this construct to include other facets such as students' self-assessment of their language proficiency and academic success and faculty members' evaluation of student academic performance and language problems. Such a multi-faceted conceptualization of the research problem enabled the researchers to genuinely exploit and mix methods from the two research approaches.

The multi-dimensional conceptualization of the construct of 'academic performance and success' and 'language proficiency' allowed Lee and Greene to use a variety of quantitative and qualitative data sources and analyses. The findings from different data sources and analyses, in turn, enabled the researchers to make quantitative and qualitative inferences, and to integrate these two types of inferences in favour of a more comprehensive meta-inference about students' language proficiency and their academic performance and success.

Challenges facing researchers

Designing and conducting MMR studies with complementarity purpose is much more demanding and challenging compared with other types of MMR studies. As Mason (2006) notes, putting into practice the complementary purpose is a great deal more challenging regarding the range of skills required on the part of the researchers. It requires researchers to integrate the two strands at all stages in the research process, demanding higher levels of theoretical and methodological expertise and skills. The researcher should, therefore, be:

1. familiar with the key theories and concepts relating to the topic of the study and particularly the construct under study;
2. able to conceptualize the research problem as multi-dimensional, showing different aspects of the research problem and how they might interact;
3. able to formulate research questions in light of the conceptualization of the research problem, different research questions perhaps

addressing different aspects, but together eliciting information about the whole research problem;

4. able to design appropriate data collection instruments to collect the required data for each of the aspects or dimensions of the research problem;

5. capable of performing the required quantitative and qualitative data analysis based on the principles and quality standards of each of the two research approaches;

6. competent in making plausible inferences using the findings from the quantitative and qualitative data and analysis;

7. able to integrate results and inferences from each of the research approaches to make more comprehensive meta-inferences relating to the conceptualization of the research problem.

Challenges facing MMR researchers

- Familiarity with relevant and diverse theoretical backgrounds of the research phenomenon.
- Ability to conceptualize the research problem to address different aspects and dimensions related to the research problem.
- Ability to collect and analyze different data sources.
- Ability to make plausible inferences on the basis of findings from each strand and to integrate them for a more holistic explanation of the research problem.

Based on the above requirements and challenges, it might not be easy for all researchers to embark on MMR studies with complementarity purpose. According to Mason (2006), this kind of MMR study is immensely challenging because by nature it pushes at the boundaries of social science philosophy and knowledge at the conceptualization level and then through all other stages in the research process. If not carefully and skillfully designed and implemented, the study may turn into an expansion purpose with a parallel logic underpinning different strands, as will be discussed later.

One possible solution to compensate for the complexity involved in this type of research is collaborative research. Through collaborative research, it would be possible to form research teams composed of different skilled researchers from different theoretical and methodological orientations to work with each other at all stages in the research process. Collaboration among researchers with different theoretical backgrounds and research skills will lessen the burden of the research load as well as the challenges inherent in this type of study (Creswell & Plano Clark, 2011).

Complementarity purpose as used in this book

The conception of complementarity purpose advanced and advocated in this book is thus a theoretically multi-layered or multi-dimensional defined construct that could be understood through different methodological approaches. This perspective on complementarity is also advocated by researchers from other disciplines, such as health (see, for example, Carroll & Rothe, 2010). As Carroll and Rothe explain, this perspective of complementarity corresponds to Weber's conceptualization in which he advocates 'the importance of both "rational or objective" (as in quantitative research) and "empathic or subjective" (as in qualitative research) dimensions for understanding human phenomena' (Weber, 1949, cited in Carroll & Rothe, 2010, p. 3481). From this perspective, each research paradigm has its own capability to expand our knowledge, but when integrated they could develop a complementary understanding of the research phenomenon.

Mason (2006) also emphasized that a multi-dimensional logic informs MMR studies of this kind. The argument is that different methods from different methodological approaches have distinctive strengths and can therefore help researchers to address the multi-dimensionality of complex social phenomena. The integrative logic underlying complementarity purpose is thus there from the starting point of conceptualization of the research problem as multi-dimensional. Researchers sometimes explicitly state their assumptions about how they viewed different parts and dimensions of the research problem and how they form a whole when put together, but sometimes less so. This conception of complementarity also corresponds to Morse's (1991) 'methodological triangulation' and Howe's (2012) broader definition of triangulation.

In line with the above elaboration, the complementarity purpose can also be seen as an integration of the 'etic' and 'emic' perspectives. An etic perspective is linked to quantitative methodology in which the researcher is presumably detached from the researchee (object of the study), seeking an objective explanation of the phenomenon as discussed in Chapter 1. In contrast, an emic perspective, also discussed in Chapter 1, considers such detachment impossible and thus pursues a subjective account about the participants' behaviours and experiences. The complementarity purpose intends to bring these two perspectives together in favour of a more complete understanding of the research problem. The two research approaches are distinct, but when used together they help researchers to create a whole and mutually dependent explanation of the research phenomenon. Teddlie and Tashakkori (2006) also elaborate on the confirmatory and exploratory roles of quantitative and qualitative research and how these two roles can be mixed in a single study in MMR. Further elaboration and discussion of how MMR designs can accommodate the confirmatory and exploratory roles is presented in the next chapter.

Initiation purpose

Greene *et al.* (1989) identified MMR studies with an initiation purpose as those in which researchers addressed paradoxes and contradictions in findings by recasting of questions or results from one method with those from the other. Mathison (1988) also elaborated on the use of initiation purpose to address inconsistent results that arise when different data sources are used. The inconsistent results, as Mathison argued, can point to either methodological or both methodological and substantive issues in the data. The observed inconsistencies or issues need to be resolved by either initiating further analysis of the available data sources or designing and implementing an MMR study that could address those issues through more comprehensive data and analyses (Bazeley, 2012).

Figure 3.3 presents a schematic diagram for the initiation purpose that begins with an observation of contradictory findings and aims at designing an MMR study to provide further explanation of the observed issues.

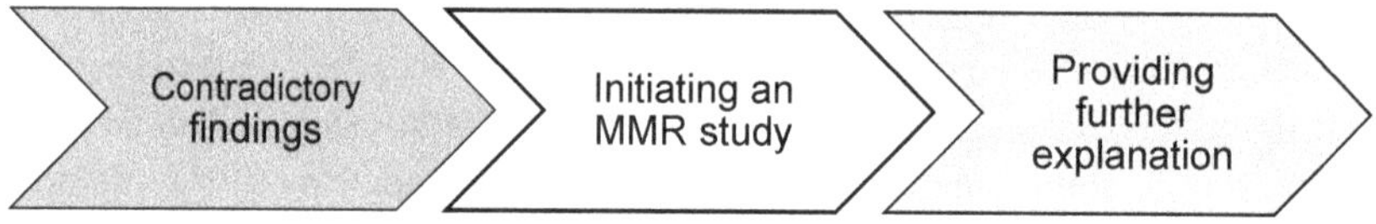

Figure 3.3 Initiation purpose in MMR studies

Like complementarity purpose, MMR studies with an initiation purpose might be represented through different design structures. However, the main purpose would be to especially resolve contradictory outcomes attributed to methodological approaches by designing and implementing a more comprehensive and appropriate MMR study that can explain the observed paradoxes. The initiation may begin while a research project is still in progress, or it may be started after a project is completed. In some situations, MMR studies with initiation purpose may be designed when the researcher observes contradictory results in the existing literature on a particular topic. The contradictions may be due to different methodological approaches used by researchers, or they may be substantially explored in the data sources. An MMR study can address the observed issues and contradictions and shed more light on the observed contradictions.

Highlights

Initiation purpose allows MMR researchers to:

- design new phases of data collection and analysis when they observe contradictions in different strands;
- seek further elaboration and provide more comprehensive explanation of the observed contradictions and paradoxes in the literature;
- extend the scope of their studies.

Examples of MMR studies with initiation purpose

An example of an MMR study with initiation purpose, which is also reviewed in Part Three of this book, is Wesely's (2010) study in which the researcher used mixed methods research to explore contradictions in findings regarding early adolescents' motivation to learn foreign languages. Wesely refers to McInerney (1998), who argues that the construct of motivation has posed an 'emic–etic dilemma', which has divided researchers in approaching and investigating this construct using either a positivist or a constructivist orientation (see Chapter 1 for an explanation of these orientations to research in language teaching and learning). Wesely considers this either–or approach as a problem that has prevented researchers from developing a more comprehensive understanding of the issues related to this construct. Consequently, Wesely decided to initiate an MMR study through which the researcher could integrate both approaches to produce a more comprehensive understanding of students' motivational problems.

The initiation purpose allowed Wesely to identify and address not only issues and paradoxes in the existing literature but also contradictions observed in her own data sets about L2 learning motivation. Wesely sought further explanations from her data sources and was thus able to shed more light on the observed inconsistencies. Surprisingly, for example, she noticed that those participants who left the immersion programmes developed slightly more positive attitudes towards learning the language than those who remained in the immersion programmes. More surprisingly, participants from the programmes with the highest attrition rates indicated more positive attitudes towards learning the language in the sub-scales of the attitudes questionnaire. These rather unexpected and paradoxical findings extended the scope of Wesely's study to further interrogate the data sources. Full details and discussion of Wesely's study can be found in Chapter 11.

Challenges facing researchers

MMR studies with initiation purpose are used either to address observed contradictions in the existing literature on a particular topic or to address contradictory findings and/or paradoxes in a study in progress. The former type of initiation purpose is especially attractive if the observed contradictions and paradoxes could be attributed to different methodological approaches used by previous researchers. The challenge facing MMR researchers would then be to design a study that can clearly address the sources of the observed contradictions and how these could be resolved through an MMR study. This requires researchers to draw on and apply higher levels of theoretical and methodological expertise and experiences. This level of expertise and skills is, in many cases, beyond the capabilities of novice researchers and thus requires more experienced researchers or groups of researchers to design and conduct such studies.

The second challenge facing MMR researchers when pursuing initiation purpose is usually observed when graduate and doctoral students are conducting their thesis projects following a triangulation purpose. In many cases, and despite the initial plans, these researchers may come across contradictory findings emerging from different methods of data collection and analysis. As discussed earlier, these paradoxes in the findings could either be attributed to different methods producing different findings or could be inherent in the data sources and interpretations. In either case, the researcher needs further time and budget to design and conduct additional phases of data collection and analysis to be able to elaborate on the contradictions and clarify the explanations. However, given the restricted resources graduate and doctoral students face when they are completing their degrees, this may not prove feasible. Many universities in Australia, for example, are not ready to extend doctoral students' scholarships beyond the designated three years and they urge students and their supervisors to ensure that the doctoral projects are completed within the time and budget frames. As discussed above, in such cases, researchers can alternatively recommend fruitful directions for further research rather than initiating new phases of data collection and analysis. Future researchers hopefully may take up these suggestions and design further studies.

Finally, embarking on new phases of study while a project is still in progress would lead to an emergent (initiation) purpose and thus would be more demanding in terms of resources such as time and budget. A case in point would be when the results of the two strands of an MMR study initially designed with a triangulation purpose turned out to be contradictory. The researcher might then initiate a new phase of research to seek further explanation for the observed inconsistencies. However, this would require enough resources (time and money) for the researcher to initiate new phases of the study, which might not prove feasible, especially in graduate and doctoral programmes where resources are restricted. In such cases, the researcher could make suggestions for further research.

Notwithstanding these challenges, initiation purpose is appealing to researchers because it is a catalyst through which inconsistencies could be addressed and further and more comprehensive explanations could be presented.

Initiation purpose as used in this book

In the literature on initiation purpose (see, for example, Greene *et al.*, 1989; Teddlie & Tashakkori, 2009), initiation is mostly used to provide further explanation of the observed discrepancies between quantitative and qualitative results in a study. This realization of initiation purpose is recognized and used in this book. However, two types of initiation are recognized in this book: emergent and planned. The emergent type is used when a study is in progress and the researcher notices contradictions in findings of different strands. The researcher can then plan and conduct another phase of data collection and analysis or even a whole new strand to account for the observed contradictions. The planned representation of initiation purpose is particularly important when researchers find that existing contradictions and paradoxes within the reported findings related to a particular topic are rooted in conceptual and methodological differences. Different camps of researchers (quantitative and qualitative) conceptualize social and educational constructs differently and use different methodological approaches to investigate them. Consequently, they may obtain different and sometimes contradictory findings.

When faced with the situations described above, planning MMR studies with an initiation purpose to address the observed contradictions could further elaborate on the construct of the study. Therefore, in this book both types of initiation purposes – emergent and planned – are recognized and recommended.

Development purpose

Greene *et al.* (1989) defined MMR studies with a development purpose as those in which researchers used the results of one strand (quantitative or qualitative) to inform, design and conduct the other strand. Since in MMR studies with a development purpose results from one strand are used to develop and implement the next strand, they are sequential in nature. Figure 3.4 presents a schematic diagram of MMR studies with a development purpose.

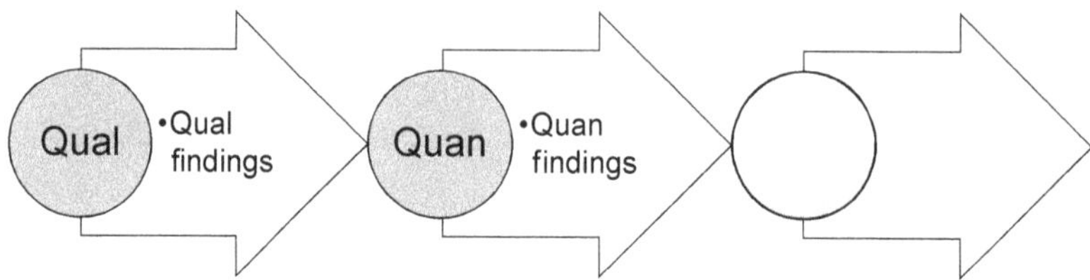

Figure 3.4 MMR studies with a development purpose

As Figure 3.4 illustrates, MMR studies may have only two strands, each may include different phases of data collection and analysis, or they may have more than two strands. An exemplar of an MMR study with development purpose with more than two strands could be the Delphi method (Riazi, 2016) in which there are usually three to five sequentially designed strands.

The Delphi method is a useful research method through which consensus among experts is sought on a particular issue. It is mostly used in futurist research and technological forecasting, but it has been used in a variety of other disciplines. In education, for example, the Delphi method is used for curriculum development and for setting assessment criteria. The Delphi method is designed and implemented through iterative phases of data collection and analysis, usually three to five rounds. Each phase of data collection and analysis may constitute one strand based on one methodological approach, or some strands may represent independent MMR studies initiated and developed on the bases of contradictory findings obtained from a previous strand. As such, studies with the Delphi method may be designed with development purpose or a combination of development and initiation purposes. The final conclusions and inferences are made mainly from the results of the last strand in the study, but also in light of the results from different strands.

> ## Highlights
>
> Development purpose allows MMR researchers to:
>
> - design new strands based on the results of a previous strand;
> - seek generalization of the qualitative results or in-depth explanation of quantitative results from different strands;
> - design their MMR studies with two or more strands;
> - combine development and initiation purposes when one or more strands is MMR.

As indicated above, since subsequent strands are built on the results obtained from the previous strands, MMR studies with development purpose are by nature sequential. They may be represented by different permutations of QUAL → QUAN or QUAN → QUAL, as presented and discussed in the next chapter.

Examples of MMR studies with development purpose

Studies with a development purpose are implemented either to seek generalization of findings from a qualitative strand through a quantitative strand, or to provide deeper explanations of quantitative findings through a qualitative strand. The key difference from triangulation purpose, for example, is the sequence, designing one strand based on the outcomes of a previous one. When more than two strands are involved, as in the Delphi method, then the results of the final strand are used to provide evidence for consensus, or disagreement, among experts.

A typical example of a study with a development purpose where the researcher seeks deeper understanding of quantitative findings is when a survey questionnaire is conducted with a large sample of language teachers or learners using closed-ended questions as the method of data collection. The completed questionnaires will be analyzed quantitatively and patterns of responses will be identified. For example, if the questionnaire was related to language learning motivation, based on factor analysis, language learners might be classified into three categories of intrinsic, extrinsic and amotivated language learners. The researcher could then use the outcomes of the quantitative strand and design a qualitative strand in which participants from each of the three motivational categories would be asked to elaborate and provide more in-depth explanation about their motivational propensities. The qualitative strand expands the understanding of the language learners' motivational tendencies.

To seek generalization for the results obtained from a qualitative strand, a quantitative strand with a large sample can be designed using the results from the qualitative strand. For example, a small number of teachers may be interviewed to elicit information about their beliefs and attitudes towards a communicative language teaching (CLT) approach. The qualitative interview data will then be analyzed following a thematic analysis of the qualitative data for attitudinal themes to emerge from the data. If there is any intention for generalization of the obtained results, the researcher can use the results from the qualitative strand to design and develop a questionnaire survey. Each attitudinal theme achieved from the qualitative strand can be used as one section in the questionnaire and relevant coded data from the qualitative data can be used to formulate individual questions in each of the sections. The questionnaire can then be administered to a larger sample of teachers for the data to be analyzed quantitatively and to provide evidence for generalization inferences. The second, quantitative strand is thus developed based on the outcomes from the first, qualitative strand and may inform another qualitative strand. Even the sampling and data collection and analysis rely on the results of the first strand. The two strands in MMR studies with a development purpose are sequentially ordered because unless the first strand is completed and conclusions are drawn, it is not possible to develop and design the second strand. The Christ and Makarani (2009) study reviewed in Chapter 11, in which the researchers investigated Indian English language teachers' attitudes towards and practices of CLT, is similar to the above scenario.

In the above examples, the attempt has been to mix the exploratory and confirmatory roles of qualitative and quantitative research, thus adding to the rigour of research. This aspect of development purpose will be further discussed in the next chapter, where different designs and especially sequential designs are discussed.

Challenges facing researchers

MMR studies with development purpose are the most straightforward among the five purposes. This is mainly because each strand in the overall design is developed based on the results obtained from a previous strand. Therefore, there do not seem to be any serious challenges facing researchers when designing and implementing studies with a development purpose. There are no theoretical controversies around the legitimacy of the development purpose as there might be around triangulation and expansion purposes. However, like any other purpose, researchers need to design each strand very carefully based on the quality principles and standards of each approach.

Regarding different sequential design configurations presented in the next chapter, QUAL → QUAN or qual → QUAN design may turn out to be more challenging for researchers. The challenge relates to the construction of a questionnaire based on the results obtained from a major or minor previous qualitative strand. The qualitative strand usually provides researchers with some themes or categories inductively extracted from qualitative data collected from a small sample of participants. The researcher then needs to create a questionnaire based on the results of the qualitative data and analysis. The construction of the questionnaire and its validation is a demanding task. The sub-sections in the questionnaire can correspond to the categories or themes identified in the qualitative strand. It would, however, be more difficult to write specific items for each section in the questionnaire. The researcher can indeed use the specific segments in the interview data coded under each category or theme to think about and write individual items for each section of the questionnaire. Nevertheless, this may not be a straightforward task. The questions need to be carefully formulated so that each represents an issue related to the construct of the sub-section in the questionnaire. In addition, the questions need to be written clearly so that participants can understand them with no ambiguity.

Another level of challenge is the validation of the constructed questionnaire. Once the questionnaire is developed, it needs to be piloted – that is, administered to a smaller sample but similar to the main sample of the study. The purpose of this is to check that (a) the instructions are clear and participants can understand what they are required to do, (b) the wording of individual questions is clear and understandable, and (c) the questionnaire is reliable and valid. The reliability of the questionnaire and each of its sub-sections can be calculated using internal consistency measures. This is a simple procedure and can be run through different methods using statistical software packages. One common method is to check the internal consistency of the questionnaire that seeks relationship between the items and whether there is consistency in participants' responses. There are also different methods for checking the validity of the questionnaire and its sub-constructs, but factor analysis (Riazi, 2016) is mostly used and reported.

The pilot study of questionnaires gives researchers the opportunity to make any necessary changes in the questionnaire before it is administered to the target sample. The whole process might thus be challenging, especially for postgraduate students.

Finally, designing and conducting a study using the Delphi method with development and initiation purposes may be quite challenging for researchers. These types of studies require higher levels of theoretical and methodological expert knowledge and experiences and are thus most probably conducted by more experienced researchers who can draw on their accrued knowledge and expertise.

Development purpose as used in this book

Development purpose is used in its original definition in this book, that is, one strand built on a previous one. The literature on MMR makes no mention of the Delphi method as a potential representation of MMR studies with development purpose. However, this use of development purpose is acknowledged and included in this book. The potential combination of development and initiation purposes in studies using the Delphi method seems a particularly attractive option that more experienced researchers could aspire to undertake for certain topics of their interest using innovative designs.

Expansion purpose

In MMR studies with expansion purpose, the two strands of the study are usually designed, conducted and reported in parallel, each based on its methodological standards and principles. The purpose is to expand the scope of a study by adding and incorporating another set of data and analysis, most often without necessarily integrating the two strands. Figure 3.5 presents a schematic diagram of studies with an expansion purpose.

MMR studies with expansion purposes are similar to those with triangulation purpose in terms of design and can thus be represented as QUAN + QUAL, though depending on the level of emphasis put on each strand, one of the strands may be represented with lower case letters. However, the two purposes differ especially in regard to the final stage, the inferential stage. In MMR studies with triangulation purpose, after the independent quantitative and qualitative inferences are presented, they are integrated for the purpose of corroboration and cross-validation – that is, to show how findings from one strand might support findings from the other strand. This integration of inferences is most likely absent in MMR studies with expansion purposes.

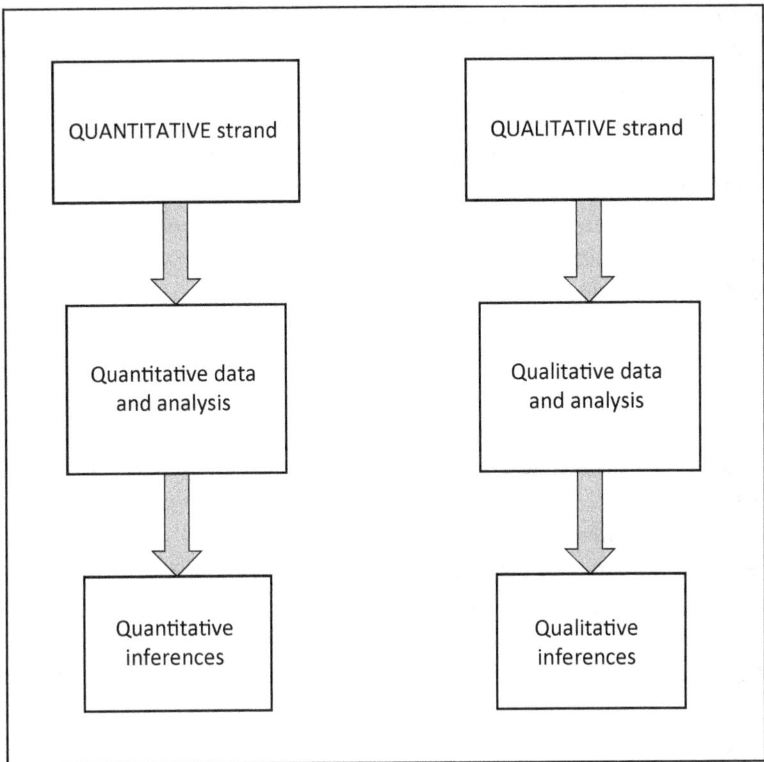

Figure 3.5 Studies with an expansion purpose

Highlights

In MMR studies with an expansion purpose the aim is to:

- expand the breadth of a study by adding another strand to it;
- design, conduct and report the two strands in a parallel way;
- leave each strand independent, often with no attempt to integrate them even at the inferential level.

Examples of MMR studies with expansion purpose

With an expansion purpose, researchers seek to extend the breadth and range of inquiry by adding another set of data and analysis. Some of the classroom-based research studies with an MMR orientation represent this type of purpose. The Vogel *et al.* (2011) study, which is reviewed in Part Three, is an example of a study with an expansion purpose. Vogel *et al.* intended to investigate whether a guided inductive or a deductive approach to the teaching of French grammar could prove more effective for intermediate-level college students' learning of French grammatical structures. A secondary goal of the study was to determine participants' preference for grammar instruction and to determine whether there was a relationship between students' preference and their performance in the grammar tests.

As can be judged from the design of the study (the experimental design) and the data collection and analysis, this MMR study was quantitative-dominant. The quantitative strand included participants' scores on immediate tests after each three sessions, that is, after teaching three grammatical structures, and pre- and post-treatment grammar test scores. In addition, after the experiment was over, participants completed a learning preference questionnaire, which included both closed-ended and open-ended questions. The qualitative strand included the open-ended questions of the questionnaire and post-study interviews with six participants. Quantitative and qualitative data were analyzed and the results were used to answer the research questions.

Results of the quantitative and qualitative data analysis were presented separately and in parallel in the research report. The qualitative data and analysis played a minor role compared with the quantitative data and analysis and were used to expand the study through some supplementary qualitative explanations.

Although Vogel *et al.* described their MMR study as sequential, perhaps because the qualitative data were collected after the experiment, the actual design of the study represents QUAN + qual and an expansion purpose. This is based on the grounds that the qualitative strand was not built on the results from the quantitative strand. In other words, the two strands were independent of each other.

Challenges facing researchers

The main challenge, and perhaps the main issue, confronting researchers who mix methods for expansion purposes is the lack of rigour. Designing and implementing an MMR study with an expansion purpose is easy to do with no serious challenges facing researchers, but it does not take the researcher very far in terms of integration and thoroughness. Greene *et al.* (1989) observed that expansion was the most flexible of the five purposes of MMR in which researchers used the two methods side by side, with less integration than research with other purposes.

Most often, MMR studies with expansion purpose are either quantitative- or qualitative-dominant and the researcher is most skilful in one of the two research methodologies. The explanatory logic in the whole study also remains either chiefly quantitative or qualitative. The other strand is then used to expand the breadth or the depth of the study using some supplementary data and analysis. Even in those MMR expansion studies in which the two strands might have equal weights, the two are conducted as independent (mini) projects and then presented in parallel in the research report, with a minimum or no attempt on the part of the researcher to integrate the two strands. Bazeley (2004) also states that in MMR studies representing expansion purpose, the different methodological approaches are kept separate, thus allowing each to stick to its own paradigm and design requirements. Bazeley then questions whether such a design could be categorized as mixed methods research, considering that the two strands are not genuinely integrated at any stage in the research process. Based on Greene *et al.*'s (1989) observation, 'Even in the stronger expansion studies reviewed, the qualitative and quantitative methods were kept separate throughout most phases of the inquiry' (p. 269).

Based on the above observations, studies with an expansion purpose would not be received strongly by research communities and would be less likely to be accepted for publication by journal editors. When designing research projects with an MMR orientation, language teaching and learning researchers therefore need to keep this issue in mind. They might then decide to opt for stronger purposes and designs that might be better worth their time and other resources.

Expansion purpose as used in this book
In this book, expansion purpose is used with its original definition as suggested by Greene *et al.* (1989). This definition and description is used especially in Part Three of the book where published MMR studies are analyzed and reviewed. Some researchers may explicitly state the purpose of their studies as expansion, while others may not. However, it should not be difficult to distinguish the expansion purpose from the details of data collection and analysis and the way results are presented in research reports.

Concluding remarks

The MMR purpose framework suggested by Greene *et al.* (1989) and discussed in this chapter, as well as alternative design typologies to be discussed in the next chapter, can help readers better understand MMR reports. In addition, the discussion of different purposes, including examples and challenges and different design typologies in the next chapter, may help them design and implement their own studies more effectively and efficiently. However, readers should be reminded that, in reality, while there may be a primary purpose of an MMR study, there is likely to be some overlap or fuzziness among different purposes. In many cases, researchers may start from scratch without designing everything in advance and let their research purpose and design develop over the course of the research. Once the research project is well progressed, they may then think of 'the best fit' in terms of purpose and design rather than force their study to fit certain purposes and designs. It would be worthwhile for both researchers and readers to include a narrative of how the purposes and designs were developed over time and how different personal and contextual factors influenced the development of the methodology. This reflective narrative would help advance methodological discussions in the researcher's field.

References

Allen, P., Frohlich, M. & Spada, N. (1984). The communicative orientation of language teaching: An observation scheme. In J. Handscombe, R.A. Orem, & B. Taylor (Eds.), *On TESOL '83: The question of control* (pp. 231–252). Washington, DC: TESOL.

Bazeley, P. (2004). Issues in mixing qualitative and quantitative approaches to research. In R. Buber, J. Gadner & L. Richards (Eds.), *Applying qualitative methods to marketing management research* (pp. 141–156). Basingstoke: Palgrave Macmillan.

Bazeley, P. (2012). Integrative analysis strategies for mixed data sources. *American Behavioral Scientist, 56*(6), 814–828.

Bryman, A. (1988). *Quantity and quality in social research.* London: Unwin Hyman.

Bryman, A. (1992). Quantitative and qualitative in social research: Further reflections on their integration. In J. Brannen (Ed.), *Mixing methods: Quantitative and qualitative research* (pp. 57–58). Aldershot: Avebury.

Buber, R., Gadner, J. & Richards, L. (Eds.) (2004). *Applying qualitative methods to marketing management research* (pp. 141–156). Basingstoke: Palgrave Macmillan.

Campbell, D.T. & Fiske, D.W. (1959). Convergent and discriminant validation by the multitrait–multimethod matrix. *Psychological Bulletin, 56*(2), 81–105.

Carroll, L.J. & Rothe, J.P. (2010). Levels of reconstruction as complementarity in mixed methods research: A social theory-based conceptual framework for integrating qualitative and quantitative research. *International Journal of Environmental Research and Public Health, 7*, 3478–3488.

Christ, T.W. & Makarani, S.A. (2009). Teachers' attitudes about teaching English in India: An embedded mixed methods study. *International Journal of Multiple Research Approaches, 3*(1), 73–87.

Creswell, J.W. & Plano Clark, V. (2011). *Designing and conducting mixed methods research* (2nd ed.). Thousand Oaks, CA: Sage.

Denzin, N.K. (1978). *Sociological methods*. New York: McGraw-Hill.

Denzin, N.K. (1988). Triangulation. In J.P. Keeves (Ed.), *Educational research, methodology, and measurement: An international handbook* (pp. 51–113). Oxford: Pergamon Press.

Denzin, N.K. (2012). Triangulation 2. *Journal of Mixed Methods Research, 6*(2), 80–88.

Flick, U. (2007). *Designing qualitative research*. London: Sage.

Gorard, S. & Taylor, C. (2004). What is 'triangulation'? Building research capacity. *Journal of the ESRC Teaching and Learning Research Programme: Research Capacity Building Network, 7*, 7–9.

Greene, J.C., Caracelli, V.J. & Graham, W.F. (1989). Toward a conceptual framework for mixed-method evaluation designs. *Educational Evaluation and Policy Analysis, 11*(3), 255–274.

Howe, K.R. (2012). Mixed methods, triangulation, and causal explanation. *Journal of Mixed Methods Research, 6*(2) 89–96.

Kelle, U. (2001). Sociological explanations between micro and macro and the integration of qualitative and quantitative methods. Forum Qualitative Sozialforschung/Forum: Qualitative Social Research, *2*(1), Art. 5. Available at: http://nbn-resolving.de/urn:nbn:de:0114-fqs010159

Knafl, K.A. & Breitmayer, B.J. (1989). Triangulation in qualitative research: Issues of conceptual clarity and purpose. In J.M. Morse (Ed.), *Qualitative nursing research: A contemporary dialogue* (pp. 209–220). Rockville, MD: Aspen.

Lee, Y. & Greene, J. (2007). The predictive validity of an ESL placement test: A mixed methods approach. *Journal of Mixed Methods Research, 1*, 366–389.

Mason, J. (2006). Six strategies for mixing methods and linking data in social science research. Real Life Methods working paper, University of Manchester. Retrieved 22 June 2012 from: http://www.manchester.ac.uk/realities/resources/toolkits

Mathison, S. (1988). Why triangulate? *Educational Researcher, 17*, 13–17.

McInerney, D.M. (1998, April). Multidimensional aspects of motivation in cross-cultural settings and ways of researching this. Paper presented at the American Educational Research Association Annual Meeting, San Diego, CA.

Mertens, D.M. & Hesse-Biber, S. (2012). Triangulation and mixed methods research: Provocative positions. *Journal of Mixed Methods Research, 6*(2), 75–79.

Morse, J.M. (1991). Approaches to qualitative-quantitative methodological triangulation. *Nursing Research, 40*, 120–123.

Morse, J.M. (2003). Principles of mixed methods and multimethod research design. In A. Tashakkori & C. Teddlie (Eds.), *Handbook of mixed methods in social and behavioural research* (pp. 189–208). Thousand Oaks, CA: Sage.

Riazi, A.M. (2016). *The Routledge encyclopedia of research methods in applied linguistics: Quantitative, qualitative and mixed-methods*. London: Routledge.

Riazi, A.M. & Candlin, C.N. (2014). Mixed-methods research in language teaching and learning: Opportunities, issues and challenges. *Language Teaching, 47*, 135–173.

Teddlie, C. & Tashakkori, A. (2006). A general typology of research designs featuring mixed methods. *Research in the Schools, 13*(1), 12–28.

Teddlie, C. & Tashakkori, A. (2009). *Foundations of mixed methods research: Integrating quantitative and qualitative approaches in the social and behavioral sciences*. Thousand Oaks, CA: Sage.

Vogel, S., Herron, C., Cole, S.P. & Holly, Y. (2011). Effectiveness of a guided inductive versus a deductive approach on the learning of grammar in the intermediate-level college French classroom. *Foreign Language Annals, 44*(2), 353–380.

Webb, E.J., Campbell, D.T., Schwartz, R.D. & Sechrest, L. (1966). *Unobtrusive measures* (rev. ed.). Thousand Oaks, CA: Sage.

Weber, M. (1949). *The Methodology of the Social Sciences*. Glencoe, IL: The Free Press.

Wesely, P.M. (2010). Language learning motivation in early adolescents: Using mixed methods research to explore contradiction. *Journal of Mixed Methods Research, 4*(4), 295–312.

Woolley, C.M. (2009). Meeting the mixed methods challenge of integration in a sociological study of structure and agency. *Journal of Mixed Methods Research, 3*(1), 7–25.

4 Mixed Methods Research Designs

This chapter will:
- discuss three MMR design typologies, including the design classifications of:
  - Morse (1991, 2003)
  - Teddlie and Tashakkori (2006, 2009)
  - Creswell (2015) and Creswell and Plano Clark (2011);
- relate these design typologies to MMR purposes.

Introduction

In Chapter 3, the five main purposes for which MMR researchers mix methods from quantitative and qualitative approaches were explained and discussed. In this chapter, the focus is on research design and so the main types of designs through which researchers adjust their plans and overall aims for implementation will be presented and discussed. In the discussion of purposes in Chapter 3, the focus was on the goal of mixing methods and the logic for mixing. Greene *et al.*'s (1989) framework has provided a useful taxonomy for both analyzing and planning MMR studies. There have been, however, some ambiguities around the five purposes suggested by Greene *et al.*, as discussed in Chapter 3. These ambiguities have prompted other MMR researchers to devise alternatives to Greene *et al.*'s framework. According to Teddlie and Tashakkori (2006), typologies of MMR designs are not only useful in helping to establish a common language for the field, they can also help researchers decide how to design their MMR studies.

Alternative typologies have focused on the level of emphasis put on each strand as well as time order among different strands. Accordingly, the main criteria used by researchers to classify MMR studies are purpose, strand emphasis and time order among strands.

> ## Criteria used to classify MMR studies
>
> - The purpose or the function for which quantitative and qualitative methods are mixed – this criterion was originally used by Greene *et al.* (1989) and is discussed in Chapter 3.
> - The methodological priority or emphasis – that is, which of the strands in the MMR study receives more emphasis or priority.
> - The time order – whether the two or more strands in an MMR study are conducted concurrently (simultaneously) or sequentially.

While Greene *et al.* (1989) used the first criterion, Morse (1991, 2003) and Morgan (1998) have used the last two criteria to illustrate how different strands in an MMR study might be represented in terms of design structure. In addition, Creswell *et al.* (2003), Creswell and Plano Clark (2011) and Teddlie and Tashakkori (2006, 2009) have focused on these criteria and have suggested different families of MMR designs. This chapter therefore discusses the main design typologies presented by Morse (1991, 2003), Teddlie and Tashakkori (2006, 2009) and Creswell (2015) and Creswell and Plano Clark (2011).

Two key terms need to be distinguished from each other as they relate to MMR designs. The first is **strand** and the second is **phase**. Throughout this book, 'strand' is used to denote a methodological approach, quantitative or qualitative, and encompasses the whole process of conducting either quantitative or qualitative research, from posing questions, collecting and analyzing data and making inferences. Research studies can, therefore, be mono-strand when there is only one methodological approach (either quantitative or qualitative), or they could be multi-strand where two or more methodological approaches are involved in the study. MMR studies usually have two strands, one quantitative and the other qualitative. Nevertheless, in some MMR studies, there might be more than two strands involved, such as when one or both of the methodological approaches might be repeated to complete the process of data collection and analysis. In some multi-strand MMR studies, one strand might even be an MMR itself employing two strands of quantitative and qualitative approaches.

The term 'phase' or 'stage' is used in this book to refer to a particular step or component of a strand, different from Teddlie and Tashakkori's (2006, 2009) use of the term. Teddlie and Tashakkori generally use 'phase' interchangeably with 'strand' and use 'stage' for what is defined as 'phase' in this book. Here, phase and stage are used interchangeably to denote different rounds of data collection and analysis within each of the strands in MMR study. For example, in a quantitative strand, there might be three phases through which quantitative data are collected and analyzed, including, for instance, a pre- and post-test within an experimental phase, a survey of participants' attitudes, and a test or task completion. Similarly, in a qualitative strand, there might be two phases of data collection and analysis: a qualitative case observation and qualitative interviews. This distinction between strand and phase is made to prevent unnecessary confusion.

Morse's design typology

Morse (1991, 2003) used two criteria – priority or emphasis and chronological order between strands – in MMR studies to classify design structures. To represent priority and dominance, Morse used capital letters (e.g. QUAL or QUAN) and to show chronological order she used the plus sign (+) for simultaneous and the arrow sign (→) for sequential order. Table 4.1 summarizes Morse's design typology. As noted earlier, this typology was intended to provide an alternative to Greene *et al.*'s purpose framework.

Table 4.1 Design structures using Morse's (1991, 2003) notation system

Design	*Description*	*Potential purpose*
QUAL + QUAN	Simultaneous strands with equal status	Triangulation, complementarity or expansion
QUAL + quan	Simultaneous strands with more emphasis on the qualitative strand	Triangulation, complementarity or expansion
QUAN + qual	Simultaneous strands with more emphasis on the quantitative strand	Triangulation, complementarity or expansion
QUAL → QUAN or QUAN → QUAL	Sequential strands with equal status	Development
QUAL → quan or quan → QUAL	Sequential strands with more emphasis on the qualitative strand	Development
QUAN → qual or qual → QUAN	Sequential strands with more emphasis on the quantitative strand	Development

The potential link between each design and purpose is suggested in the last column of the table.

To identify the dominance of a strand in an MMR study, Morse suggested determining whether the research problem is primarily a quantitative or a qualitative one. She elaborated on this criterion by asking whether the theory that drives the research is to be applied deductively to the data (as in quantitative research) or is to be developed inductively and from the data (as in qualitative research). In other words, whether the research problem leads to testing hypotheses related to existing theories using empirical data, or whether the research problem encourages developing theoretical explanations from the data.

Methodological triangulation

Morse (1991) defined methodological triangulation as 'the use of at least two methods, usually qualitative and quantitative, to address the same research problem' (p. 120). It is not clear from her brief definition of methodological triangulation, however, whether she conceived triangulation in its broader sense and as suggested by Howe (2012) and Mathison (1988), discussed in Chapter 3, or in its narrower sense as one of the five purposes of mixing methods, as suggested by Greene *et al.* (1989). Nor is it clear from the above definition how methodological triangulation might relate to the four triangulation methods suggested by Denzin (1978, 1988) – triangulation through different data sources, different methods, different investigators and different theories or theoretical orientations – as she does not make any reference to Denzin in her article either. It is likely that by using 'methodological triangulation' Morse intended to cover all the four methods of triangulation suggested by Denzin. The following section proposes (a) a link between Morse's design structures with different purposes of mixing methods, and (b) and elaboration on Morse's use of methodological triangulation to delineate it from the common sense of triangulation purpose.

Linking designs to MMR purposes
Triangulation purpose
Simultaneous designs including equal emphasis, such as QUAL + QUAN, or main emphasis on one of the strands, such as QUAL + quan or QUAN + qual, may potentially follow one of the three purposes of triangulation, complementarity and expansion, as suggested in Table 4.1. In practice, researchers usually use simultaneous design structures to achieve a triangulation purpose, that is, to support and corroborate the findings of one strand with those of another strand. The order is not important in simultaneous

designs because the two strands are conducted independently and reported separately, and the mixing or integration occurs at the interpretation stage in the research process where the researcher could cross-validate findings from the two strands. The requirement for pursuing and achieving a triangulation purpose, as discussed in Chapter 3 and as clarified by Morse, is that both strands address the same research problem. For example, if the quantitative strand used survey questionnaires, and the qualitative strand used interviews, the same questions should inform data collection and analysis in the two strands so that the findings could be compared.

Expansion purpose

When researchers do not attempt to integrate the two strands even at the interpretation stage in the research process, the outcome of the MMR study will reflect an expansion purpose. This happens frequently, particularly with novice researchers who may not yet be able to focus on and see the forest rather than the trees. As discussed in Chapter 3, some MMR researchers (e.g. Bazeley, 2012) are doubtful about recognizing studies with expansion purpose as MMR. This is mainly because the researcher does not attempt to integrate the two strands at any stage in the research process except that two mini projects are included in a research report. In terms of challenge, expansion purpose poses the slightest challenge to researchers. This has resulted in a high prevalence rate of purported MMR studies with expansion purpose in different disciplines including language teaching and learning (Riazi & Candlin, 2014). The high prevalence rate of purported MMR studies with expansion purpose could be related to the ease of conducting and reporting this type of study as well as a misconstruing of the true nature of MMR.

Complementarity purpose

The most challenging form of simultaneous design would be to aim for complementarity purpose (Riazi, 2016b; Riazi and Candlin, 2014). As discussed in Chapter 3, to achieve a complementarity purpose, researchers need to conceptualize research problems as multi-dimensional and/or multi-layered. Each dimension or layer may require a certain methodological approach so that when the outcomes are put together a more comprehensive explanation of the research problem can be provided. As discussed in Chapter 3, MMR studies with complementarity purpose are highly demanding and challenging for researchers in terms of theoretical orientation and methodological expertise. This has resulted in researchers pursuing complementarity purpose far less frequently, and it generally being conducted only by more experienced researchers. Designing and conducting MMR studies with complementarity purpose requires some levels of innovation: at the conceptualization stage (definition of the construct of the study as multi-dimensional) and at the methodological and inferential stages in the research process.

Development purpose

All sequential designs suggested by Morse could be related to development purpose. This can be justified in light of the basic characteristic of sequential order in MMR studies. In sequential designs, the argument is that a subsequent strand is developed on the basis of the results achieved from a previous strand. The next strand in an MMR study with development purpose cannot be conducted unless the previous strand is completed so that results are used to design the next strand. As Table 4.1 illustrates, there are six potential scenarios in which an MMR study may be designed with a development purpose. These six design structures depend on the weight and level of emphasis placed on each of the two strands.

An example of a sequential design can be represented by QUAN → QUAL, in which the two strands are of equal emphasis. This design may be used to investigate the effect of instruction on student learning. In the quantitative strand, the researcher may collect student performances on different tests during and after the course of instruction. Quantitative analysis of the test scores may help the researcher to provide an explanation of the effect of instruction on student learning. To provide a more in-depth explanation of how student learning might be affected by instruction, the researcher may use the findings from the quantitative strand to design and conduct a qualitative study. For example, the researcher could use critical case sampling (Riazi, 2016a) and conduct a critical case analysis to provide more in-depth explanations about how instruction might affect student learning. The critical case sampling procedure would allow the researcher to choose high, low and intermediate performers to reflect on and elaborate on their experiences of learning from instruction. Unless the first quantitative strand is completed and student test scores are identified, it is not possible to design and conduct the second qualitative strand.

Initiation purpose

Initiation purpose is not suggested in Table 4.1 as one of the potential purposes that could be linked with Morse's design structures. As discussed in Chapter 3, there might be two scenarios leading researchers to follow an initiation purpose. The first is when researchers are able to attribute the observed contradictions and paradoxes in the reported findings on a particular topic to methodological approaches. For example, based on a literature review on motivation for learning a foreign language, a researcher may notice paradoxes in the reported findings from quantitatively and qualitatively oriented research studies. The researcher may then design an MMR study with both quantitative and qualitative strands to provide a richer and fuller explanation of the motivation for learning a foreign language.

The second scenario would be when the researcher starts off with either a quantitative or a qualitative strand, or even a mixed methods design, but obtains some contradictory findings. The researcher may then design a more sophisticated MMR study to provide further and nuanced explanations of the observed contradictions. In the first scenario, the initiation purpose was planned and based on the observed contradictions in the literature, while in the second scenario it was emergent based on the observed paradoxes from a study in progress. In neither of these cases might it be possible to represent initiation purpose using the design notation system suggested by Morse.

One possible variation would be to combine development and initiation purposes and suggest a design such as QUAN # QUAL $\rightarrow$ MMR to represent the first scenario discussed above. It can be implied from this design structure that the findings from quantitative and qualitative studies were contradictory and led the researcher to develop an MMR study to address the observed paradoxes in a more sophisticated MMR study.

The next design typology to be discussed is that of Teddlie and Tashakkori (2006, 2009), who used the method-strand criterion to classify MMR studies.

Teddlie and Tashakkori's design typology

Using their extensive theoretical and practical experiences as well as the rich background literature on MMR, Teddlie and Tashakkori provided another design typology in 2006 and 2009. Their typology included a matrix of methods and strands resulting in five design typologies: concurrent (parallel), sequential, conversion, fully integrated and multilevel. Teddlie and Tashakkori used the terms 'concurrent' and 'parallel' interchangeably. Morse (1991, 2003) used 'simultaneous', while Creswell and Plano Clark (2007) used 'concurrent'. Teddlie and Tashakkori (2009) contended that they used parallel since simultaneous and concurrent imply that the two strands in an MMR study are conducted at the same time while this may not be the case in many studies. They found parallel to be more inclusive than either of the two terms used by Morse and Creswell and Plano Clark, and defined it to apply to the strands in an MMR study that are conducted 'either simultaneously or with some time lapse' (p. 151). The criterion used in this book to distinguish between simultaneous (concurrent) and sequential is whether the two strands are independently conducted or one strand is built on the other.

Teddlie and Tashakkori explained that their design typology was based on the three key criteria of (1) number of strands in the research design, (2) type of implementation process, and (3) stage of integration. They intended to provide an alternative to Greene *et al.*'s framework, and considered also 'methodological triangulation' as the main goal underlying their design typology, as did Morse. They argued that one of the advantages of MMR is that it enables researchers to simultaneously ask both confirmatory and exploratory questions and thus pursue both theory verification and theory generation goals in one study.

The concept of 'methodological triangulation' suggested by Morse is more clearly elaborated in Teddlie and Tashakkori's design typology. In fact, they use the theoretical (methodological) discussion of research paradigms to explain methodological triangulation. This is indeed surprising because of the predominantly pragmatic orientation of these two researchers, as discussed in Chapter 2. Tashakkori and Teddlie (Morse, 2003) started off with a call to put aside the theoretical (methodological) discussion of research paradigms and a recommendation to stick to a pragmatic approach of using research methods to answer specific research questions.

The five MMR designs in Teddlie and Tashakkori's (2006) typology are explained and discussed in the following sections.

Concurrent designs

Teddlie and Tashakkori's (2006) explanation of concurrent designs is similar to Morse's (1991, 2003) simultaneous designs. They elaborated that in concurrent designs there are at least two independent strands, one with qualitative research questions and the other with quantitative research questions. Concurrent mixed designs therefore allow researchers to ask and answer confirmatory questions (usually through the quantitative strand) and exploratory questions (usually through the qualitative strand). To answer the research questions, researchers collect and analyze appropriate data using the standards of each methodological approach. The integration of the two strands in concurrent designs happens at the inferential stage where the researcher synthesizes the inferences made on the basis of the results from each strand to form a more comprehensive meta-inference that could provide a fuller explanation about the research problem.

Teddlie and Tashakkori suggested that a concurrent mixed design such as QUAN + QUAL enables researchers to include both methodological approaches in a single MMR study. In other words, different concurrent designs, as presented in Table 4.1, allow researchers to simultaneously ask exploratory and confirmatory questions about a research phenomenon. Teddlie and Tashakkori provided a sample study (Lopez & Tashakkori, 2006) with a concurrent mixed design. In that study, Lopez and Tashakkori investigated 'the effects of two types of bilingual education programs on attitudes and academic achievement of fifth-grade students' (p. 20). However, this exemplar study is more in line with the triangulation purpose suggested by Greene *et al.* (1989) than that of methodological triangulation suggested by Teddlie and Tashakkori as discussed above.

In Lopez and Tashakkori, the quantitative strand of the study 'included standardized achievement test scores in various academic subjects, as well as linguistic competence in English and Spanish' (p. 20). In addition, the researchers utilized a questionnaire with a Likert-type scale to measure participants' self-perceptions and self-beliefs in relation to bilingualism. The qualitative strand consisted of interviews with a randomly selected sample of 32 participants in the two bilingual programmes. Each strand was conducted and reported independently and conclusions were drawn on the basis of data analysis in each strand. The integration of the two strands was made at the inferential stage where 'findings of the two studies were integrated by (a) comparing and contrasting the conclusions, and (b) trying to construct a more comprehensive understanding of how the two programs impacted the children' (p. 21).

As the above discussion shows, sometimes the concepts and terms used do not reflect what exactly happened in practice. Put differently, there are usually discrepancies between theory and practice. Teddlie and Tashakkori used 'methodological triangulation', which covers a broader scope than the narrow triangulation purpose, as the underlying criterion for their design typology. Nevertheless, in practice, the example they provided for a concurrent design represented the narrower definition of triangulation, the one suggested by Greene *et al.* as one of the purposes for mixing methods from the two research approaches.

Sequential designs

Teddlie and Tashakkori's definition of sequential designs accords with Greene *et al.*'s (1989) definition of development purpose and follows

Morse's (1991) notation system. They considered sequential designs to comprise at least two strands (one quantitative and one qualitative) to occur chronologically, such as QUAL → QUAN. All the six sequential designs presented in Table 4.1 represent Teddlie and Tashakkori's definition of sequential designs. They elaborated that in sequential designs, the results of the first strand are used to develop the next strand. However, they considered that methodological triangulation (mixing exploratory and confirmatory roles) could also be realized in sequential designs. As such, they avoided using Greene *et al.*'s concept of 'development' as the main purpose in sequential designs.

Conversion designs

Conversion designs are one of the design structures suggested by Teddlie and Tashakkori (2006, 2009). In conversion designs, data collected through one methodological approach (quantitative or qualitative) are transformed into another type for further analysis using qualitizing and quantitizing procedures. It can be said, therefore, that a mono-strand research is converted to a multi-strand research through data transformation. Conversion designs are represented in Figure 4.1.

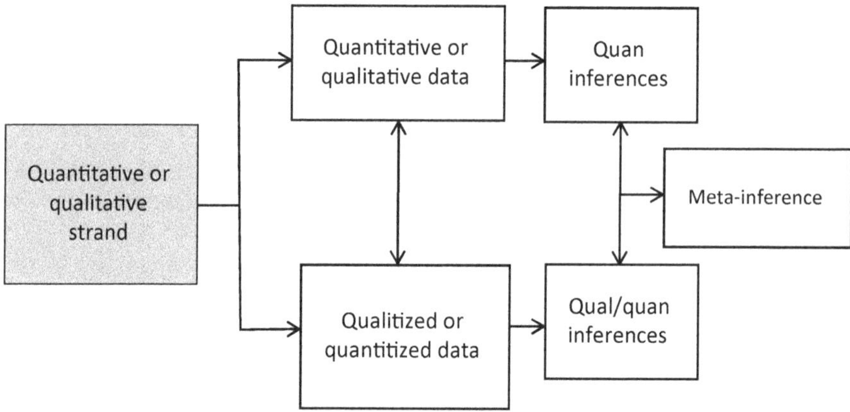

Figure 4.1 Conversion designs

Data conversion or transformation occurs when quantitative numerical data are converted into narrative data or qualitative narrative data are converted into numerical data for appropriate analysis (Teddlie & Tashakkori, 2009). Qualitizing and quantitizing, therefore, refer to the process of data conversion and analysis. It is usually easier to quantitize than to qualitize data. For example, researchers can quantitize qualitative data collected through interviews by searching for and counting certain key words or phrases in the data and preparing frequencies and/or percentages of these key terms, then subjecting the observed frequencies to an appropriate statistical analysis such as Chi-square. However, it might not be as easy and straightforward to qualitize quantitative data.

One technique for qualitizing quantitative data is to form narrative profiles (Tashakkori & Teddlie, 1998; Teddlie & Tashakkori, 2009). A narrative profile is to form categories of participants based on their test scores or their responses to questionnaires. Usually, these narrative profiles are formed using a norm or a standard. For instance, based on the mean of a standardized test of language proficiency, participants in a study may be categorized as high-, low- and intermediate-proficiency language learners. Or based on participants' responses to a questionnaire on motivation for learning a foreign language, they may be categorized as highly motivated, poorly motivated and moderately motivated. These categories or profiles are then used for further analysis. It can be said that conversion designs are particular forms of concurrent designs.

Fully integrated designs

The fourth type of MMR design suggested by Teddlie and Tashakkori is fully integrated designs. They called it fully integrated because they believed in this family of designs – integration of the two research approaches occurs at all stages in the research process. They therefore used characteristics such as interactive, dynamic and reciprocal to describe this family of designs. In fully integrated designs, the research problem needs to be conceptualized as multi-layered or multi-dimensional. The multi-layered conceptualization of the research problem will then lead to the formulation of reciprocal quantitatively and qualitatively oriented research questions, which in turn will lead to interactive quantitative and qualitative data and analysis. The outcomes of the interactive data analysis give researchers the opportunity to produce integrative inferences about the research problem. Figure 4.2 presents a schematic diagram for fully integrated designs.

Different strands involved in a fully integrated study can be carried out simultaneously, sequentially or as a combination of both. In terms of purpose, fully integrated designs follow a complementarity purpose by nature given the multi-dimensional construct of the study. They may, however, embrace other purposes, such as development if one strand is built on the results of another, triangulation or initiation.

As Figure 4.2 illustrates, ultimately inferences drawn from the quantitative and qualitative data and analysis will be mixed to produce

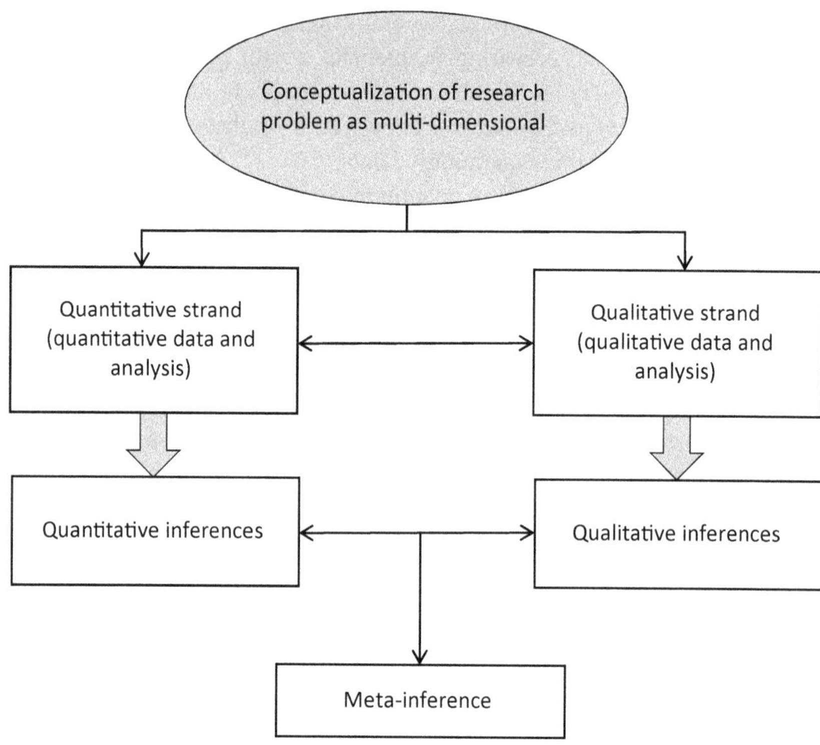

Figure 4.2 Fully integrated designs

meta-inferences that can provide a more comprehensive understanding of the research problem.

Multilevel designs

Multilevel mixed designs are, in fact, an example of fully integrated designs. This design family is used when researchers intend to investigate issues related to hierarchical social organizations such as schools, universities and hospitals. The designs can be parallel (simultaneous), in which the two or more strands are conducted independently. Or they may be sequential, where one or more strands might be developed based on the results from other strands. It is even possible to have a multilevel design with both simultaneous and sequential components. They are called multilevel because different levels of a social institution are addressed and included in the study.

An example of a multilevel MMR design would be when researchers investigate language policy and practice in a university or several universities.

Four different organizational levels can be defined in each university relating to language policy and practice, including the management, the academic staff, the administration and the students. Both quantitative and qualitative data regarding language policy and practice can be collected and analyzed as related to each of the four levels. For example, quantitative data may include students' language proficiency scores, questionnaire surveys administered to both staff and students, and records of language facilities and resources available to students. Qualitative data may include interviews with the management and administrative bodies in addition to a content analysis of policy documents.

As indicated above, quantitative and qualitative strands might be conducted simultaneously and independently, or one may be built based on the results obtained from the other. It is even possible that some phases of data collection are conducted independently, while other phases are conducted sequentially. An imaginary multilevel mixed design can be represented as (QUAL+QUAN) $\rightarrow$ QUAN $\rightarrow$ QUAL. In the above example, through a qualitative strand, policy documents might be analyzed and interviews conducted with the management and the administrative bodies while records of students' language proficiency scores and language facilities and resources (QUAN) are also collected. Based on the results of the qualitative strand, a questionnaire can be developed with two versions, to be administered to the staff and to students. Results of the quantitative analysis of the questionnaires may then be used to identify and conduct interviews with selected groups of staff and students.

The units of analysis in multilevel mixed designs are different levels of the social organization from which both quantitative and qualitative data may be collected through different research methods. As indicated in the above example, both types of data may be collected and then analyzed at each level in the social institution to answer different research questions.

Depending on the purpose and research questions of a multilevel mixed design study, quantitative and qualitative inferences can be made from the quantitative and qualitative data analysis. In addition, the two types of inferences can be integrated to make meta-inferences and provide more comprehensive explanations about the research problem.

How can multilevel designs be related to MMR purposes suggested by Greene *et al.* (1989)? Multilevel designs lend themselves to four MMR purposes: triangulation, development, complementarity and initiation. Findings from different data sources and different methods may be cross-validated in multilevel designs if convergence is observed. Otherwise, if any contradictions are observed in the findings, an MMR strand could be initiated corresponding to both development and initiation purposes. In addition, as indicated in the above example, the multilevel nature of these designs represents a multi-dimensional conceptualization of the construct of the study, thus representing a complementarity purpose. It goes without saying, then, that designing and conducting a multilevel MMR study is highly demanding and challenging in terms of theoretical knowledge and research expertise, and in need of the collaboration of a team of researchers. Nevertheless, the complexity of the design opens a window for the innovativeness of the design.

Creswell and Plano Clark's design typology

Creswell and Plano Clark (2007, 2011) used the four criteria of implementation or time order, strand priority or emphasis, stage of integration and theoretical perspective, and introduced six mixed designs. These designs have been described in the authors' other publications, including Creswell (2015). These six mixed designs include three concurrent and three sequential designs as follows.

1. Concurrent triangulation.
2. Concurrent nested.
3. Concurrent transformative.
4. Sequential explanatory.
5. Sequential exploratory.
6. Sequential transformative.

The terms 'concurrent' and 'sequential' are used by Creswell and Plano Clark in the same sense as used by Morse and Teddlie and Tashakkori.

Regarding implementation or the time order criterion, concurrent applies to those MMR studies in which the two strands are conducted simultaneously and independent of each other. Sequential applies to those MMR studies with a chronological order, that is, one strand is built on the basis of the results obtained from another strand. Considering strand priority or level of emphasis, all priority variations presented in Table 4.1 also hold true in Creswell *et al.*'s (2003) design typology. That is, the two strands can be of equal weight, or one strand may receive more emphasis in any single design. Concerning the integration criterion, Creswell *et al.* believed that in four of the six suggested designs (all the sequential designs and concurrent triangulation), integration happens at the interpretation stage. In the concurrent nested design, integration occurs at the data analysis stage, and in the concurrent transformative design usually at the data analysis stage, but can also be during the interpretation stage. Finally, regarding the theoretical perspective criterion, this certainly exists in transformative (concurrent and sequential) designs, but may be present or not in other designs.

Triangulation is used in its narrow definition, that is, the purpose defined by Greene *et al.* (1989). Creswell and his colleagues, however, used some new terms to define concurrent and sequential designs. These supplementary terms included 'nested', 'transformative', 'explanatory' and 'exploratory'. Concurrent nested designs are used when one of the two strands is dominant (priority criterion) and the other strand is implemented within the dominant strand for further elaborations on the results obtained from the dominant strand. For example, in an MMR study, the dominant strand might be an experimental design (QUAN); however, interviews may be conducted with a sub-sample of participants, as they are involved in the experiment to reflect on their experiences. Transformative is used by Creswell *et al.* (2003) to refer to the particular research orientation or worldview presented by Mertens (see references and discussions in Chapter 2).

Creswell *et al.* (2003) used the terms 'explanatory' and 'exploratory' in their original meanings, as discussed in Chapter 1. In sequential explanatory designs, usually a quantitative strand is done using survey questionnaires. Once the data are collected and analyzed and certain categories are developed, a sub-sample of the participants will be interviewed to elaborate on the patterns of their responses as were revealed by the quantitative analysis. The qualitative data (elaborations) are analyzed and results are used by the researcher to explain the observed patterns in participants' responses. In sequential exploratory designs, the purpose is to explore different aspects of a construct and how these different aspects might be related to each other. In its simplest form, a sequential exploratory design will include a small-scale qualitative strand in which data collected from a small sample will be analyzed and results will be used to design a second quantitative strand. This design is very common in constructing and validating new questionnaires and inventories.

Concurrent designs suggested by Creswell *et al.* (2003) can pursue any of the four purposes suggested by Greene *et al.*: triangulation, complementarity, expansion or initiation. The potential purpose that could be achieved through concurrent designs will depend on how the research problem is conceptualized, how the study is implemented, how different stages in the process of research emerge, and indeed how the researcher manages the whole process. Sequential designs, meanwhile, lend themselves absolutely to development purpose given the chronological order between the strands, but also to initiation purpose depending on the results of data analysis and the researcher's capabilities to build on contradictory findings from data analysis.

Seeing the forest and the trees

Four main typologies of MMR studies were presented and discussed in Chapters 3 and 4. The first typology was Greene *et al.*'s (1989) framework, which focused on the purpose for which MMR researchers might mix quantitative and qualitative methods. The other three typologies – those of Morse (1991, 2003), Teddlie and Tashakkori (2006, 2009), and Creswell (2015) and Creswell and Plano Clark (2011) – were initiated to provide an alternative to Greene *et al.*'s framework to account for some of the controversies over the purpose framework as well as for some of the nuances of mixed designs that were absent in Greene *et al.*'s earlier framework. As such, and as could be seen from the above discussions, these three typologies had a lot more in common. In fact, it can be said that Morse's design typology was built on and expanded by Teddlie and Tashakkori on the one hand, and Creswell and his colleagues on the other. The variety of typologies presented by different MMR researchers may confuse readers of MMR studies as well as prospective MMR researchers. It would therefore be very helpful if the purpose and design typologies were put together so that readers and future researchers could make better sense of how purposes for mixing methods and design typologies might be related. Table 4.2 presents a possible matrix of purpose-design based on the four typologies presented and discussed in these two chapters.

Table 4.2 The purpose-design matrix

	Concurrent (parallel)	*Sequential*	*Conversion*	*Fully integrated (e.g. multilevel)*
Triangulation	✓			
Complementarity	✓			✓
Initiation		✓		✓
Development		✓		
Expansion	✓		✓	

Multilevel design suggested by Teddlie and Tashakkori is not included in Table 4.2 because, as discussed before, it is in fact an example of a fully integrated design. The relationship between purpose and design as suggested in the table is based on the discussions of the four typologies as presented in Chapters 3 and 4 and may have exceptions in practice. However, based on the features of each purpose and design, the matrix presents most potential links. For example, if a researcher decides to design and conduct an MMR study to explain the contradictions reported or observed in the findings, they will most probably need to design a sequential MMR study. The reported or observed paradoxes will be used to design a more comprehensive multi-strand MMR study that could shed more light on and unfold the reported or observed contradictions. If a researcher decides to design and conduct a fully integrated MMR study, they need to know that can be achieved through complementarity and initiation purposes. It would be hard for other purposes to lend themselves to a fully integrated design. This is mainly because the level of theoretical/conceptual and methodological sophistication involved in designing and conducting studies with complementarity and initiation purposes would require researchers to integrate different strands and their related phases of data collection and analysis at different stages in the research process.

Further clarifications on purpose/design typologies

The presentation and discussion of the four typologies related to the purposes and designs of MMR studies in Chapters 3 and 4 have revealed some ambiguities in the use of terminology and concepts. These ambiguities include the use of:

- triangulation in narrow and broad senses;
- various terms to explain MMR design variations.

It therefore proves useful to elaborate on these ambiguities and to provide further clarification for readers. Each of these ambiguities will thus be discussed in the last section of this chapter.

Triangulation in narrow and broad senses

As discussed in Chapter 3, triangulation had precedents in both quantitative and qualitative research and was also being applied and used in MMR. It was noted that triangulation is used in two senses in the MMR literature, a narrow sense and a broad sense. The narrow sense of the term was used by Greene *et al.* (1989) to identify those MMR studies in which findings achieved from one or more methods in one strand of the study (quantitative, for example) could be corroborated with findings obtained from one or more methods in another strand (qualitative, for example). This meaning of triangulation was based on two of the four types or methods suggested by Denzin (1978, 1988) for achieving triangulation and thus enhancing credibility of research. These two methods were triangulation through data sources and triangulation through methods. It was also argued that another type of triangulation suggested by Denzin, investigator triangulation, could be realized in MMR studies given that either two investigators with different methodological perspectives collaborate or one researcher applies two methodological perspectives in the two strands. Denzin (2012), however, criticized the extrapolation of his triangulation framework to MMR, arguing that by triangulation he meant different data sources and methods from qualitative approaches, and not data and methods from different, if not opposing, quantitative and qualitative approaches.

Howe's (2012) discussion of triangulation as an umbrella term, and Morse (1991, 2003) and Teddlie and Tashakkori's (2006, 2009) discussion of methodological triangulation as presented in this chapter, have informed alternative MMR design typologies. These researchers recognized that the two or more strands in MMR studies draw on different theoretical (methodological) orientations. Quantitative methods are based on a (post)positivist worldview, whereas qualitative methods are based on constructivist perspectives, using their own rationalization for what can be researched, how it can be researched and what can be known about the object of research, as discussed in Chapter 1. Generally, a quantitatively oriented methodology aims for confirmatory research. A qualitatively oriented methodology, meanwhile, aims for exploratory research. MMR researchers can, therefore, argue for methodological triangulation if they are able to show how these two methodological approaches have helped them in conceptualizing the research problem, making sense of their data and interpreting findings in an integrative way to provide a fuller understanding of the research phenomenon.

Various terms to explain MMR design variations

As discussed in this chapter, different MMR researchers have used different terms to explain MMR design variations, resulting in some levels of ambiguity. These terms and their use by MMR researchers will be explained in this section to reduce any ambiguities.

One of the distinctions made in design typologies is when the two strands are implemented simultaneously or sequentially. It is conceivable when the term 'sequential' is used because it conveys chronological order, and this is exactly what happens in sequential designs. In all sequential designs with, for example, two strands, the second strand is built on the results obtained from the first strand, resulting in MMR studies with development purpose. It is therefore not possible to design and implement the second strand in MMR studies with development purposes unless the first strand is completed and results are obtained. The best example of a sequential design is when results obtained from the data analysis in a qualitative strand are used to design and implement a subsequent quantitative strand, thus a design representation such as QUAL → QUAN and its variations in terms of the level of emphasis on each strand.

The issue is not so clear when it comes to simultaneous or concurrent designs, however, when the two strands are used for triangulation, complementarity or expansion purposes. The initial understanding was that the two strands are conducted at the same time. Nevertheless, as Teddlie and Tashakkori (2009) noted, this might not be the case in many MMR studies where the two strands may be completed with time lapses. Teddlie and Tashakkori therefore suggested the term 'parallel' for simultaneous and concurrent to avoid this ambiguity. The criterion used and advocated in this book is that simultaneous and concurrent is used when the two strands are conducted independently to differentiate it from sequential. The dependent/ independent criterion might be a more useful approach because this accords with the literature on MMR. In addition, the term 'parallel' might convey 'expansion' purpose because in MMR studies with an expansion purpose, the two strands are designed and implemented in parallel, resulting in two separate projects with no genuine integrations at different stages in the research process.

The other noted ambiguity is Teddlie and Tashakkori's (2006, 2009) use of 'multilevel' as a distinct design typology. Based on their description and explanation of a multilevel study, it was argued that this design mostly represents an example of a fully integrated MMR design rather than an independent design. The advantage of a multilevel MMR study is that it lends itself to a fully integrated design since the researcher needs to conceptualize the research phenomenon as multi-dimensional and integrate different data sources and levels of analyses to provide a fuller understanding of it.

Finally, Creswell and his colleagues have used 'transformative' to describe design concurrent and sequential transformative studies. As explained and discussed in Chapter 2, transformative or critical theory is one of the underlying worldviews for MMR along with other worldviews such as pragmatism and critical realism. It is possible to design and implement different types of MMR designs within any of the worldviews. For example, it is possible to design and implement concurrent and sequential designs within a pragmatist worldview, as it is possible to do so within a transformative worldview. Including the underlying philosophies or worldviews to define design structures may therefore cause unnecessary complexity and ambiguity.

Based on the above reflections, it is possible to summarize the two design typologies suggested by Teddlie and Tashakkori and Creswell and Plano Clark in Table 4.3.

Table 4.3 A summary of design typologies and potential purposes

	Time order	
	Concurrent (independent)	Sequential (dependent)
Fully integrated	Complementarity, multilevel	Initiation
Not fully integrated	Triangulation, expansion, conversion	Development, explanatory, exploratory

Hashemi (2012) and Hashemi and Babaii (2013) found that concurrent designs were used more frequently (71.71%) than sequential designs (24.88%) in 205 MMR articles they surveyed in seven applied linguistics journals. In addition, they found that concurrent designs with a triangulation purpose formed a high percentage (66.34%) among the whole number of articles. They noted that other categories did not appear to be very common in applied linguistics research.

In addition, the analysis of the MMR articles indicated that applied linguistics researchers did not show a tendency towards using fully integrated designs that involve mixing the two methodological approaches at all levels in the research process. Further elaborations on MMR studies in terms of their purpose, design and inferences made from quantitative and qualitative data analysis will be presented in the next section of the book (Part Three), where published MMR studies will be discussed.

References

Bazeley, P. (2012). Integrative analysis strategies for mixed data sources. *American Behavioral Scientist, 56*(6), 814–828.

Creswell, J.W. (2015). *A concise introduction to mixed methods research*. Thousand Oaks, CA: Sage.

Creswell, J.W. & Plano Clark, V. (2007). *Designing and conducting mixed methods research*. Thousand Oaks, CA: Sage.

Creswell, J.W. & Plano Clark, V. (2011). *Designing and conducting mixed methods research* (2nd ed.). Thousand Oaks, CA: Sage.

Creswell, J.W., Plano Clark, V.L., Gutmann, M.L. & Hanson, W.E. (2003). Advanced mixed methods research designs. In A. Tashakkori & C. Teddlie (Eds.), *Handbook of mixed methods in social and behavioral research* (pp. 209–240). Thousand Oaks, CA: Sage.

Denzin, N.K. (1978). *Sociological methods*. New York: McGraw-Hill.

Denzin, N.K. (1988). Triangulation. In J.P. Keeves (Ed.), *Educational research, methodology, and measurement: An international handbook* (pp. 51–113). Oxford: Pergamon Press.

Denzin, N.K. (2012). Triangulation 2.0. *Journal of Mixed Methods Research, 6*(2), 80–88.

Greene, J.C., Caracelli, V.J. & Graham, W.F. (1989). Toward a conceptual framework for mixed-method evaluation designs. *Educational Evaluation and Policy Analysis, 11*(3), 255–274.

Hashemi, M.R. (2012). Reflections on mixing methods in applied linguistics research. *Applied Linguistics, 33*, 206–212.

Hashemi, M.R. & Babaii, E. (2013). Mixed methods research: Toward new research designs in applied linguistics. *The Modern Language Journal, 97*(4), 828–852.

Howe, K.R. (2012). Mixed methods, triangulation, and causal explanation. *Journal of Mixed Methods Research, 6*(2) 89–96.

Lopez, M. & Tashakkori, A. (2006). Differential outcomes of TWBE and TBE on ELLs at different entry levels. *Bilingual Research Journal, 30*(1), 81–103.

Mathison, S. (1988). Why triangulate? *Educational Researcher, 17*, 13–17.

Morgan, D.L. (1998). Practical strategies for combining qualitative and quantitative methods: Applications to health research. *Qualitative Health Research, 8*(3), 362–376.

Morse, J.M. (1991). Approaches to qualitative-quantitative methodological triangulation. *Nursing Research, 40*, 120–123.

Morse, J.M. (2003). Principles of mixed methods and multimethod research design. In A. Tashakkori & C. Teddlie (Eds.), *Handbook of mixed methods in social and behavioural research* (pp. 189–208). Thousand Oaks, CA: Sage.

Riazi, A.M. (2016a). *The Routledge Encyclopedia of Research Methods in Applied Linguistics: Quantitative, qualitative, and mixed-methods research.* London: Routledge.

Riazi, A.M. (2016b). Innovative mixed-methods research (IMMR): Moving beyond design technicalities to epistemological and methodological realisations. *Applied Linguistics*, 37(1), 33–49.

Riazi, A.M. & Candlin, C.N. (2014). Mixed-methods research in language teaching and learning: Opportunities, issues and challenges. *Language Teaching, 47*, 135–173.

Tashakkori, A. & Teddlie, C. (1998). *Mixed methodology: Combining qualitative and quantitative approaches.* Thousand Oaks, CA: Sage.

Teddlie, C. & Tashakkori, A. (2006). A general typology of research designs featuring mixed methods. *Research in the Schools, 13*(1), 12–28.

Teddlie, C. & Tashakkori, A. (2009). *Foundations of mixed methods research: Integrating quantitative and qualitative approaches in the social and behavioural sciences.* Thousand Oaks, CA: Sage.

5 Research Questions, Sampling Procedures and Data Collection Strategies

This chapter will discuss:
- research questions:
  - in quantitative, qualitative and MMR
  - as related to concurrent and sequential designs
  - in different worldviews underlying MMR;
- MMR sampling procedure typologies;
- data collection strategies:
  - within- and between-strategies
  - instruments of data collection
  - ethical considerations.

Introduction

This chapter is composed of three sections: research questions, typologies of sampling procedures and data collection strategies. In the first section, the role of research questions in the research process will be examined. Then, to provide a context for how to write MMR questions, the nature of research questions in quantitative and qualitative research will be considered. Afterwards, formulating research questions in light of purpose and design of the study will be discussed. An important issue is how different MMR underlying worldviews consider the status of research questions in the research process. The discussion of this link is presented in the final part of the first section. In the second section, two typologies of MMR sampling procedures will be presented and discussed: those of Onwuegbuzie and Collins (2007) and Teddlie and Yu (2007). In the third section of the chapter, data collection strategies, including within- and between-strategies, instruments of data collection and ethical considerations, will be discussed. Data analysis procedures and making inferences will be considered in the next chapter.

The role of research questions in the research process

Research questions play a significant mediatory role in the research process. They directly link the conceptual stage with the methodological stage and indirectly act as a catalyst for inferences to be related to the conceptual stage, as presented in Figure 5.1.

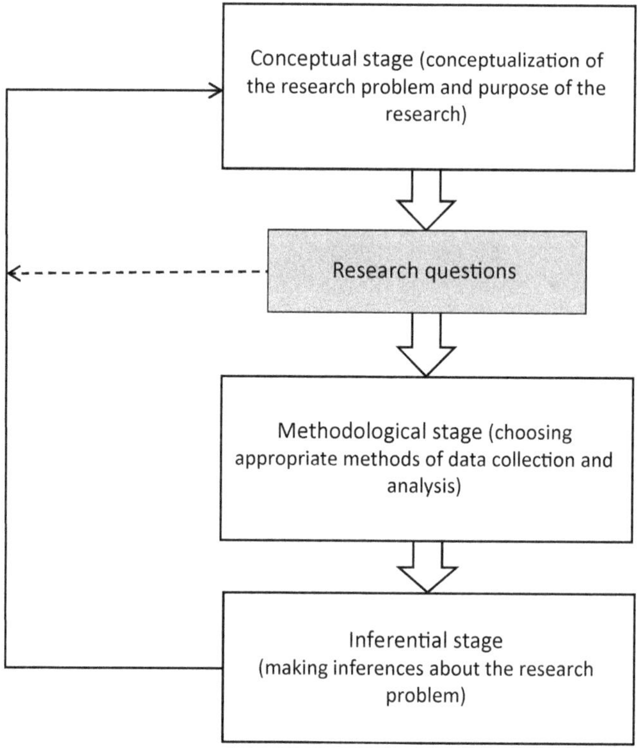

Figure 5.1 The role of research questions in the research process

As such, research questions are considered to have a 'pivotal role' in making decisions about 'research design and methods' in order to be answered (Bryman, 2007, p. 6). In addition, when a study is completed and reported, research questions 'serve as signposts for the reader, foreshadowing the specific details of the study' (Onwuegbuzie & Leech, 2006, p. 478). According to Onwuegbuzie and Leech (2006), research questions therefore have several roles in the planning, implementation and reporting of research. Some of these roles include:

- delimiting the study, revealing its boundaries;
- providing a framework for conducting the study, giving direction and coherence to the study;
- keeping the research and the researcher focused throughout the study;
- determining the type of data and analysis required to answer the questions.

Based on their pivotal role in the research process, it can be said that research questions have both backward and forward regulatory functions in the whole process. As Figure 5.1 shows, they are derived from the conceptual stage, meaning that researchers need to narrow down their conceptualization of the research problem into rather more tangible and specific research questions that could be answered by subsequent steps of data collection and analysis. Once they are formulated, research questions delineate the boundaries of the study and determine its scope. They will also provide a framework for making decisions about the design and methods of data collection and analysis. Blaikie (2000) highlighted the forward function of research questions in the research process by saying: 'Establishing research questions makes it possible to select research strategies and methods with confidence. In other words, a research project is built on the foundation of research questions' (p. 58).

Notwithstanding the importance of research questions in the research process, Onwuegbuzie and Leech (2006, p. 477) remark: 'It is surprising that an extensive review of the literature revealed no guidance as to how to write research questions specifically in mixed methods studies.' They refer to the leading textbook in mixed methods research produced by Tashakkori and Teddlie (2003), *Handbook of mixed methods in social and behavioural research*, and contend that while virtually all aspects of inquiry are included in the book, it 'does not provide any significant discussion of research questions in mixed methods research' (p. 477). There is, indeed, a chapter on research questions in Tashakkori and Teddlie's 2010 edition.

This chapter addresses this important topic. A brief discussion of research questions in quantitative and qualitative research will provide a context for the subsequent discussion of how to formulate MMR research questions.

Research questions in quantitative research

Quantitative research, as discussed in the first chapter, is generally confirmatory, seeking evidence to approve or reject hypotheses related to a theory. As such, quantitative research questions are very specific and interrogate the relationship between variables included in a study. Johnson and Christensen (2012) classify quantitative research questions as 'descriptive', 'predictive' and 'causal' questions. They explain that descriptive questions seek answers to 'How much?', 'How often?' or 'What changes over time or over different situations?' questions, while 'predictive questions ask whether one or more variables can be used to predict some future outcome' (Johnson & Christensen, 2012, pp. 74–75). Causal questions, they further explain, compare the outcomes of two groups when an independent variable is manipulated and used in the two experimental and control groups.

Onwuegbuzie and Leech (2006) as well as Creswell (2014) also categorize quantitative research questions into 'descriptive', 'comparative' and 'relationship' questions. They explain that descriptive research questions seek to quantify participants' responses to some questions and are mostly used in survey research. In survey research, a questionnaire designed to elicit information about a particular construct (for example, motivation, attitude, strategies, learning preference style, etc.) is administered to a sample selected from a target population and participants' responses are quantified and then analyzed using statistical analysis procedures. In the majority of survey studies, the questionnaire items use a Likert-type scale and participants' responses to these items are then analyzed through parametric or non-parametric statistical tests of significance (Riazi, 2016) to make generalizations about the target population. Each item in a questionnaire acts as a variable, so it is possible to seek relationships between different variables as well as between variables and participants' demographic characteristics, such as their gender, age range, level of education and so on, in addition to describing their responses to the questions. Through surveys, researchers are therefore able to answer both descriptive and relationship research questions.

Comparative or causal research questions, meanwhile, are formulated when researchers seek to compare two or more groups on some dependent or outcome variables. Comparative causal research questions are mostly used in experimental designs where the experimental and control groups are compared on an outcome or dependent variable. Researchers might, for example, be interested to investigate whether there is any significant difference between two groups of language learners when they are exposed to different language teaching methodologies. Any significant difference between the two groups in terms of the outcome (language learning) can be attributed to the teaching methodology.

> ## Highlights of research questions in quantitative research
>
> - Research questions are used in quantitative research for descriptive, predictive (relationship) and comparative (causal) purposes.
> - Descriptive and relationship research questions are mostly used in survey research.
> - Comparative (causal) research questions are mostly used in experimental designs.

> ## Learning task 5.1
>
> Find one or two quantitatively oriented articles. Focus on the research questions stated in the articles. Try to categorize the research questions as descriptive, comparative (causal) and predictive (seeking relationships).

Research hypothesis in quantitative research

In light of the overall confirmatory function of quantitative research, and in order that quantitative researchers are able to especially seek relationships among variables or investigate group differences, quantitative research questions are sometimes turned into research hypotheses. Research hypotheses are statements, in contrast to research questions, which express clearly how the theoretical framework of the research predicts relationships or group differences. Consequently, in quantitative research, research hypotheses usually play a more central role than research questions. Dornyei (2007) also explains that good quantitative research questions often identify the descriptive or causal relationships between variables to be examined in a study, and once they are formulated, they lead to the statement of research hypotheses.

In practice, however, in their research reports quantitative researchers may present research questions only, research hypotheses only, or both. Even when research hypotheses are not explicitly stated, researchers' interpretation of the quantitative results implicitly reveals their implied hypotheses.

As discussed in Chapter 1, quantitative research is also known as hypothetico-deductive or hypothesis testing research. Researchers follow a deductive or top-down approach by formulating research questions and/or stating research hypotheses related to the project's theoretical framework. Using sample statistics and through statistical procedures, researchers test their research hypotheses and draw inferences about the target population. Descriptive and inferential statistics are, therefore, the main analytical tools in quantitative research. While descriptive statistics such as mean and standard deviation are used to describe the sample characteristics, inferential statistics are used to check whether observations at the level of the sample could be generalized to the target population or not.

Learning task 5.2

In the quantitative articles you found, check whether there are:

1.   only research questions;
2.   only research hypotheses;
3.   both research questions and research hypotheses.

Research questions in qualitative research

Posing and formulating research questions in qualitative research is intrinsically different from doing so in quantitative research. While research questions still play a central role in qualitative research, they are modified at different stages in the research process due to the emergent nature of qualitative research. Qualitative researchers start with some initial and broad questions based on their conceptualization of the research problem and the purpose of the research. As the research progresses and different aspects of the research design are unfolded, researchers revisit their questions and may modify them to fit their data collection procedures. At the stage of analysis and interpretation of the results, qualitative researchers revisit their research questions once more and refine them in light of their results. Developing research questions is, therefore, a recursive and iterative process in qualitative research and not as streamlined as in quantitative research.

In terms of the nature of research questions, Onwuegbuzie and Leech (2006) state that qualitative research questions are posed to discover and explore a process or describe participants' experiences. Rather than seeking relationships between variables or group differences, qualitative research questions tend to ask 'what' and 'how' exploratory questions. Creswell

(2014, p. 139) classifies questions in qualitative research into 'central' and 'associated sub-questions'. The central research question is a broad question seeking an exploration of a research phenomenon or aspects of that phenomenon. This broad overarching research question can then be broken down into several sub-questions to address specific aspects of the central question. Creswell, however, recognizes the emergent nature of research questions in qualitative research and contends that the formulation of the qualitative research questions is consistent with the emerging methodology of the study.

Learning task 5.3

Find one or two qualitatively oriented articles. Focus on the research questions stated in the articles. To what extent are the questions general or specific? Are they exploratory or confirmatory?

Dornyei (2007) also explains that 'one characteristic feature of qualitative studies is their emergent nature and therefore QUAL research purposes and questions are often inevitably vaguer than their QUAN counterparts' (p. 74). He elaborates that in qualitative research, the purpose and the research questions often describe an overall specification of a situated phenomenon to be explored through qualitative procedures. The goal of qualitative research is thus to develop new insights about the research phenomenon through a theoretical explanation. In comparison with quantitative research questions, qualitative research questions therefore tend to be more general, 'often focusing on the big picture or the main processes that are thought to shape the target phenomenon' (Dornyei, 2007, p. 74).

Highlights of research questions in qualitative research

- Research questions are broader and more general than quantitative research questions.
- In line with the emergent nature of qualitative research, research questions will be modified and refined as the research progresses.
- Qualitative research questions mainly seek exploration of a research phenomenon or some aspects of the phenomenon.
- Qualitative research questions may be formulated as a central research question with some sub-questions.

Research questions in mixed methods research

In MMR, researchers may formulate independent quantitative and qualitative research questions, but they also usually pose questions that could be answered by an integration of the quantitative and qualitative results. Creswell (2014) asserts: 'A strong mixed methods study should contain the qualitative question, the quantitative question or hypothesis, and a mixed methods question' (p. 148). Creswell and Tashakkori (2007, p. 208) call the mixed question a 'hybrid' or 'integrated' question. It may indeed be a challenge for researchers to write the mixed research question.

Brannen and O'Connell (2015) also observe that when a mixed methods strategy is used, the implication is that a substantive issue will be addressed and investigated. They also contend that the use of MMR is 'justified in terms of its capacity to address different aspects of a research question' (p. 259). This capacity of MMR was especially discussed in Chapter 4 and as related to the complementarity purpose.

The challenge, however, would be how to write research questions 'we define as questions that embed quantitative and qualitative research questions' (Onwuegbuzie & Leech, 2006, p. 477). In their editorial in the *Journal of Mixed Methods Research*, Creswell and Tashakkori (2007) declare that current thinking calls for an explicit MMR question in addition to separate quantitative and qualitative questions. They propose two main strategies for this to happen as follows.

1. Writing separate quantitative and qualitative questions followed by an explicit mixed methods question, a question that represents the nature of integration.
2. Writing an overarching mixed, hybrid or integrated research question and then breaking it down into separate quantitative and qualitative sub-questions. Each of the separate quantitative and qualitative questions will be answered by the relevant strand in the study.

Creswell and Tashakkori (2007) suggest a third strategy in which research questions of each strand would be framed as each strand of a study evolves. The overarching mixed question can then be formulated based on the quantitative and qualitative questions. Creswell (2014) also suggests: 'An ideal format would be to write the questions into separate sections, such as the quantitative questions or hypotheses, the qualitative questions, and the mixed methods questions' (p. 148). Creswell explains that this format of writing research questions highlights the importance of all three sets of questions and can draw readers' attention to the separate questions as they relate to different strands and how they might then come together (or be integrated) in a mixed question.

Aside from the above strategies of writing mixed questions, Creswell (2014) also suggests that the mixed methods question can be written in a method-oriented, content-oriented or both method–content-oriented way. In the first orientation, the mixed question is written in a way that conveys the methods or procedures in a study. For example: 'Do the qualitative data help explain the results from the initial quantitative results of the study?' The second orientation considers writing the mixed question in a way that conveys the content of the study. For example: 'Do students' perceptions of barriers in their reading help explain their performance in reading tests?' The third approach would be to combine the methods and content orientation in writing the mixed question. For example: 'How do the qualitative interview data on student perceptions of barriers to reading further explain students' reading performance, as measured quantitatively through the reading tests?'

Learning task 5.4

Find one or two MMR articles in your own field.

1. Focus on the research questions stated in the articles and check whether there are separate quantitative and qualitative research questions.
2. Is there any overarching mixed question?

If yes:

3. Is the integrated mixed question method oriented, content oriented or method–content oriented?

Highlights of research questions in MMR

- Individual quantitative and qualitative research questions and then an integrated MMR question.
- An integrated MMR question that can be broken down into specific quantitative and qualitative research questions.
- Formulation of research questions as the MMR study develops.
- Method-oriented, content-oriented or both method–content-oriented mixed questions.

MMR questions and mixed designs

Creswell and Tashakkori (2007, p. 201) explain: 'The nature and form of research questions might be different in sequential and parallel or concurrent mixed methods studies.' While in concurrent designs, individual quantitative and qualitative questions are usually framed from the start, in sequential designs, 'the questions of a second (or later) strand emerge as a result of the findings of the first (or earlier) strand'. They also suggest that the two strategies of writing research questions, as presented above, are applicable to MMR studies with concurrent and sequential designs.

Research questions may thus be formulated using one of the above strategies for concurrent designs that might follow triangulation, complementarity or expansion purposes. For example, a mixed methods question in a concurrent triangulation study may ask: 'Do the quantitative results and the qualitative findings converge?' (Creswell & Plano Clark, 2007, p. 107). Creswell and Plano Clark (2007) encourage the inclusion of such mixed methods questions to make explicit what and how researchers intend to mix the quantitative and qualitative strands in a study.

Onwuegbuzie and Leech (2006), meanwhile, suggest that mixed methods research questions for sequential designs could be written based on the results of the two strands. For example, a study may address the question of reading comprehension among university students and their perceived barriers to reading. The study may start with a quantitative strand in which the results of students' performance on a reading test are collected and analyzed to answer specific quantitative questions. Students may then be divided into three groups of proficient readers, good readers and poor readers based on their scores on the test. A second strand can then be developed based on the results of the quantitative strand. Students from the three sub-groups identified in the quantitative strand would be invited to reflect on perceived barriers for their reading comprehension in order to answer specific qualitative research questions. A mixed question may be ultimately formulated along the lines of: 'What is the difference in perceived barriers which impact on reading comprehension of proficient, good and poor readers?'

Christ (2007) provides further explanations and examples of how to develop research questions in a sequential manner to represent the link between qualitative and quantitative findings. Christ's strong argument is that writing questions in sequential designs is a recursive process in which research questions of one strand initiate or shape the questions of another strand in a continuous manner. In sequential designs, research questions may be answered using both exploratory and explanatory approaches to research. However, Christ's sequential study is an example of an exploratory research.

Language teaching and learning researchers may use any of the above strategies to formulate and write mixed questions. However, an important issue to consider is the relationship between research questions and underlying MMR worldviews, as discussed in the next section.

Learning task 5.5

In the MMR articles you found, check whether they used concurrent or sequential designs. Check how the research questions were formulated in regard to the study's concurrent or sequential design.

Research questions and underlying worldviews

As discussed in Chapter 2, there are different worldviews underlying mixed methods research. These different worldviews were broadly divided into a-paradigmatic (pragmatic) and paradigmatic (transformative and critical realist) views. These worldviews significantly influence how researchers formulate their research questions in an MMR project. For novice researchers, however, these worldviews may still be in the process of formulation while the research is being designed or even undertaken.

The point of departure for pragmatist MMR researchers is to limit the theoretical paradigmatic discussion of the nature of research problems as represented in Guba and Lincoln's (1988, 2005) paradigm debates. In fact, some pragmatically oriented MMR researchers initiate and use MMR with a strong a-paradigmatic position. Rather than considering the epistemology–method relationship, as discussed in Chapter 2, they find the 'link as distracting or unnecessary and ignored it' (Teddlie & Tashakkori, 2009, p. 97). Rather, they concentrate on research questions and use whatever methods fit those research questions.

Using the metaphor of the 'dictatorship' of the research question, Tashakkori and Teddlie (1998, p. 20) argue that methodological considerations are of secondary importance 'to the research question itself, and the underlying paradigm or worldview hardly enters the picture' (p. 21). In other words, the conceptualization stage in the research process (see Figure 5.1) for pragmatist MMR researchers such as Tashakkori and Teddlie includes only the purpose and the research questions and not how the research phenomenon is theoretically conceptualized.

In line with the above argument, Collins, Onwuegbuzie and Sutton (2006, pp. 69–70) conceive MMR as comprising the following 13 distinct steps.

1. Determining the goal of the study.
2. Formulating the research objective(s).
3. Determining the research/mixing rationale.
4. Determining the research/mixing purpose.
5. Determining the research question(s).
6. Selecting the sampling design.
7. Selecting the mixed methods research design.
8. Collecting the data.
9. Analyzing the data.
10. Validating/legitimating the data.
11. Interpreting the data.
12. Writing the mixed methods research report.
13. Reformulating the research question(s).

As can be seen from the above conceptualization, the research questions originate from the goal, objectives and rationale for mixing methods rather than from a theoretical conceptualization of the research problem. Bryman (2006, p. 118) also noticed and commented on the primacy of the research questions in pragmatically oriented MMR:

> One of the chief manifestations of the pragmatic approach to the matter of mixing quantitative and qualitative research is the significance that is frequently given to the research question. This position with regard to the debate about quantitative and qualitative research prioritizes the research question and relegates epistemological and ontological debates to the sidelines. In doing so, it clears the path for research that combines quantitative and qualitative research.

Based on this primary principle, concurrent and sequential mixed designs were generated (see Chapter 4) to answer specific research questions through appropriate methods from the two methodological approaches. Creswell and Plano Clark (2011), for example, present a useful table on page 166 of their book to illustrate which research questions could be answered through which design structure using which methods.

While a pragmatically oriented approach to MMR has its own merits, in this book both a-paradigmatic and paradigmatic worldviews are acknowledged and used in the discussions of MMR. As such, it is argued in this book that some of the five purposes (for example, complementarity and initiation) identified by Greene *et al.* (1989) may lend themselves more to a paradigmatically rather than an a-paradigmatically (pragmatically) oriented perspective and research. In other words, purposes such as triangulation, development and expansion more readily lend themselves to pragmatically oriented MMR. For complementarity and initiation purposes, it seems, however, that researchers need to become involved in a theoretical discussion of how the research problem is conceptualized and how this conceptualization generates research questions that could be answered through different methodologies. The epistemology–method link (what can be known through which methodology) is thus able to address more complex social and educational problems as represented in complementarity and initiation purposes.

As discussed in Chapter 3, transformative and critical realist MMR researchers, who follow a paradigmatic approach, consider research questions to originate from the researcher's conceptualization of the research problem. Mertens (2007), for example, discusses how a researcher's transformative worldview might or should affect his or her research questions, which in turn will affect data collection and analysis procedures and the conclusions reached. She clarifies that the transformative paradigm 'provide[s] a framework that is useful for raising questions about the assumptions that underlie research and the contribution of research to enhancing human rights' (p. 224).

Similarly, from a critical realist perspective, social and educational phenomena are multi-layered and multi-dimensional. The multi-layered and/or multi-dimensional conceptualization of research phenomena will allow for research questions to originate from and address different layers and dimensions and to be answered by different methodologies, and provide a fuller understanding of the research problem when results are integrated.

Learning task 5.6

In the MMR articles you found, check whether:

1. they stated research questions based on research purpose (a-paradigmatic); or
2. they formulated research questions based on a conceptual framework of the research problem (paradigmatic).

Regardless of whether researchers formulate their research questions using a-paradigmatic or paradigmatic perspectives, once the questions are formulated the questions will determine the specific methods to be used in each strand. The methods include sampling and data collection and analysis procedures. The components of methods used in MMR studies are basically the same as those used in independent quantitative and qualitative research projects. However, some levels of interaction and integration of these components are involved in MMR projects. In the following section, the different components of methods including sampling procedures, strategies for data collection and ethical considerations will be discussed. Where relevant, how the components related to different methods in the two strands might interact or integrate with each other will be elaborated on. Data analysis procedures and drawing inferences will be discussed in the next chapter.

Sampling procedures

Since in an MMR project at least two strands, a quantitative and a qualitative, are involved, two types of sampling procedures are usually present. The first is probability sampling (Riazi, 2016), affiliated to the confirmatory role of the quantitative strand, and the second is non-probability sampling (Riazi, 2016), associated with the qualitative strand. Regardless of whether the MMR project is concurrent or sequential, some forms of the two sampling procedures are usually employed to collect the required data from the participants. However, the sampling procedures in the two strands are related to each other in MMR projects. How the two sampling procedures are used in each strand and how they may be related is discussed below with reference to prominent theorists. Recommendations will also be made regarding the most appropriate models for language teaching and learning research. The assumption is that readers are already familiar with probability quantitative and non-probability qualitative sampling procedures, so the main focus will be on mixed methods sampling procedures. That is, how probability sampling procedures such as simple random, stratified, or cluster and non-probability sampling procedures like purposive sampling are used in mixed methods projects.

Typologies of MMR sampling procedures

Onwuegbuzie and Collins (2007) use two criteria, time order between the two strands (concurrent vs. sequential) and relationship of the qualitative and quantitative samples, and suggest a typology of MMR sampling procedures. Table 5.1 presents their MMR sampling framework.

Table 5.1 Onwuegbuzie and Collins' (2007) typology of MMR sampling procedures

Time order between the two strands	*Design*	*Sampling type*
Concurrent	QUAN + QUAL	Identical
	QUAN + qual	Parallel
	QUAL + quan	Nested
	quan + qual	Multilevel
Sequential	QUAN → QUAL	
	QUAL → QUAN	
	QUAN → qual	
	QUAL → quan	
	quan → QUAL	
	qual → QUAN	

As can be seen from Table 5.1, Onwuegbuzie and Collins suggest four types of samples applicable to both concurrent and sequential designs: identical, parallel, nested and multilevel. An identical sampling type might be used, for example, when a randomly selected sample of participants respond to both closed- and open-ended questions on a questionnaire. Such a study may follow a triangulation purpose if the researcher aimed at and was able to cross-validate participants' responses to the closed- and open-ended items. Or the study may follow an expansion purpose if the closed- and open-ended questions and the resultant data and analysis were reported separately as two mini projects with no attempt to integrate them.

An example of a parallel sampling procedure in a concurrent study with a triangulation purpose would be when two similar samples of raters (e.g. in terms of their level of education, English language proficiency and experience) are recruited to rate 50 essays using two different rating scales (e.g. a quantitative analytical scale and a qualitative impressionistic one). The researcher may then be able to establish correlations between the two sets of scores and argue for cross-validation of the rating scales. Nested sampling procedures in concurrent designs can best be exemplified when participants in an experiment are then interviewed to provide more in-depth information about the experiment processes and how they might have affected them. Finally, a multilevel sampling procedure is used when a multilevel mixed design, as explained in Chapter 4, is used to collect data from different levels and units in an organization.

> **Learning task 5.7**
>
> 1. In the MMR articles you found, identify the sampling procedure used and see whether it can be mapped against one of the four sampling procedures presented above.
> 2. Can you provide examples or describe scenarios for each of the four sampling procedures for sequential designs?

Collins, Onwuegbuzie and Jiao (2006, 2007) analyzed 121 MMR studies from nine different fields in the social or health sciences and found that identical sampling designs were the most prevalent, followed by nested sampling, multilevel sampling and parallel sampling, respectively. They also found that 66.1% of the studies used concurrent and 33.9% used sequential designs.

The second sampling typology was suggested by Teddlie and Yu (2007) and Teddlie and Tashakkori (2009), who indeed referred to Onwuegbuzie and Collins' (2007) typology and built their own. Teddlie and his colleagues suggested the following provisional (as they called it) sampling typology.

1. Basic mixed methods sampling strategies.
2. Concurrent mixed methods sampling.
3. Sequential mixed methods sampling.
4. Multilevel mixed methods sampling.
5. Sampling using multiple mixed methods sampling strategies.

Teddlie and his colleagues explained that 'basic mixed methods sampling' is used when a combination of a probability and non-probability sampling procedure is used. An example provided by Teddlie and Yu (2007) is stratified purposive sampling procedure. The stratified part is the characteristic of probability sampling, whereas the purposive part is the characteristic of non-probability sampling. In a stratified sampling procedure (Riazi, 2016), the researcher first divides the sample selected from a target population (e.g. undergraduate students) into relevant strata (e.g. freshmen, sophomore, junior and senior). The researcher then uses a criterion (e.g. high performers) to select a small number of participants to study intensively within each of the four strata. It is not clear, however, how this sampling procedure is different from a sequential mixed methods sampling procedure such as QUAN → QUAL or QUAN → qual, or even a concurrent QUAN + QUAL, as will be discussed below.

The above sampling framework has been presented in both Teddlie and Yu (2007) and Teddlie and Tashakkori (2009). The only difference is that in Teddlie and Tashakkori (2009) the word 'parallel' substitutes 'concurrent' in the second sampling procedure. This is in line with Teddlie and Tashakkori's use of 'parallel' for 'concurrent' in their design typology, as discussed in Chapter 4. However, their use of the term 'parallel' is different from Onwuegbuzie and Collins' use of the term, who use it in its common sense, while Teddlie and Tashakkori use it as an alternative for 'concurrent' in MMR designs. They explain that by 'parallel mixed methods sampling' they meant that both probability and non-probability sampling procedures are used simultaneously. In other words, one type of sampling procedure does not set the stage for the other to be defined and selected as is the case in sequential mixed methods sampling. 'In sequential mixed models studies, information from the first sample (typically derived from a probability sampling procedure) is often required to draw the second sample (typically derived from a purposive sampling procedure)' (Kemper *et al.*, 2003, cited in Teddlie & Yu, 2007, p. 89).

The above description of sequential mixed methods sampling applies only to QUAN → QUAL or QUAN → qual designs. In QUAL → QUAN or qual → QUAN designs, the initial non-probability (purposive) sampling procedure informs the selection of a larger probability sample in the second strand. When one of the above designs is used, the researcher will need to decide how to choose an appropriate probability sampling procedure so that the results of the quantitative strand could be generalized to a relevant target population.

Multilevel mixed methods sampling is, in fact, used with a multilevel mixed design, as discussed in Chapter 4. Multilevel designs are used when researchers focus on hierarchical and nested organizations, such as schools, universities and hospitals. Collecting data from different units in the organization requires both probability and purposive sampling techniques for different levels of analysis (Tashakkori & Teddlie, 2003). Indeed, it was argued in Chapter 4 that multilevel design could be considered as an example of a fully integrated MMR rather than an independent design framework. Depending on the research problem and research questions, collecting and analyzing data from different units and at different levels may require both concurrent and sequential designs and sampling procedures.

Surprisingly, there is no description and/or explanation of the last sampling procedure (sampling using multiple mixed methods sampling strategies) either in Teddlie and Yu (2007) or in Teddlie and Tashakkori

(2009). Only in Teddlie and Yu (2007, p. 78) has this sampling procedure been worded as a 'combination of mixed methods sampling strategies', which does not make much sense because MMR sampling procedure itself is already a combination of probability and non-probability sampling procedures. In light of the above discussion, Teddlie and his colleagues' MMR sampling typology could thus usefully be reframed and reduced to the following two sampling procedures.

1.   Concurrent mixed methods sampling.
2.   Sequential mixed methods sampling.

The exclusion of three sampling procedures – basic mixed methods sampling strategies, multilevel MM sampling and a combination of MM sampling – is based on the three arguments presented above. First, the basic MM sampling strategy is not different from a sequential or concurrent MM sampling procedure. The main type of a basic MM sampling strategy suggested by Teddlie and his colleagues is stratified purposive sampling. As discussed above, it is possible to use a stratified purposive sampling procedure in both concurrent and sequential MM sampling procedures. Second, it was argued that where a multilevel sampling procedure is required it could be a combination of concurrent and sequential MM sampling procedures depending on the purpose and research questions of the study. Third, the fifth sampling procedure suggested by Teddlie and his colleagues (using multiple MM sampling strategies) is, in fact, not different in nature than those of the above two sampling procedures.

Overall, therefore, Teddlie and his colleagues' typology of MMR sampling is related to the two general design structures, concurrent and sequential. The implication of this for researchers is that they just need to use appropriate combinations of probability and non-probability sampling procedures depending on the purpose of their studies and whether the studies follow concurrent or sequential designs. This is recognized by Teddlie and Yu (2007), who state: 'Concurrent and sequential MM sampling procedures are based on design types, and those design types are based on strands (QUAL and QUAN)' (p. 96).

If any MMR sampling typology is to be considered and recommended for language teaching and learning researchers to consider when designing their studies, it seems that Onwuegbuzie and Collins' (2007) typology is more relevant and meaningful than the one suggested by Teddlie and his colleagues. Collins (2013) further elaborates on the four MM sampling procedures – identical, parallel, nested and multilevel.

- **Identical** sampling procedure involves using the same sample of participants or units in both the quantitative and qualitative strands of the study. Identical sampling procedure may be used for all the MMR purposes except development, in which the sample of the second strand is usually a subset or an expanded form of the sample used in the first strand. Even in the Delphi method, which can be a particular MMR study with a development and initiation purpose, identical sampling procedure is used.
- **Parallel** sampling procedure uses similar samples of different participants or units selected from the same population of interest (e.g. university undergraduate students). Each of the two samples is then used to collect data for one strand in the MMR study. This type of sampling procedure may be used in studies with triangulation, complementarity, initiation and expansion purposes.
- **Nested** sampling procedure involves using a subset of the sample from the quantitative strand to provide data for the qualitative strand. Nested sampling procedure may be used in MMR studies with triangulation, complementarity, initiation, development and expansion purposes.
- **Multilevel** sampling procedure selects samples from different units or levels in a multilevel organization representing different populations (e.g. students, academic staff, professional staff, management). This type of sampling is mainly used in multilevel designs that could be used to investigate more complex research problems. MMR studies with complementarity and initiation purposes lend themselves to multilevel design and thus multilevel sampling. These types of studies are usually fully integrated because researchers need to follow an integrated approach at the conceptual, methodological and inferential stages in the research process.

Data collection strategies

Within- and between-strategy data collection

Teddlie and Tashakkori (2009, p. 207) classify data collection procedures in MMR as 'within-strategy' (using a single data collection strategy) and 'between-strategy' (using more than one data collection strategy). The criterion they use for this distinction is whether both quantitative and qualitative data are collected using methods from one methodological approach (one research strategy) or using methods from different methodological approaches (two research strategies). An example of a within-strategy data collection is when identical sampling procedure is used to collect both quantitative and qualitative data using a survey questionnaire that includes both closed- and open-ended questions. Survey questionnaires usually include items using Likert or other types of scales and are thus used to produce quantitative data. It is, however, possible to add some open-ended questions in a survey questionnaire so that respondents can express detailed answers that could be treated as qualitative data.

Meanwhile, Teddlie and Tashakkori consider collecting quantitative data using only closed-ended questionnaire items and qualitative data using unstructured interviews as a between-strategy data collection procedure. They call it between-strategy because the two instruments of data collection are selected from quantitative and qualitative research strategies.

Instruments of data collection

When collecting data for an MMR project, researchers use a set of data collection instruments that could elicit the required data from the participants to enable researchers to answer research questions. Except for a conversion design (see Chapter 4), in which only one instrument of data collection is used, for all the other MMR designs a combination of instruments is used. In conversion design, either a quantitative instrument (an instrument that can collect numerical data) or a qualitative instrument (an instrument that can produce narrative data) is used, and then qualitizing or quantitizing procedures are employed to produce both types of data and analysis. In other MMR designs, depending on the purpose and design of the study, appropriate instruments of data collection are used. Some examples of quantitative data collection instruments include tests (placement, achievement, proficiency, diagnostic, etc.) and questionnaires, inventories or checklists. Some examples of qualitative data collection instruments include semi-structured and unstructured interviews, individual or focus group interviews, field notes, and participant and non-participant observations.

In concurrent designs in which the two strands are conducted independently, different independent quantitative and qualitative data collection instruments are used. For example, in the quantitative strand, data may be collected from participants through achievement tests and questionnaires with closed-ended items, while in the qualitative strand, data may be collected through field notes and individual semi-structured interviews. In sequential designs with development purposes where a subsequent strand is built on the results of a previous strand, instruments of data collection for the subsequent strand may also be developed based on the outcomes of the previous strand. For example, in a qual → QUAN design, results of interviews with a small sample of teachers on their beliefs, perceptions and attitudes towards communicative language teaching may be used to construct a questionnaire on CLT to be administered to a larger sample of teachers.

Learning task 5.8

In the MMR articles you found:

1. Which data collection instruments were used to collect data for the quantitative and qualitative strands?
2. Were within- or between-strategies used for data collection?

Ethical considerations

Before researchers are entitled to collect any data from potential participants, they need to seek ethics clearance from authoritative bodies or review panels of their institutions. Institutes of higher education usually have ethics committees that are responsible for reviewing research proposals and ensuring that researchers are following codes of ethics as defined in relevant documents. Some of the codes of ethics are generic and broad to cover issues at international and national levels. There are, however, more specific codes of ethics developed by specific professional organizations to address particular issues related to the professional conduct of research. Researchers including postgraduate and doctoral students need to submit their research proposal to and obtain ethics clearance from review panels or ethics committees before they commence their data collection from participants.

The terms 'ethics' and 'morals' are used interchangeably, 'but sometimes morality is limited to conventional expectations for what is good and bad whereas ethics is the broader attention to standards and principles for making good decisions and reflecting on what standards are applicable to given situations' (Preissle *et al.*, 2015, p. 145). Researchers are therefore required to comply with the codes of ethics in practice in their relevant institutions and professions.

Once research proposals are submitted, review panels or ethics committees attend to different aspects related to researchers' compliance with codes of ethics. The review panels particularly seek evidence that researchers have considered and addressed the three main issues of coercion, conflict of interest and confidentiality (Roger, 2013) as they relate to participants. The appropriate management of these three issues will ensure participants' rights. Coercion usually happens where and when there is a perceived power relationship between the researcher and the participants so that participants feel they must take part in the research and provide data for the researcher. For example, in some language teaching and learning research, it was observed that researchers had collected data from students of their own classes. In such situations, students may have felt they had to participate in the research given the perceived power relationship between students and the teacher.

If the research activity places an individual in real, potential or perceived conflict between the individual's duties and the research interests, a conflict of interest may arise. When submitting a research proposal to review panels, researchers shall disclose any real, potential or perceived individual conflicts of interest of which they are aware and that may have a bearing on their research. One example of conflict of interest is researchers' dual roles, such as researcher and teacher, advisor, or supervisor, which can lead to coercion as discussed above. Where there is a real or potential conflict of interest, researchers should think of and suggest alternative management for data collection to avoid any real or perceived conflict of interest.

Finally, confidentiality means not disclosing any information gained from an interviewee deliberately or accidentally in ways that might identify an individual. In a research context, confidentiality means (1) not discussing information provided by an individual with others, and (2) presenting findings in ways that ensure individuals cannot be identified (chiefly through anonymization) (Wiles *et al.*, 2008). According to Walford (2005), anonymity simply means that we do not name the person or research involved, and is reasonably straightforward. However, in research, it is usually extended to mean that we do not include information about any individual or research site that will enable that individual or research site to be identified by others. While this is not usually observed in the published papers, it should be remembered that even this level of anonymization does not cover all the issues raised by concerns for confidentiality. When applying for ethics clearance, researchers are required to provide a copy of the research information and consent form along with interview questions and questionnaires. Researchers thus need to take note of this and prepare all documents for submission to ethics committees.

Learning task 5.9

In the MMR articles you found:

1. Have the researchers discussed ethical issues related to their projects?
2. Did the researchers use any particular strategies to ensure the integrity of their reported research?

Research integrity

Preissle *et al.* (2015) contend that research ethics involves more than how scholars treat participants of their study. They refer to other researchers' use of integrity as a more global term for the quality or the goodness of the research. According to them, research integrity covers issues related to the significance of the research topic, criteria on which research practices could be defended, researchers' honesty in terms of their viewpoints, interests and procedures, and whether the reported studies come under suspicion of some violations such as falsification, fabrication or plagiarism. Falsification and fabrication can occur at the data collection and analysis stages in the research process, and plagiarism may happen if researchers do not give due credit for the materials attributed to others from whom they have borrowed. Accordingly, providing adequate information and details in both research proposals and research reports regarding significance of the topic, research criteria as well as procedures of recruiting participants and following appropriate citation procedures in line with ethical guidelines can ensure the integrity of research.

Ethical challenges in MMR sampling procedures

Drawing on Teddlie and Yu (2007), Preissle *et al.* (2015) describe the compromise MMR researchers must make when using both probability and non-probability (purposive) sampling techniques within a mixed methods study. The compromise relates to fulfilling the standards of the two types of sampling. Probability sampling aims to achieve representativeness, while non-probability (purposive) sampling aims to achieve saturation for a rigorous qualitative component. Preissle *et al.* (2015) contended 'If the ultimate strength of MMR is the ability to compensate for the weaknesses of individual methods by creating a balance, then compromises should provide some kind of specified balance in sampling. However, in real-settings, researchers must make decisions based on limited resources, time, and other pressing concerns that result in sampling imbalances' (p. 150). Such sampling trade-offs can, therefore, pose ethical challenges if they compromise the integrity of studies, as Preissle *et al.* (2015) note. They suggest that researchers must consider the ethical implications of reporting results based on incongruent sampling, and recommend that 'researchers should strive to develop evenly scaled sampling strategies that provide external validity while also addressing key search questions and remaining accountable requirements of each sampling method' (p. 150).

The next chapter will discuss data analysis procedures and drawing conclusions and inferences based on the results of the data analysis.

References

Blaikie, N. (2000). *Designing social research.* Oxford: Blackwell.

Brannen, J. & O'Connell, R. (2015). Data analysis I: Overview of data analysis strategies. In S. Hesse-Biber & R.B. Johnson (Eds.), *The Oxford handbook of multimethod and mixed methods research inquiry* (pp. 257–274). Oxford: Oxford University Press.

Bryman, A. (2006). Paradigm peace and the implications for quality. *International Journal of Social Research Methodology Theory and Practice, 9*(2), 111–126.

Bryman, A. (2007). The research question in social research: What is its role? *International Journal of Social Research Methodology, 10*(1), 5–20.

Christ, T.W. (2007). A recursive approach to mixed methods research in a longitudinal study of postsecondary education disability support services. *Journal of Mixed Methods Research, 1*(3), 226–241.

Collins, K.M.T. (2013). Sampling: Mixed methods. In C.A. Chapelle (Ed.), *The encyclopedia of applied linguistics.* Oxford: Wiley-Blackwell Publishing Ltd.

Collins, K.M.T., Onwuegbuzie, A.J. & Jiao, Q.G. (2006, April). Prevalence of mixed methods sampling designs in social science research and beyond. Paper presented at the meeting of the American Educational Research Association, San Francisco.

Collins, K.M.T., Onwuegbuzie, A.J. & Jiao, Q.G. (2007). A mixed methods investigation of mixed methods sampling designs in social and health science research. *Journal of Mixed Methods Research, 1*(3), 267–294.

Collins, K.M.T., Onwuegbuzie, A.J. & Sutton, I.L. (2006). A model incorporating the rationale and purpose for conducting mixed methods research in special education and beyond. *Learning Disabilities: A Contemporary Journal, 4,* 67–100.

Creswell, J.W. (2014). *Research design: Qualitative, quantitative, and mixed methods approaches* (4th ed.). Thousand Oaks, CA: Sage.

Creswell, J. & Plano Clark, V.L. (2007). *Designing and conducting mixed methods research.* Thousand Oaks, CA: Sage.

Creswell, J. & Plano Clark, V.L. (2011). *Designing and conducting mixed methods research* (2nd ed.). Thousand Oaks, CA: Sage.

Creswell, J. & Tashakkori, A. (2007). Editorial: Exploring the nature of research questions in mixed methods research. *Journal of Mixed Methods Research, 1*(3), 207–211.

Dornyei, Z. (2007). *Research methods in applied linguistics.* Oxford: Oxford University Press.

Greene, J.C., Caracelle, V.J. & Graham, W.F. (1989). Toward a conceptual framework for mixed-method evaluation designs. *Educational Evaluation and Policy Analysis, 11*(3), 255–274.

Guba, E.G. & Lincoln, Y.S. (1988). Do inquiry paradigms imply inquiry methodologies? In D.M. Fetterman (Ed.), *Qualitative approaches to evaluation in education* (pp. 89–115). New York: Praeger.

Guba, E.G. & Lincoln, Y.S. (2005). Paradigmatic controversies, contradictions, and emerging confluences. In N.K. Denzin & Y.S. Lincoln (Eds.), *The Sage handbook of qualitative research* (3rd ed., pp. 191–215). Thousand Oaks, CA: Sage.

Johnson, B. & Christensen, L. (2012). *Educational research* (4th ed.). Thousand Oaks, CA: Sage.

Kemper, E., Stringfield, S. & Teddlie, C. (2003). Mixed methods sampling strategies in social science research. In A. Tashakkori & C. Teddlie (Eds.), *Handbook of mixed methods in social and behavioral research* (pp. 273–296). Thousand Oaks, CA: Sage.

Mertens, D.M. (2007). Transformative paradigm: Mixed methods and social justice. *Journal of Mixed Methods Research, 1*(3), 212–225.

Onwuegbuzie, A.J. & Collins, K.M.T. (2007). A typology of mixed methods sampling designs in social science research. *The Qualitative Report, 12*(2), 281–316.

Onwuegbuzie, A.J. & Leech, N.L. (2006). Linking research questions to mixed methods data analysis procedures. *The Qualitative Report,* 11(3), 474–498. Retrievable from: http://www.nova.edu/ssss/QR/QR11-3/onwuegbuzie.pdf

Preissle, J., Glover-Kudon, R.M., Rohan, E.A., Boehm, J.E. & DeGroff, A. (2015). Putting ethics on the mixed methods map. In S. Hesse-Biber & R.B. Johnson (Eds.), *The Oxford handbook of multimethod and mixed methods research inquiry* (pp. 144–163). Oxford: Oxford University Press.

Riazi, A.M. (2016). *The Routledge Encyclopedia of Research Methods in Applied Linguistics: Quantitative, qualitative, and mixed-methods research*. London: Routledge.

Roger, P. (2013). Understanding research ethics. Handout presented to the 'Research Methods in Language Study' course. Sydney, NSW: Macquarie University.

Tashakkori, A. & Teddlie, C. (1998). *Mixed methodology: Combining the quantitative and qualitative approaches*. Thousand Oaks, CA: Sage.

Tashakkori, A. & Teddlie, C. (Eds.) (2003). *Handbook of mixed methods in social and behavioural research*. Thousand Oaks, CA: Sage.

Tashakkori, A. & Teddlie, C. (Eds.) (2010). *Sage handbook of mixed methods in social and behavioral research*. Thousand Oaks, CA: Sage.

Teddlie, C. & Tashakkori, A. (2009). *Foundations of mixed methods research: Integrating quantitative and qualitative approaches in the social and behavioural sciences*. Thousand Oaks, CA: Sage.

Teddlie, C. & Yu, F. (2007). Mixed methods sampling. *Journal of Mixed Methods Research, 1*(1), 77–100.

Walford, G. (2005). Research ethical guidelines and anonymity. *International Journal of Research & Method in Education, 28*(1), 83–95.

Wiles, R., Crow, G., Heath, S. & Charles, V. (2008). The management of confidentiality and anonymity in social research. *International Journal of Social Research Methodology, 11*(5), 417–428.

6 Analyzing Data and Making Inferences

This chapter will discuss:

- data analysis in relation to MMR purposes, designs and research questions;
- computer assisted data analysis (CADA);
- inferences made from the results of data analysis.

Introduction

This chapter is divided into two main sections. In the first section, data analysis in MMR studies will be discussed. This section will be organized according to the topics of the three previous chapters to provide a more coherent discussion. As such, data analysis will be looked at in relation to the purpose, design and research questions of the research project. A brief introduction and discussion of computer assisted data analysis (CADA) will complete the first section. In the second section, different types of inferences that MMR researchers can make based on the results of data analysis will be discussed.

MMR projects include at least two strands, one quantitative and one qualitative. Accordingly, two types of analysis are fundamentally carried out in any MMR study. Researchers need to ensure that they analyze quantitative and qualitative data according to the standards of each methodology. Except for a few MMR studies, usually those with an expansion purpose in which there is little or no integration of the two strands, researchers attempt to integrate the two or more strands at some levels in the research process. Data analysis is one of the levels at which researchers strive to do this in light of the study's purpose and design. Integration of the strands at data analysis level also prepares researchers to integrate findings and make meta-inferences, as will be discussed in the second part of this chapter. The link between the four chapters (Chapters 3, 4, 5 and 6) is illustrated in Figure 6.1.

It is assumed that readers are already familiar with the fundamentals of quantitative and qualitative data analysis, or if necessary they can consult other references related to these types of analyses. The chapter, therefore,

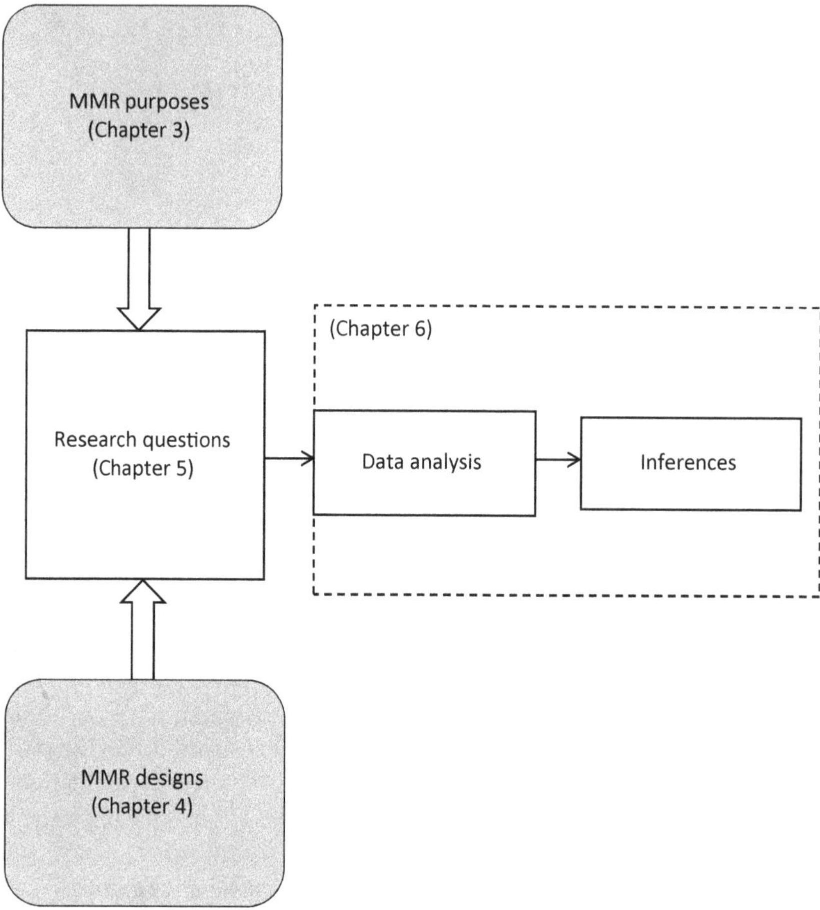

Figure 6.1 The link between purpose, design, research questions, data analysis and inferences

does not discuss details of how quantitative and qualitative data might be analyzed. Rather, the main focus will be on how these types of analyses might be employed in MMR projects to achieve certain goals.

Data analysis

The majority of published MMR studies typically present quantitative and qualitative data analysis and results separately or side by side and attempt to integrate at the level of interpretation or conclusions (Bryman, 2006; Greene *et al.*, 1989). As Bazeley (2006) observes: 'Mixing of methods, particularly at the stage of data analysis, has a lesser history, however, perhaps in part because of lack of tools to undertake all but the simplest forms of it' (p. 64).

Onwuegbuzie *et al.* (2009) rightly observe that the data analysis stage in the research process can make or break an MMR study. They explain that the level of integration researchers are able to apply to their data analysis will determine how integrated the two strands of the study are. Obviously, researchers could make more coherent conclusions and inferences if they were able to perform some levels of integration at data analysis level. In contrast, failure to appropriately integrate and embed the quantitative and qualitative analyses could lead to interpretive inconsistency (Collins *et al.*, 2007), or a lack of analytic adequacy (Teddlie & Tashakkori, 2009). Such interpretive inconsistency and analytic inadequacy may signify lack of appropriate links between data analysis, purpose, design, research questions and inferences in a study. In the next parts, these links will be discussed.

Data analysis and purpose

An essential issue to consider when analyzing quantitative and qualitative data in MMR studies is the purpose the researcher wishes to achieve from the overall study. Each of the five purposes discussed in Chapter 3 greatly influence the data analysis stage in the research process. Researchers are thus required to consider the compatibility between the units of analysis in the quantitative and the qualitative strands of the study (Brannen & O'Connell, 2015) and how these will help achieve the designated purpose. If, for example, the researchers seeks corroboration of findings through different methods and thus aims at a triangulation purpose, they need to ensure that the construct of the study has been operationalized in a similar way in the quantitative and qualitative data and analysis. The results of the quantitative and qualitative data analysis could then be compared for cross-validation. Plano Clark *et al.* (2008) refer to this as 'merging data' and explain that 'researchers attempt to merge their quantitative and qualitative data in triangulation designs by bringing the two data types together during analysis and/or interpretation' (p. 379).

The fact is, however, that in studies with triangulation purpose the integration most likely happens at the interpretation or conclusion stages and not at the data analysis stage. Caracelli and Greene (1993) also contend that integration at the data analysis stage is inconsistent with triangulation purpose that is defined as corroboration and cross-validation, which requires independence of methods up until the comparison and conclusion stages.

MMR studies with expansion purpose are similar to triangulation except that the integration of the results at the interpretation and conclusion stages may not be present either.

If a researcher began to investigate different aspects of a social or educational phenomenon, she or he might be addressing different constructs and/or aspects of the research phenomenon. When it came to the data analysis stage, different types of data analysis would be done to answer different research questions related to those different aspects of the phenomenon. This is usually the case in complementarity and initiation purposes. In other words, here the purpose of data analysis is not to seek overlaps but to address different aspects of a research problem using different types of data and conducting different types of analyses. In such studies, researchers may attempt to integrate at the level of data analysis, especially in fully integrated studies. Caracelli and Greene (1993) as well as Greene *et al.* (1989) realized that evaluation MMR studies with initiation purpose most frequently lent themselves to integration at the data analysis stage in their attempt to discover contradiction and paradoxes and suggest fresh perspectives.

Finally, when researchers are interested in developing and validating a questionnaire, for example, they need to think of an MMR study with a development purpose. This will allow them to collect qualitative data from a small purposive sample and to perform appropriate qualitative data analysis so that the findings (different themes) could be used to define different sub-sections in the construction of a questionnaire and to use components of each theme to write appropriate and relevant items in each sub-section.

In reality, however, things might not be as straightforward and initial plans might change. A researcher may initially think of an MMR project with a triangulation purpose, but end up with a complementarity or initiation purpose. The initial identification of purpose should therefore be used as a guideline but revisited and revised if necessary at later stages in the research process. The recursive nature of the research process encourages amendments of the goals and procedures at different stages. As such, it can be said that MMR is to some extent recursive and iterative, like some of the qualitative research designs, before it attains its final shape. As stated before, it is essential for researchers to use a macro or wide-angle lens at different stages in the research process so that they can find the optimal link between their data, purpose, design, questions and analysis, and the type of inferences they make based on the results.

Data analysis in different mixed designs

Data analysis in conversion designs

The intended mixed design can also influence data analysis. The simplest design introduced in Chapter 5 was conversion design. Here, only one type of data (qualitative or quantitative) is collected from participants, but the data are then transformed into another type and the researcher then analyzes the two types of data in a single study. The common procedures for data analysis in a conversion design are quantitizing and qualitizing. According to Fakis *et al.* (2014), qualitative researchers have always tended to use simple quantitative procedures to quantify some parts of their data. Quantifying means attributing numbers to some observed qualities, behaviours or experiences, and it is a popular procedure in quantitative research. The assignment of numbers to qualitative variables is done according to four measurement scales (Riazi, 2016).

1. Nominal scale.
2. Ordinal scale.
3. Interval scale.
4. Ratio scale.

Detailed explanation of these measurement scales is beyond the scope of this book. Readers may want to consult other sources (e.g. Dornyei, 2007; Mackey & Gass, 2016; Paltridge & Phakiti, 2015; Riazi, 2016) for these and other main concepts and procedures related to quantitative and qualitative data and analysis. Nevertheless, quantifying is different from quantitizing, as explained in the next section.

Quanititizing and qualitizing in conversion designs

The term 'quantitizing' was originally used by Miles and Huberman (1994) to refer to 'the process of converting qualitative data into numbers that can be statistically analysed' (Teddlie & Tashakkori, 2009, p. 27). Quantitizing thus covers both quantifying and using appropriate statistical analysis. An example of a quantitizing procedure would be counting the frequency of occurrence of different codes, categories and/or themes in a qualitative research and subjecting them to appropriate statistical analysis such as Chi-square. The quantitizing procedure will allow researchers to check whether there are any significant differences in the frequency counts of codes or categories for confirmation or generalization purposes. Depending on the purpose of the study and research questions, the results of the quantitizing may be used to triangulate qualitative findings with quantitative findings, confirm the patterns observed within the qualitative results by corresponding quantitative analysis, or enhancing and illustrating qualitative results with quantitative data and analysis.

Qualitizing data is a process through which quantitative (numerical) data are transformed into some forms of qualitative categories or narratives for further analysis (Teddlie & Tashakkori, 2009). The simplest form of qualitizing is when, based on the results of statistical analysis of a variable such as language proficiency, participants are categorized into elementary, intermediate and advanced. This type of categorization is very common in language teaching and learning research and is usually done using sample statistics of mean and standard deviation. Similarly, participants might be categorized according to their motivational propensities into 'intrinsic' and 'extrinsic' groups based on their responses to a Likert-type motivation questionnaire.

A more advanced form of qualitizing is employed in factor analysis. Through factor analysis, quantitative researchers reduce a significant number of variables into some underlying factors based on the observed correlations between different variables as they load on a particular factor. Once the factor analysis is completed and the underlying factors are identified, researchers need to apply meaningful names to the underlying factors and explain them in light of the observed correlations among variables and factor loadings. Canale and Swain (1980) is an example of how researchers qualitized their quantitative data through factor analysis. Using participants' performance on different types of tests, and analyzing test scores through factor analysis, the researchers identified the underlying factors of the construct of communicative competence and named them 'grammatical competence', 'sociolinguistic competence' and 'strategic competence'.

Once the researchers have identified and labelled the categories, it will be possible for them to conduct more in-depth qualitative analysis, resulting in fuller explanations of the research problem.

The above discussion and explanation of quantitizing and qualitizing data could be realized in conversion designs. Although researchers who use quantitizing or qualitizing may not refer to their study as MMR, nor identify it as a conversion design, studies like the one mentioned above represent this type of mixed design. Some of the above examples could even be represented as 'exploratory' or 'explanatory' designs. For example,

Canale and Swain's (1980) study can be considered as an exploratory conversion study and can be represented as either [QUAN (QUAL)] or [quan (QUAL)], depending on the level of emphasis put on each strand. In the hypothetical example of the questionnaire survey about participants' motivational tendencies, sub-samples of the two identified groups (intrinsic vs. extrinsic) could be invited to provide more in-depth information about their motivational patterns as they relate to their language learning. The qualitizing process can thus lead to an explanatory design.

Data analysis in other mixed designs

Data analysis can also be discussed in terms of concurrent and sequential designs. Bryman (2006), for example, found that concurrent gathering of quantitative and qualitative data and concurrently (independently) analyzing them appears to be a common approach in MMR. Onwuegbuzie *et al.* (2007) also explain that 'when quantitative and qualitative analytical techniques are utilized concurrently (i.e. concurrent mixed analysis), results stemming from one data analysis phase (e.g. quantitative analysis) do not inform the results stemming from the other phase (e.g. qualitative analysis)' (p. 5). Conversely, Onwuegbuzie *et al.* explain: 'When quantitative and qualitative analytical techniques are utilized sequentially (i.e. sequential mixed analysis), the qualitative phase is conducted first, which then informs the subsequent quantitative phase, or vice versa' (p. 6). In other words, in sequential mixed designs, analysis of the data involves some or all of the findings stemming from data analysis in one strand to drive or inform the analysis in the second strand. In contrast, in MMR studies with expansion purposes, quantitative and qualitative data are collected, analyzed and reported separately.

In embedded or nested mixed designs, which as explained in Chapter 4 are mostly applied to experimental designs, researchers mix the data analysis by embedding one type of data analysis into the other. As Plano Clark *et al.* (2008) note, in embedded data analysis, most often, qualitative data are embedded within a quantitative design, such as experimental or correlational studies. It is also possible for researchers to embed quantitative data analysis within qualitative designs, such as when, for example, descriptive statistics are incorporated within a case study design. According to Plano Clark *et al.*, in either case the embedded data and analysis usually serve a secondary purpose.

Research questions, data source and data analysis

In Chapter 5, three strategies for formulating research questions in MMR studies were discussed.

1. Formulating individual quantitative and qualitative research questions related to each strand and then writing a final mixed methods question that integrates the separate quantitative and qualitative research questions.
2. Formulating an overarching mixed methods question, then writing separate quantitative and qualitative research questions.
3. Developing quantitative, qualitative and mixed methods research questions as the study progresses.

The distinction between the first two strategies is whether to write individual quantitative and qualitative research questions and then a mixed question, or vice versa. The third strategy suggests that researchers postpone the formulation of exact research questions until they collect data and perform some preliminary analysis. At that stage, researchers may again use one of the first two strategies to write research questions. As will be discussed later in this chapter, even when researchers use one of the first two strategies, they may need to revise and modify the questions as they progress in their research and even at the time of writing up the research.

The main focus now is on how the collected data are analyzed in light of the initial research questions. Table 6.1 summarizes how the first strategy of writing research questions led to the collection and analysis of data. The order of presentation will be different when the second strategy of writing research questions is used.

Table 6.1 Research questions, data sources and data analysis

Research question	Data source	Data analysis
Quantitative	Numerical data collected through quantitative instruments	Descriptive and inferential statistical analysis
Qualitative	Narrative data collected through qualitative instruments	Thematic analysis
Mixed	A combination of numerical and narrative data	An integration of statistical and thematic analyses

Quantitative data sources and analysis

Depending on the purpose of studies and research questions, a variety of instruments may be used to collect the required quantitative and qualitative data. Quantitative data collection instruments in the language teaching and learning field may include all types of tests, both standardized and teacher-made, used for different purposes such as diagnostic and feedback, placing students in appropriate levels of language instruction, and assessing participants' level of language proficiency and/or achievement. In addition to tests, questionnaires with different types of rating scales are used widely to collect quantitative data from participants, including data regarding their attitudes and beliefs, personality type, learning preference styles and language learning strategies. Data collected through tests and questionnaires are then subjected to both descriptive and inferential statistical analysis. Descriptive statistics are used to describe the sample characteristics using such statistics as mean, median, mode and standard deviation. Inferential statistics are used to make inferences about the parameters of the target population based on the observed sample characteristics and statistics.

As discussed in Chapter 5, quantitative research questions may be categorized into descriptive, comparative or causal, and predictive or relationship. Depending on which of these three types of research questions is the focus in an MMR study, appropriate types of statistical analysis must be used. For example, if the quantitative strand was used to describe a particular group of participants' responses and/or to find the relationship between their responses and their personal characteristics, then descriptive statistics and correlational analysis must be used. However, if the quantitative strand was used to investigate group differences through comparative or causal research questions, then researchers must use t-tests (for comparing the performance of two groups), or analysis of variance (ANOVA) (for comparing the performance of more than two groups).

As stated earlier, an important issue is that researchers justify their use of particular statistical analysis based on the principles and standards underlying certain methods. It is therefore imperative for researchers to explicitly describe their data and explain how they fulfilled the underlying assumptions for the particular statistical procedures used. For example, if the quantitative data do not meet the underlying assumptions for parametric tests, researchers should explain this clearly and explain the equivalent non-parametric statistical procedures they selected to analyze their data.

Highlights of quantitative data and analysis

- A variety of instruments may be used to collect quantitative data.
- Quantitative instruments include, but are not limited to, all types of tests and questionnaires.
- Quantitative data are analyzed in light of the research questions using descriptive and inferential statistics.

Qualitative data sources and analysis

Qualitative data are collected through instruments such as participants' responses to open-ended questions in the questionnaires or interviews as well as personal journals and diaries that may record participants' recollections and reflections on their experiences. Researchers may also observe classes, and produce field notes, memos and self-reflections to augment the data collected from the participants. Participants' responses to open-ended questionnaire items and interviews as well as any other qualitative data are analyzed using data coding and thematic analysis, sometimes called content analysis. Video and audio qualitative data, if there are any, are often transcribed for coding and analysis.

Depending on the purpose of the qualitative strand in the MMR study, researchers need to apply appropriate types of analysis to their qualitative data. Researchers may, for example, use exploratory approaches to develop a theoretical explanation of a construct that could then be substantiated through a confirmatory study. In the qualitative strand, they may therefore use constant comparative analysis (Riazi, 2016) to develop their theoretical explanation of the research phenomenon. Constant comparative analysis allows researchers to collect and analyze data and produce hypothetical explanations in a recursive and iterative way until they reach data saturation, that is, when the new data do not contribute to further development of the theoretical explanation. This is when the researcher has developed an adequate theoretical explanation about the research phenomenon and the collection of new data does not contribute to the modification of the theoretical explanation any more.

Alternatively, researchers may use a grounded theory (Riazi, 2016) approach to develop a theoretical explanation about the construct of the study or the research phenomenon. Through grounded theory, researchers would be able to inductively code the data, develop categories or themes, and merge the themes to develop a theory or a theoretical explanation about the research phenomenon. Caracelli and Greene (1993) suggest that MMR researchers could use extreme case analysis (Riazi, 2016), in which extreme cases in one data set are excluded from statistical analysis because of their impact on the analysis. Outliers could be identified and investigated in more depth to refine the overall theoretical explanation developed in the study. An example of extreme cases are 'outliers' in quantitative research, which are usually very higher achievers or very low achievers based on participants' performance on tests or questionnaires. Using box plots, quantitative researchers identify outliers and exclude them from their statistical analysis to prevent their impact on the analysis. Qualitative researchers, however, find extreme cases as good sources of information and collect in-depth data from them to modify and refine their theoretical explanations.

Highlights of qualitative data and analysis

- A variety of instruments may be used to collect qualitative data.
- Quantitative instruments include, but are not limited to, interviews, observations, field notes and diaries.
- Qualitative data are analyzed in light of the research questions using data coding and thematic analysis.

The whole point of research is to produce new knowledge and understanding that could help human beings in making better decisions and improving quality of life. As such, the more systematically that studies are designed and implemented, the more credible and useful their findings will be. Methodological discussions such as those presented in this chapter, and more broadly in this book, will therefore help researchers to design and implement their studies more systematically with more rigorous outcomes. The discussions also help readers to better analyze research reports in the literature and identify potential flaws and gaps that could be addressed and filled through subsequent and more systematic research projects.

With regard to mixing methods, Plano Clark *et al.* (2008) recommend that researchers should utilize the type of mixing that best matches their research problem and the overall design they have chosen for their study. As a practical guide and to ensure that the mixing is explicit and clear, they recommend that 'researchers state a mixed methods research question, in addition to quantitative and qualitative questions, within their mixed methods studies. These mixed methods questions foreshadow and direct the mixing that will occur within the selected design' (p. 380). With regard to principles of best practice, researchers need to consider the kind of knowledge they aim to produce and use the type of research questions, designs and data analysis procedures that match their aim.

Computer assisted data analysis (CADA)

There are now very useful computer programs for both quantitative and qualitative data analysis. The two main programs frequently used by researchers are SPSS and NVivo for quantitative and qualitative data analysis, respectively. These programs help researchers to organize and analyze their data in more systematic and reliable ways. Quantitative software programs such as SPSS have a longer history in research, while qualitative programs such as NVivo are relatively younger. As Johnston (2006) states: 'Software programs have arguably increased the popularity of qualitative research among those from traditionally positivistic backgrounds and they have brought with them different ways of approaching qualitative data analysis' (p. 384). Qualitative programs facilitate data storage and organization, coding and retrieval of codes, writing memos and annotations, and developing categories and themes in systematic and reliable ways.

It is beyond the scope of this chapter and book to provide details of how quantitative and qualitative software programs might be used in data analysis. There are a significant number of manuals and guidebooks that explain how to analyze data using these programs. Readers may want to consult, for example, Pallant (2016) to learn how to conduct statistical analysis with SPSS. For reviews on computer assisted qualitative data analysis, readers may consult Bazeley (2007, 2009, 2012) and Richards (2002). Also, Bazeley and Jackson (2013), Leech and Onwuegbuzie (2011) and Richards (2009) can be used as guides for conducting qualitative data analysis with software programs such as NVivo.

It is important to consider the use of software programs for data analysis from the beginning of the research and as an integral part of the design and methodology. This will allow researchers to use the programs more efficiently and effectively at all stages in the research process. It requires researchers, especially novices, to develop and improve technological and methodological learning curves (Johnston, 2006). On the one hand, researchers need to improve their understanding of the technicalities, and on the other, enhance their methodological understanding so that they are able to incorporate the programs into different stages of the research process.

Qualitative data analysis programs like NVivo are now efficiently used for literature review and transcription of audio and video files in addition to other useful facilities such as coding and analysis of the data. Incorporating and using software programs at different stages of the research process has resulted in what Richards (2005, 2009) has called 'method revolution'. Rather than using traditional and inefficient manual data analysis procedures, computer programs have facilitated this important stage in the research process. As a result, researchers are now able to address more complex problems since computer programs are able to handle more complex data and analysis. However, the point should be made that it is always important that the research questions drive the use of CADA and not the technology that drives the process.

Quantitative and qualitative data analysis may be conducted separately using relevant computer programs and appropriate procedures, or they might be integrated and performed together. For qualitative and mixed data analysis using software programs, readers may consult Bazeley (2006, 2007), Bazeley and Jackson (2013), Johnston (2006), Richards (2002, 2009) and Welsh (2002). One possible technique for conducting mixed analysis is to import tabular data from statistical software packages into qualitative software packages that could then be used for more advanced types of analysis. The tabular data may include all the demographic information about the participants. The imported information or attributes about participants would enable researchers to compare and contrast themes that have emerged from qualitative data analysis across those attributes. Richards (2002) calls this type of mixed analysis 'pattern analysis'. Richards also believes that many researchers who claim they are using grounded theory are, in fact, conducting a form of pattern analysis.

In summary, using CADA has a lot of advantages, which will enable researchers to approach their data analysis in more systematic and reliable ways. However, using computer programs brings its own challenges, especially in MMR and particularly if some techniques such as pattern analysis are to be used. To face and overcome these challenges, researchers need to develop and improve their technological and methodological learning curves to obtain the necessary skills and knowledge for incorporating and using CADA in their research projects. Where resources are limited, researchers may conduct the analyses in collaboration with more experienced researchers and data analysts.

Challenges facing researchers to mix at data analysis stage

Caracelli and Greene (1993) were concerned about why MMR researchers do not integrate at the data analysis stage and before interpretation and discussion of their results. They considered the following three issues.

1. The impact of the paradigm debates and the implication this might have had for researchers that the two methodological approaches should be used independently.
2. The commonly implied association of mixing methods with triangulation and by extension expansion purposes, and that the strands should be implemented independently and then corroborated or cross-validated only at the discussion and conclusion sections.
3. The view that integration of results is a theoretically driven activity and thus independent of data analysis.

In addition to the above three challenges facing researchers, Bazeley (2006, p. 65) observed and added four more practical reasons.

1. Mixing at the data analysis level requires a breadth of skills that has not been commonly available in a single researcher, or even in a multi-skilled team.
2. It requires the capacity to imagine and envision what might be possible – to tread new paths – along with the logic (and skills) to bring that about.
3. Students (and others) are frequently encouraged to write results from different components of their studies separately (integration in a dissertation is in the 'too hard' basket, or is seen as 'risky').
4. Integration is greatly benefited by data handling technology (computer software), which, until relatively recently, has not been readily available.

Based on the above observations, Bazeley (2006) suggests two strategies researchers might use to face some of the challenges and achieve mixing at the data analysis stage.

1. Using categorical data or variables for both statistical analysis and comparison of qualitative data.
2. Converting data within a conversion design, as discussed above.

An example of the first strategy is when both closed-ended and open-ended questions are used in a survey questionnaire. Researchers may then use participants' gender (a categorical variable) to compare male and female participants' responses across different items or sections of the questionnaire. This is usually done through frequency counts and running a non-parametric test of significance, Chi-square. Simultaneously, researchers can code the participants' answers to open-ended questions and compare the codes or code categories across male and female participants. This may also be done in sequential designs when, for instance, questionnaire data analysis might be mixed with interview data analysis. 'The matrix function in NVivo facilitates this kind of comparative querying by allowing multiple comparisons at one time, with or without restrictions on what data are considered within each query' (Bazeley, 2006, p. 67).

Details of the second strategy were discussed earlier in this chapter and included quantitizing and qualitizing. Overall, therefore, CADA can greatly help researchers to convert data and to use categorical data related to the participants not only to make comparisons across participants' attributes but also to detect any discrepancies and outliers through the matrix function and statistical analysis. As discussed earlier in the chapter, outliers, and negative or deviant cases, can be used for further in-depth analysis to achieve data handling and mixing. Once the data are properly analyzed, results can be used to make inferences.

Making inferences

The word 'inference' generally means claims or conclusions researchers make on the basis of evidence obtained from the data analysis results and applying plausible reasoning. The process of making inferences from the data is called informal argument (Toulmin, 2003) and is depicted in Figure 6.2.

In the informal argument structure, as suggested by Toulmin, the inference or claim is the statement of an argument (e.g. good readers use a variety of reading strategies) and the data are the raw information based on which the argument is presented. The structure therefore includes a process (argumentation: using data and analysis) and a product (argument: claim or inference). As Figure 6.2 shows, claims and data are linked by 'warrants', which are general rules, principles or accepted procedures which authorize the making of inferences from the data. Warrants are also supported by 'backing', any evidence that can be collected in favour of the warrants. The type of backing required to support a warrant depends on the field in which the argument is

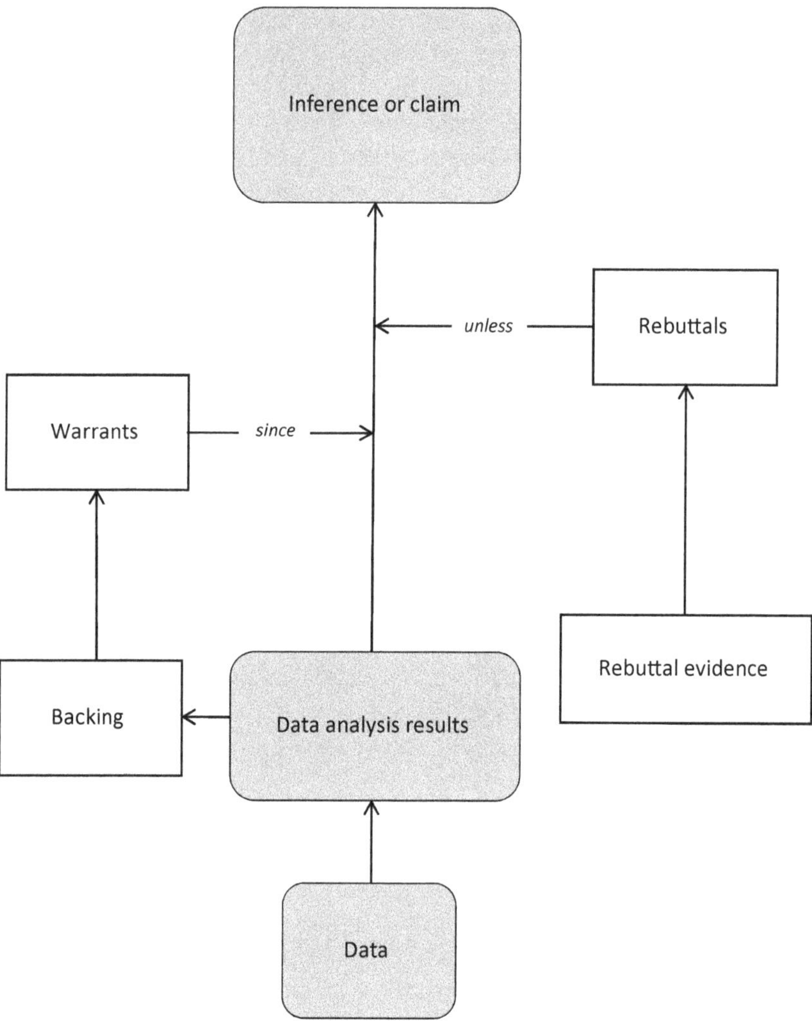

Figure 6.2 Informal argument structure (adapted from Toulmin, 2003)

used and may include relevant scientific theories, laws, precedents, results of quantitative statistical or qualitative thematic analysis, or other forms of evidence available to researchers. In addition, conditions or exceptional circumstances resulting in refuting the lnferences are known as 'rebuttals', negation of warrants. Given that no researcher can claim full certainty in the arguments they propose, inferences are usually hedged, with the use of some qualifiers such as 'most likely', 'almost certainly', and so on.

Inferences in MMR

In MMR, usually three types of inferences are made: quantitative, qualitative and integrated or meta-inference. All three types should follow the informal argument structure presented in Figure 6.2.

A simple hypothetical example of making a quantitative inference is when a researcher claims that good readers are strategic readers, that is, those who employ a variety of reading comprehension (RC) strategies have a better reading performance. Underlying this argument or inference is that there is a common variance between reading comprehension and RC strategy use. Using Toulmin's informal argument structure presented in Figure 6.2, the researcher may select a representative sample of participants from the population of university undergraduate students. The researcher then administers both an RC test and an RC survey questionnaire to the selected sample and checks for correlation between participants' RC test scores and their reported RC strategy use. The correlation coefficient turns out to be 0.87 and significant at 0.05 levels. The warrant here applies to the underlying assumptions and principles for correlational analysis. Four principles related to the interpretation of correlation coefficients are as follows.

1. **The sign of the correlation coefficient.** A positive sign shows a direct relationship between the two variables and a negative sign shows an indirect relationship between the two variables.
2. **The magnitude of the correlation coefficient.** The range for correlation coefficients is 0–1 and the closer the coefficient is to 1 (1.0), the stronger the relationship between the two variables will be.
3. **The level of significance.** Conventionally, in social and educational research the level of significance is set at 0.05, meaning that if a correlation was significant at or lower than 0.05 levels, the relationship is meaningful and not due to sampling error or chance.
4. **The coefficient of determination or common variance.** When the correlation coefficient is squared, the outcome shows the common variance between the two variables – in other words, the amount of variance in one variable that can be accounted for by the other variable.

Using the warrants as stated above, the researcher could claim that there is a relatively common variance between reading performance and RC strategy use. The warrants are backed up or supported by the results of the statistical analysis. First, the correlation between the two variables was found to be positive, showing a direct relationship between the two. Second, the magnitude of the correlation coefficient was found to be 0.87, which is a relatively high correlation, indicating a rather strong relationship between the two variables (close to 1.0). Third, the relationship between the two variables was found to be significant at the 0.05 level, showing that it is not by chance and that it could be generalized to the target population of university undergraduate students. Further, when the correlation coefficient is squared and rounded ($r^2 = 0.76$), it shows that 76% of variance in reading comprehension can be accounted for by readers' RC strategies. The other 24% of the variance in reading performance relates to other variables not included in the analysis.

The quantitative inference as presented above is then considered plausible because the argument can be supported by warrants as backed up by the statistical analysis evidence. However, if in a hypothetical situation a researcher made the above claim based on non-significant results, this could be used as a rebuttal to refute the claim. Similarly, a cause-and-effect rather than a relationship inference between the use of RC strategies and reading performance based on the above scenario would be considered implausible. The rebuttal used here is that there is no cause-and-effect relationship among the underlying principles related to the warrants for correlational studies.

The process for making qualitative inferences may not be as straightforward as explained above for quantitative research. However, there are now enough standards and principles underlying different qualitative research methods to enable researchers to develop plausible inferences from their data. For example, when researchers produce theoretical explanations and make claims about the nature of a research phenomenon through either constant comparative analysis or grounded theory, they need to illustrate how they applied the informal argument structure so that their claims are considered plausible. For example, in grounded theory, researchers use three levels of coding – open, axial and selective – to develop their theoretical explanation about the research phenomenon. They need to illustrate how their theoretical explanation (selective coding) emerged from the open and axial coding. This is why detailed explanation of qualitative data analysis procedures is deemed essential in both qualitative and mixed research.

The integration of quantitative and qualitative inferences in favour of a more comprehensive meta-inference is a goal to be achieved by MMR researchers. Making meta-inferences requires some background in the research process. This background may be provided through the conceptualization of the research problem, formulation of research questions, collection of appropriate data, and analysis of the data using appropriate analytical procedures. Some levels and forms of integration might be required at earlier stages in the research process so that researchers can generate meta-inferences in the last stages. As discussed above, for example, if some forms of integrated quantitative and qualitative data analysis are performed, this will set the scene for the researcher to make more comprehensive meta-inferences. Figure 6.3 shows a fully integrated MMR and how quantitative, qualitative and meta-inferences might be produced in such fully integrated mixed research.

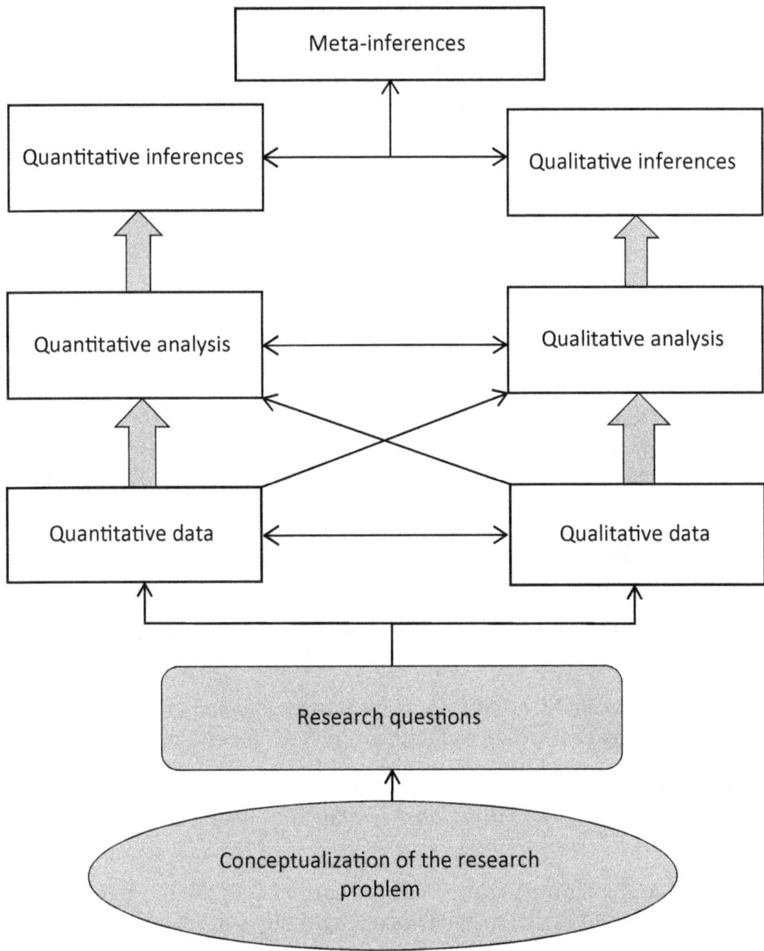

Figure 6.3 Making inferences in a fully integrated MMR

The next chapter will discuss presenting and reporting MMR projects. Issues related to preparing MMR proposals and reports for publication will be covered in this final chapter of Part Two. In the last section of the book a framework, FRAMMR, will be presented and applied to examples of MMR studies published in journals as research articles. In addition, learning tasks will be given so that readers can practise the analysis of MMR studies by using the FRAMMR framework.

References

Bazeley, P. (2006). The contribution of computer software to integrating qualitative and quantitative data and analyses. *Research in the Schools, 13*(1), 64–74.

Bazeley, P. (2007). *Qualitative data analysis with NVivo* (2nd ed.). Thousand Oaks, CA: Sage.

Bazeley, P. (2009). Analysing qualitative data: More than 'identifying themes'. *Malaysian Journal of Qualitative Research*, 2, 6–22.

Bazeley, P. (2012). NVivo 10 reference guide. Retrievable from: http://www. researchsupport.com.au/NV_10_notes.pdf

Bazeley, P. & Jackson, K. (2013). *Qualitative data analysis with NVivo* (2nd ed.). London: Sage.

Brannen, J. & O'Connell, R. (2015). Data analysis I: Overview of data analysis strategies. In S. Hesse-Biber & R.B. Johnson (Eds.), *The Oxford handbook of multimethod and mixed methods research inquiry* (pp. 257–274). Oxford: Oxford University Press.

Bryman, A. (2006). Integrating quantitative and qualitative research: How is it done? *Qualitative Research, 5*(1), 97–113.

Bryman, A. (2007). Barriers to integrating quantitative and qualitative research. *Journal of Mixed Methods Research, 1*(1), 8–22.

Canale, M. & Swain, M. (1980). Theoretical bases of communicative approaches to second language teaching and testing. *Applied Linguistics, 1*(1), 1–47.

Caracelli, V.J. & Greene, J.C. (1993). Data analysis strategies for mixed-method evaluation designs. *Educational Evaluation and Policy Analysis, 15*(2), 195–207.

Collins, K.M.T., Onwuegbuzie, A.J. & Jiao, Q.G. (2007). A mixed methods investigation of mixed methods sampling designs in social and health science research. *Journal of Mixed Methods Research, 1*, 267–294.

Dornyei, Z. (2007). *Research methods in applied linguistics*. Oxford: Oxford University Press.

Fakis, A., Hilliam, R., Stoneley, H. & Townend, M. (2014). Quantitative analysis of qualitative information from interviews: A systematic literature review. *Journal of Mixed Methods Research, 8*(2), 139–161.

Greene, J.C., Caracelli, V.J. & Graham, W.F. (1989). Toward a conceptual framework for mixed-method evaluation designs. *Educational Evaluation and Policy Analysis, 11*, 255–274.

Johnston, L. (2006). Software and method: Reflections on teaching and using QSR NVivo in doctoral research. *International Journal of Social Research Methodology, 9*(5), 379–391.

Leech, N.L. & Onwuegbuzie, A.J. (2011). Beyond constant comparison qualitative data analysis: Using NVivo. *School Psychology Quarterly, 26*(1), 70–84.

Mackey, A. & Gass, S.M. (2016). *Second language research: Methodology and design* (2nd ed.). London: Routledge.

Miles, M.B. & Huberman, A.M. (1994). *Qualitative data analysis: An expanded sourcebook* (2nd ed.). Thousand Oaks, CA: Sage.

Onwuegbuzie, A.J., Slate, J.R., Leech, N.L. & Collins, K.M.T. (2007). Conducting mixed analyses: A general typology. *International Journal of Multiple Research Approaches, 1*, 4–17.

Onwuegbuzie, A.J., Slate, J.R., Leech, N.L. & Collins, K.M.T. (2009). Mixed data analysis: Advanced integration techniques. *International Journal of Multiple Research Approaches, 3*, 13–33.

Pallant, J. (2016). *SPSS survival manual: A step by step guide to data analysis using IBM SPSS* (6th ed.). Melbourne: Allen & Unwin.

Paltridge, B. & Phakiti, A. (Eds.) (2015). *Research methods in applied linguistics: A practical resource* (2nd ed.). London: Bloomsbury.

Plano Clark, V.L., Creswell, J.W., O'Neil Green, D. & Shope, R.J. (2008). Mixing quantitative and qualitative approaches: An introduction to emergent mixed methods research. In S.N. Hesse-Biber & P. Leavy (Eds.), *Handbook of emergent methods* (pp. 363–387). New York: Guilford Press.

Riazi, A.M. (2016). *The Routledge Encyclopedia of Research Methods in Applied Linguistics: Quantitative, qualitative and mixed-methods research*. London: Routledge.

Richards, L. (2002). Qualitative computing: A methods revolution? *International Journal of Social Research Methodology, 5*(3), 263–276.

Richards, L. (2005). *Handling qualitative data: A practical guide*. London: Sage.

Richards, L. (2009). *Handling qualitative data: A practical guide* (2nd ed.). London: Sage.

Teddlie, C. & Tashakkori, A. (2009). *Foundations of mixed methods research: Integrating quantitative and qualitative techniques in the social and behavioral sciences.* Thousand Oaks, CA: Sage.

Toulmin, S. (2003). *The uses of argument* (2nd ed.). Cambridge: Cambridge University Press.

Welsh, E. (2002). Dealing with data: Using NVivo in the qualitative data analysis process. *Forum: Qualitative Social Research, 3*(2), 1–9.

7 Writing Proposals for MMR Studies

This chapter will:
- discuss writing thesis proposals for MMR studies;
- present a template structure for writing proposals;
- discuss each section in the proposed structure.

Introduction

Postgraduate and doctoral students are typically required to submit a proposal for a research project they will be conducting and then reporting as a thesis in partial fulfilment of their degree requirements. The proposal constitutes one of several documents these students need to submit to a review panel. However, the applicant's prospective supervisors will read the applicant's proposal and make judgements about their research capabilities. The research proposal thus needs to be written as carefully and precisely as possible so that candidates demonstrate their capacity to engage in genuine and authentic research in their research degree.

Conventionally, and indeed depending on the applicant's research background, they may suggest conducting and reporting a quantitative or a qualitative research project. However, with the increasing attention to mixed methods research, this type of proposal may be considered more positively if it is well prepared. This chapter therefore focuses on how to prepare and write a thesis or research proposal with an MMR orientation in the field of language teaching and learning.

First, a template structure for writing proposals will be presented, then each section in the template will be explained and discussed. Although there are different sections in a proposal, these sections should be written in close relationship with each other so that the whole proposal represents a coherent idea. It is, therefore, important to attend not only to the specific function of each section but also to the overall goal of the proposal. The other important point to remember is that like any other academic genre, proposals must be written in a persuasive style. Readers of proposals should be convinced that the proposed study is worth doing and that the outcomes will fill the identified gaps and contribute to the knowledge of the field. In so doing, any claims made in the proposal about the gaps in the literature, significance of the proposed study and plausibility of the data collection and analysis procedures need to be adequately argued for and supported with relevant warrants for the assumptions made. These points will be further discussed in relation to each section of the proposal template.

The structure or organization of a thesis proposal

There is no fixed structure, number of sections or way in which different sections might be organized for thesis proposals. The structure, sections and organization of the sections could be different for different proposals depending on many factors, but basically on the research field, topic and researchers' methodological orientation. However, there seem to be some core sections in all proposals, including those with an MMR orientation. These core sections are presented in Figure 7.1. Depending on the researchers' field of study, the topic of investigation and the research community's orientation, these sections may be added to or reduced in number, and/or reorganized to meet the specific conventions of the research community.

Each of the main sections in Figure 7.1 acts as a signpost and has a particular function or purpose. Each should be written with that purpose in mind; together, however, they enable the researcher to focus on and define their plans in a coherent and formal way. This coherent and formal presentation and discussion of different sections in a proposal creates an argument as to why the research problem is significant and worthy of investigation, how it will be investigated and understood, and how the outcomes might contribute both theoretically and practically to the current body of knowledge on the topic. The research proposal and subsequently the whole thesis must, therefore, be considered as an argument that is created and written with a persuasive tone. Readers of the proposals, who are more experienced members of the field, must see adequate argumentation with proper evidence in the proposal to ensure the student researcher's capacity for embarking on a genuine research project, whose results would benefit different stakeholders in the field. It is thus imperative to write different sections and the whole proposal in a way that clearly communicates the significance of undertaking the proposed study and its potential contributions for promoting both the current knowledge base and the practical expertise related to the topic and research problem.

Readers must be reminded that like any other writing task, producing and writing a quality thesis proposal requires it to be recursive, with quite

> **Introduction**
>   o   Statement of the research problem
>   o   Conceptualization of the research problem
> **Literature review**
> **Purpose of the study along with research questions**
> **Methods**
>   o   Design of the study
>   o   Participants and sampling procedure
>   o   Instruments of data collection
>   o   Data collection and analysis procedures
> **Ethical issues**
> **Feasibility**
>   o   Timeline
>   o   Budget plan
>   o   Risk management
> **Potential contributions to the field**
> **References**
> **Appendices**

Figure 7.1 Typical structure and sections of a thesis proposal

a lot of revising and editing and thus multiple drafting. The initial draft of a proposal may not exceed one or two pages, but through regular feedback from more experienced people, and especially students' supervisory panel, it will develop into a full proposal. The feedback from supervisory panels includes written feedback on different drafts; however, students also need to have substantive conversations with their supervisory panels so that they can get insight into how they should clearly explain and articulate the main arguments in the proposal.

Each of the suggested sections in Figure 7.1 will be explained briefly so that readers can see how to achieve the specific function designated for each section and can envisage how to write these sections, and the whole proposal, more effectively and with more confidence.

Introduction

The introduction section of a proposal is very important because it is the readers' first encounter with the proposed project. Readers get their first impression of the potential researchers and their proposed study from the introduction, so it is vital to write it as carefully and effectively as possible. The main function or purpose of the introduction section in thesis proposals is to establish an overall context for the proposed study. As Figure 7.1 shows, this section typically covers two important aspects of the research, the statement of the research problem and its conceptualization. Together, the two sub-sections fulfil the function of introduction as 'create-a-research-space' (CARS) (Swales, 1990; Swales & Feak, 2014).

Swales (1990, 2004) and Swales and Feak (2014) present a useful framework for writing the research introduction section and creating a research space. The framework includes four standard rhetorical moves to create a context for the proposed study. The first move helps the researcher to establish a territory by introducing the research topic and demonstrating its importance. The second move allows the researcher to create a narrower context by selecting and reviewing a few key published research studies relevant to the topic. The third move puts the researcher in a position to create a research niche by showing the gaps in the key literature. Finally, the fourth move enables the researcher to discuss why the proposed research is a timely and appropriate filler of the gap identified and presented in the third move.

For example, a researcher might be proposing a new research project related to first-year university students' challenges with academic writing. Using the first move, the researcher must introduce the topic (issues related to academic writing as they relate to first-year university students) and discuss its importance (why writing academically appears to be so important for these students). Authors may refer to a few selected empirical research studies here to support their argument about the significance of the topic, followed by a review of another set of key empirical studies to show how different aspects of this topic have been investigated by previous studies. In the next move, authors should be able to draw on their concise critical review presented in the second move to identify some gaps in the research on academic writing as related to first-year university students.

The gaps could be identified in relation to the content or methods employed by previous researchers. That is, authors might be able to identify some aspects of the topic (academic writing as related to first-year students) that have been neglected by other researchers. The authors' critical review may also reveal that previous research studies were conducted predominantly within particular methodological orientations. When the authors find out that previous researchers have used either quantitative or qualitative methods to examine different aspects of the topic, they can suggest a more comprehensive MMR study to produce a fuller understanding of the research problem. The identification of content and methodological gaps in the third move must be followed by a reasoning as to why addressing these gaps can contribute to the current knowledge base.

The last two moves in the introduction section either establish or lead the researcher to conceptualize the research problem. In other words, the researcher needs to delineate and demonstrate how the new gap(s) is conceptualized in light of the key literature reviewed and how the outcomes of the proposed study might contribute to the current knowledge base. As such, the conceptualization of the research problem may be incorporated within the introduction, or it may be presented under an independent title, especially if the researcher intends to emphasize this section. It can be said that those MMR studies that aim for complementarity and initiation purposes might preferably have an independent section for the conceptualization of the research problem.

Highlights of the introduction section in research proposals

- The main function or purpose of the introduction section is to establish a context for the proposed study.
- The introduction section usually includes a discussion of the topic and its importance, the research gap and how the proposed study can fill the gap.
- The four-move framework suggested by Swales and his colleagues can help researchers write an effective introduction.

A practical strategy for writing effective introduction sections is to postpone them and write them after all the other sections are completed. This is mainly because once the other sections of the proposal are ready, the researcher will be able to draw on those sections and structure and write the introduction section to fulfil the functions discussed above.

Literature review

The literature review section in the proposals, and subsequently in the thesis presented in a whole chapter, should tell a research story (Feak & Swales, 2009), the story of the topic being researched. The analogy of literature review with a story has implications for both the writer and the readers. Like any other story, it should have a plot, characters, setting and climax. The overall plot of the literature review should help readers understand how the topic has developed over time through different empirical studies. The characters should include the key researchers who have done substantial research on the topic and the way their findings have contributed to the knowledge base on the topic. The setting must delineate the contexts in which previous studies were conducted and the similarities and/or differences of those contexts, and how the similarities and/or differences might have influenced the findings of the studies. Finally, the climax in a literature review is where the researcher identifies one or several gaps in the previous studies and shows how the proposed study would fill one or some of those gaps.

Considering the whole process of writing a literature review as telling a story will help student writers to position themselves within the whole story. In other words, writers will be able to reflect on what has been investigated, by whom, how and with what significant findings, and where their proposed study will fit in the larger picture representing the topic.

Based on the above reflection, it is generally observed that postgraduate and doctoral students mistake the literature review for a list of summaries of different studies. Usually, novice researchers' literature reviews include a set of paragraphs, each summarizing one of the empirical studies included in the literature review. To avoid falling into this trap, student researchers should be reminded that a good literature review is the basis of both theoretical and methodological sophistication of the newly proposed research project (Boote & Beile, 2005). It therefore requires authors to go much beyond summarizing studies and treating the summaries as sufficient for a literature review.

A good strategy for preparing and writing the literature review as a story and a coherent piece that can inform the theoretical and methodological sections of the proposed research is to consider the literature review as a research project by itself. It is obvious, then, that the literature review would be secondary research because the researcher uses already reported studies. Like primary research, however, this secondary research can also be conceived at three levels:

- conceptual;
- methodological;
- inferential.

At the conceptual level, a literature review must be considered as proof of knowledge (Boote & Beile, 2005) through which the researcher identifies a research family, or as Swales (1990) calls it, a discourse community, and what the chief members of the community have done in regard to the topic. Another aspect of the literature review would be to identify what has been neglected by this particular research family that could be addressed through new research projects. To emphasize the importance of a literature review, Boote and Beile titled their article 'Scholars before researchers' and they explained that future researchers must first develop a relatively full understanding of the literature on the topic before they begin their own research. Conceptually, therefore, a literature review must show that the researcher is familiar with the background of the research topic, including key concepts and theories.

At the methodological level, the researcher must approach the literature review as a research project. That is, relevant articles found through systematic search into related databases should be considered as new data. These data need to be organized and then analyzed by the researcher in order to make plausible references (claims) about the research background. As discussed in Chapter 6, one of the advantages of computer assisted data analysis is that researchers can incorporate such programs into different stages in their research process. It seems, then, that conducting a literature review using a software program like NVivo would not only help researchers to improve their experiential hands-on learning of the software (enhancing their technological learning curve) but also prepare them to perform their own data analysis using the primary data collected in subsequent stages of the research process. For example, a researcher may upload all the relevant articles searched and obtained from databases on the academic writing related to first-year university students to NVivo. The researcher can then code these articles based on the key arguments found in them to develop categories for higher-level analysis. By finding relationships between different categories the researcher should be able to produce the main themes in the literature and use these to write a theme-based literature review.

Finally, looking at the literature review at an inferential level, the researcher should be able to present a coherent argument (see Toulmin's 2003 model presented in Chapter 6) and make claims about previous studies. The claims or inferences developed by the researcher are, in fact, represented in the critical review of the previous studies. Using information in the reported studies, the researcher finally would be able to make inferences about the gaps in the literature and how these gaps may be filled with new research projects, especially MMR studies.

Highlights of the literature review section in research proposals

The main function of the literature review section is to extend the context of the proposed study by:

- critically reviewing related literature through a systematic search of relevant articles, organizing and analyzing them
- writing a coherent story by presenting a theme-based critical review and making claims about the neglected aspects of the research topic.

Obviously, it is not possible to include a full and comprehensive literature review in a thesis proposal because of limitations on the length of the proposal, which is generally only 10–15 pages. However, a full and comprehensive literature review is expected in the theses where researchers usually have a whole chapter to devote to this important section. In addition, a full and comprehensive literature review develops over the course of one's master's or doctoral thesis and takes time for its preparation and regular revisions. Accordingly, when preparing and writing proposals, researchers are required to include selected but significant studies that have contributed to the understanding of the topic. They can use this selected set of literature to argue for potential observed gaps in need of further research.

As noted earlier, the literature review can inform both theoretical and methodological aspects of the newly proposed research project. Researchers should thus ensure that the literature review section of their proposal and subsequently of their thesis is of high quality and written carefully. There are now useful checklists and frameworks in the literature that can be used to check the quality of the literature review. These include criteria for the evaluation of the quality of the reviews and a taxonomy suggested by Cooper (1988, 1989), specific criteria recommended by Boote and Beile (2005), and a useful checklist suggested by Feak and Swales (2009). These resources provide useful discussion points and guidelines about producing quality literature reviews and readers are encouraged to consult them before, during and after they have written theirs.

Purpose of the study and research questions

The purpose section of research proposals logically follows the literature review. This is because once the claims about the gaps in previous research have been identified, researchers need to clearly state the purpose of the study they propose. The statement of the purpose is usually brief, one or two paragraphs, and is used as a road map for the whole research. It is geared to the identified research gap(s) on the one hand, and why the proposed project is timely on the other. In some research proposals there is another section called 'significance of the study' in which researchers enunciate the importance of doing the research project and the contributions the outcomes will have for different stakeholders. However, researchers may merge the purpose and the significance sections and not only address how the proposed study would fill the identified gaps in the literature, but also explain the ways in which conducting the research would benefit different stakeholders theoretically and practically.

One of the features of purpose in MMR proposals and studies that is absent in other purposes relates to the identification of one of the five MMR purposes for the proposed study. Ultimately, an MMR study should be able to make a claim for one of the five purposes discussed in Chapter 3. The purpose may indeed change based on the data collection and analysis procedures as well as other unforeseen factors that might occur during the course of research. It is, however, useful to both researchers and their audience (usually supervisory panels) to be able to envisage a particular purpose for the proposed study and how the other sections of the proposal help to achieve this purpose. The recommendation, then, is that researchers state the intended MMR purpose of their proposed study in addition to the general purpose of the study.

In addition to clarifying the perceived MMR purpose, it is desirable to briefly link the purpose to the design of the study. For example, as discussed in Chapter 4, sequential designs may be exploratory or explanatory. It would therefore help the researcher and the readers to explain how the perceived purpose might be realized in certain designs. There is, indeed, a sub-section in the 'Methods' section where researchers can identify and explain the design of the proposed study. However, it will not harm and may even enhance coherence of the proposal to reiterate the link between the purpose and design in this part.

> ## Highlights of the purpose section in research proposals
>
> - The purpose in research proposals is a general statement of the overall goals to be achieved by the proposed study.
> - It is usually one or two paragraphs and is geared to the identified gaps in the literature.
> - In addition to the overall goals, the timeliness of the research is discussed in the purpose section.
> - An additional feature is the identification of one of the five MMR purposes that applies to the proposed study.

Research questions

At a more specific level but related to the general purpose of the study, research questions and/or research hypotheses are presented. Research questions/hypotheses may come under an independent sub-heading or they may be presented right after the purpose with no sub-headings but a signalling sentence.

As discussed in Chapter 5, research questions in MMR studies generally follow one of two patterns.

1. Presenting independent quantitative and qualitative research questions related to different strands, then formulating a mixed question that can be answered by mixing the answers to the two independent questions.

Or:

2. Presenting a mixed question first that could be answered by a synthesis of results, then breaking it down into relevant quantitative and qualitative questions that could be answered by the results of the data analysis in the two strands in the study.

There is not much difference between the two strategies. In essence, quantitative questions are answered by the results of quantitative data analysis, qualitative questions are answered by the results of qualitative data analysis, and mixed questions are answered by a synthesis of the two sets of results. In Chapter 5 it was also explained that sometimes researchers state hypotheses related to quantitative research questions to be tested using the results of statistical analysis. Researchers may therefore decide to state research hypotheses in addition to quantitative research questions if they find it important in their research design. Otherwise, researchers may state only research questions.

Formulating research questions can routinely follow one of the above two strategies when researchers design their studies and plan to achieve one of the three purposes of triangulation, development or expansion. To plan studies with complementarity and initiation purposes, writing research questions may not be as streamlined as for other purposes. Researchers need to be more creative in formulating research questions to achieve these two purposes because research questions should be derived from a more complicated conceptualization of the research problem. The research questions may, therefore, need several iterations during the course of research until the final versions are written.

Highlights of research questions in thesis proposals

- Research questions are more specific compared with the purpose.
- Quantitative research questions may be accompanied by research hypotheses.
- There needs to be a mixed question to show how the quantitative and qualitative results may be mixed for a fuller understanding of the research problem.
- Writing research questions for complementarity and initiation purposes is not as streamlined as with other purposes and may require several iterations.

Methods

Another important section in each proposal is the methods section. Researchers have the opportunity to explicate all aspects and issues related to the methodology of their study in this section. Accordingly, this section includes several sub-headings, as presented in Figure 7.1, to be written carefully with the required details. Each of these sub-headings will be discussed in this section.

Design of the study

In the design sub-section, researchers have the opportunity to discuss all issues related to the design of their study. Depending on the purpose of the study and the research questions, researchers should be able to clearly explain what type of design they foresee their study will follow. This section does not need to be lengthy, but researchers need to clarify and indeed justify the design they think matches their purpose and research questions. In particular, they need to communicate with their readers whether, based on their purpose and research questions, a concurrent or a sequential design better fits their study.

As discussed earlier, researchers need to provide arguments and convince their readers of the plausibility of those arguments. One strategy for sound arguments is to support them with reliable sources and justifications. Researchers may thus rely on the reviews and discussion of mixed designs presented in Chapter 4 to develop an argument for their choice of design. It is recommended that they support their arguments with available sources on design structures, such as Creswell and Plano Clark (2011) or Creswell (2014). Another useful strategy is to use diagrams such as those in this and other books to explain the design of the study. Researchers should, however, be careful to use graphs appropriately and accurately to represent their studies.

Participants and sampling procedure

This sub-section relates to the study's participants and how they were chosen. There are several issues researchers need to consider and address when they make decisions about their sample of participants.

1. The quality and quantity of participants in each strand.
2. The overall sampling procedure and how the samples of different strands are related to each other.

Based on the purpose and research questions, researchers need to justify their choice of particular cohorts as participants in their study. Thus, researchers need to explain the characteristics of the potential participants and how the selected cohort is able to provide the required data for the study. In addition to explaining the quality of the potential participants and justifying their selection, it is equally important to discuss the quantity of participants and to justify the suggested numbers.

The discussion of the quality and quantity of the potential participants for the proposed study must be augmented with the sampling procedure. Explanation and discussion of sampling procedure in MMR proposals and studies are different from those of pure quantitative and pure qualitative studies. While some similar sampling procedures might be employed in

MMR studies, the overall sampling procedure and the link between the samples in different strands need further discussion in MMR studies. The recommendation here is, therefore, for researchers to consult the MMR sampling typology suggested by Onwuegbuzie and Collins (2007) to discuss their overall sampling procedure and to delineate the relationship between the samples in the two strands of the proposed MMR study. Onwuegbuzie and Collins suggest four sampling procedures – identical, parallel, nested and multilevel – as explained and discussed in Chapter 5. These sampling procedures are applicable to both concurrent and sequential designs.

Instruments of data collection

The required data for the proposed study must be collected within the two strands and through particular data collection instruments. The data collection instruments in MMR studies are basically the same as those used in quantitative and qualitative studies. However, their selection and appropriateness for the designated purpose and design need to be explained and discussed. This is particularly important because in MMR studies the mixing may happen at different stages in the research process – at the data collection stage (collecting both quantitative and qualitative data using one instrument) or after data are collected and through data transformation. How these strategies might help researchers to collect their data needs to be clearly explained and discussed in the proposal. Two data collection strategies, within- and between-strategy (Teddlie & Tashakkori, 2009), were discussed in Chapter 5 along with a variety of data collection instruments. Researchers are thus encouraged to consult the data collection strategies and instruments section in Chapter 5 when they are writing this section in their proposals.

An important issue to be explained and discussed in the instruments sub-section is the reliability and validity of quantitative data collection instruments and dependability and credibility of qualitative data collection instruments. Instruments of data collection are either borrowed from previous studies or developed in the context of the proposed study. In case the researcher is borrowing instruments from previous studies they need to cite and report how previous researchers validated these instruments. For quantitative instruments such as tests and questionnaires, researchers may need to re-check the reliability and validity of these instruments with their own data, even if there is already some evidence for this. When instruments are developed for the proposed study, researchers must explain the procedures through which they attempted to validate these instruments. They may, for example, propose to conduct a pilot study through which the reliability and validity of the instruments could be checked.

Data collection and analysis procedures

Another essential sub-section in the methods section relates to the procedures of data collection and analysis. Details of how the required data for the study will be collected and analyzed should be explained and discussed in this part and related to the design of the study.

In concurrent designs, quantitative and qualitative data are collected independently, while in sequential designs data collection in the second strand depends on the result of the first strand. If, for example, the proposed study lends itself to a sequential design, researchers need to explain how data will be collected and analyzed in the first strand and how the results of the data analysis in the first strand inform the development and procedures of data collection in the second strand. If a study is to use a conversion design, the researcher needs to explain how the quantitizing or qualitizing of the data will be performed.

If researchers foresee a pilot study through which they could check the feasibility of their data collection instruments as well as validation of those instruments, this should also be included and explained.

Finally, details of both quantitative and qualitative data analysis must be presented in this sub-section. The analysis of the data should correspond to the research questions and the type of evidence needed to answer them. It is, therefore, advisable to present a table in this sub-section, like the example in Table 7.1, to explicate the relationship between research questions, data sources and data analysis.

Table 7.1 **An example of how to relate research questions, data sources and data analysis**

Research question	*Data source*	*Data analysis*
RQ1	Test performance	Descriptive analysis + Inferential parametric tests (t-test or ANOVA)
RQ2	Survey questionnaire	Descriptive analysis + Non-parametric statistical test of significance (Chi-square)
RQ3	Interviews + Extreme case analysis	Transcription of audio files → coding of the data → generation of categories → linking categories and producing themes
RQ4	Synthesis of quantitative and qualitative data	Comparative analysis of quantitative and qualitative data and results

Ethical issues

When thesis proposals are finalized and approved by supervisory panels, researchers need to apply for ethics approval before they embark on data collection. It is thus desirable for researchers to foreshadow ethical issues in the proposal. It is sufficient for the researchers to discuss whether or not they predict any serious ethical issues relating to the collection of data from their participants. Generally, conducting research in the field of language teaching and learning is considered low risk, with no serious ethical issues. However, researchers need to show they are aware of the ethical issues and that they will do their best to respect participants' rights and that there would be no violation of those rights.

It is thus desirable if researchers can discuss how they will inform potential participants, how they will obtain consent from participants and how they will ensure participants' rights to withdraw from their project at any stage in the research process.

Feasibility

Master and doctoral theses are completed within limited resources. Currently, for example, master of research programmes must be completed within 2 years and doctoral projects must be completed within 3.5–4 years. Scholarships are also geared to these time frames and in most cases they cannot be extended. It is therefore imperative for researchers to demonstrate how their proposed study could be completed on time and in accordance with available resources. Three areas that could contribute to the feasibility of the proposed studies are a reasonable timeline, a budget plan and risk management.

Timeline

In the contemporary candidature culture and in the context of limited resources, the need to meet milestones for predetermined tasks is obligatory. Researchers need to develop specific strategies to enable them to conduct their research and write up their thesis within the allocated time frame. Some universities provide time management templates such as Excel files in which certain milestones and deliverables are identified for researchers to adapt and append to their proposals. Where such templates are not available, researchers need to design timelines for their studies. The timeline could be broken down into six-month intervals, identifying which research or writing tasks will be exactly completed when. For example, the first six months may be devoted to writing and finalizing the research proposal, with three deliverables of a final copy of the proposal, a completed ethics form to be submitted to the ethics committee, and a commencement review and report. Other milestones could be included in the timeline depending on the stage of the research or writing in the whole programme.

Gantt charts are very useful for the preparation of timelines and can be created using Excel. If researchers do not have access to Excel or they find it difficult to use, it is possible to create a table in Word and populate it with various research and writing activities at appropriate time intervals. All this needs to be done in consultation with supervisory panels.

Budget plan

The majority of universities provide some financial support to their postgraduate and doctoral students to help them achieve their milestones. Such financial support is usually allocated for certain research activities such as payments to participants, travel fares if data are to be collected from a different location, purchasing certain hardware and software, and attending data analysis workshops and conferences. But this type of support is not allocated automatically. Rather, student researchers need to include it in their budget plan initially to accompany their proposals and to be approved by the relevant authorities in the department. Students must therefore predict potential costs that might be incurred over their degree and include them in their budget plan.

Like timeline templates, departments might provide templates for a budget plan. Otherwise, students may create their own budget plan using Excel or Word programs and in consultation with their supervisors.

Risk management

Another aspect of feasibility of studies is risk management. Risks include all potential barriers that may impede or prevent the planned objectives. These risks may occur at any stage in the research process. Researchers need to consider and suggest solutions if such risks may arise. The impact of potential risks on one's study can vary from severe to not substantial, and the likelihood may range from quite likely to highly improbable. In any case, researchers need to have a plan for how they might encounter and overcome these risks.

Some of the foreseeable risks relate to sample size and data collection, especially if researchers suggested they would collect a large amount of data from a large sample. In reality, they may not be able to achieve their targets. It is thus wise to explain in the proposal alternatives for data collection if the targets are not achieved. Although in qualitative strands the sample might be small, there is still the risk that even the small sample size does not provide further data. This possibility needs to be acknowledged and alternatives considered, especially if this is the only source for the qualitative data.

Other potential risks may relate to the identified resources and time frames. For example, student researchers may anticipate they will attend different workshops related to data analysis to enable them to analyze their qualitative data within certain time periods. Experience shows students usually underestimate the time they need for the organization and analysis of their qualitative data. A similar issue may arise regarding the time required for writing different chapters, receiving feedback from supervisors and revising the chapters. Researchers thus need to show that they have allowed for some flexibility in their timeline to account for unforeseen delays and unachieved targets.

Potential contributions to the field

Conventionally, theses at master's levels are considered research practice, giving students the opportunity to independently plan, implement and report a piece of research. It is, therefore, not expected that theses at this level will make a significant contribution to knowledge in the field. In some universities where students are given a 'bundle' offer, that is, first doing a master of research and then promoting to doctoral, the master's thesis may be planned as a pilot study for the doctoral one.

Nevertheless, one of the premises of doctoral research is that it makes a significant contribution to the knowledge of the field. In order to achieve this goal, student researchers need to understand what is known about their topic and how their proposed study will contribute to this knowledge base. New research projects are planned and proposed to fill conceived gaps in the literature, as discussed earlier. It is thus desirable if researchers can add one or two paragraphs at the end of their proposals and explain how their proposed study might resolve some of the current problems. In addition to potential theoretical contributions to the knowledge, researchers might be able to discuss the practical contributions of their proposed study and how different stakeholders might benefit from the outcomes.

References

At the conclusion of the proposal there must be a list of references for all works which have been cited in the body of the text. This list should be prepared according to the writing style conventions in practice in the departments where students are studying. Some departments may use the sixth edition of the American Psychological Association (APA, 2010) writing style manual; others may use other guidelines and manuals. Student researchers should therefore determine the common practice in terms of writing and citation styles and adhere closely to those conventions and seek advice from their librarians.

Generally, the list of references at the end of the proposals is arranged in alphabetical order so that readers can easily locate the cited work in the body of the proposal in the reference list. One of the requirements in preparing references is that there should be one-to-one correspondence between the works cited in the body of the proposal and those included in the reference list. That is, every individual source cited in the proposal should have been included in the reference list, and there should not be any source listed in the reference list that is not referred to in the proposal.

Appendices

The appendices in a proposal should include all extra documents that researchers feel readers need to see but which could not be included in the main sections of the proposal. These may include, for example, a copy of the instruments of data collection if they are ready at the time of writing proposals. The conventions in some departments may require students to supply the research timeline and budget plan as appendices.

References

American Psychological Association (2010). *Publication manual of the American Psychological Association* (6th ed.). Washington, DC: APA.

Boote, D.N. & Beile, P. (2005). Scholars before researchers: On the centrality of the dissertation literature review in research preparation. *Studies in Higher Education, 34*(6), 3–15.

Cooper, H. (1988). Organizing knowledge synthesis: A taxonomy of literature reviews. *Knowledge in Society, 1*, 104–126.

Cooper, H. (1989). *Integrating research: A guide for literature reviews*. Newbury Park, CA: Sage.

Creswell, J.W. (2014). *Research design: Qualitative, quantitative and mixed methods approaches* (4th ed.). Thousand Oaks, CA: Sage.

Creswell, J.W. & Plano Clark, V. (2011). *Designing and conducting mixed methods research* (2nd ed.). Thousand Oaks, CA: Sage.

Feak, C. & Swales, J. (2009). *Telling a research story: Writing a literature review*. Ann Arbor, MI: University of Michigan Press.

Frels, R.K. & Onwuegbuzie, A.J. (2010). Typology lists of verbs for scholarly writing. Unpublished manuscript. Huntsville, TX: Sam Houston State University.

Onwuegbuzie, A.J. & Collins, K.M.T. (2007). A typology of mixed methods sampling designs in social science research. *The Qualitative Report, 12*(2), 281–316.

Randolph, J. (2009). A guide to writing the dissertation literature review. *Practical Assessment, Research & Evaluation*, 14(13). Available online: http://pareonline. net/getvn.asp?v=14&n=13

Swales, J. (1990). *Genre analysis: English in academic and research settings*. New York: Cambridge University Press.

Swales, J. (2004). *Research genres: Explorations and applications*. New York: Cambridge University Press.

Swales, J. & Feak, C.B. (2014). *Academic writing for graduate students: Essential skills and tasks* (2nd ed.). Ann Arbor, MI: University of Michigan Press.

Teddlie, C. & Tashakkori, A. (2009). *Foundations of mixed methods research: Integrating quantitative and qualitative approaches in the social and behavioural sciences*. Thousand Oaks, CA: Sage.

Part Three

Review and Analysis of Published MMR Studies

8 A Framework for Analyzing MMR Studies

This chapter will:

- present a framework for the analysis and review of MMR studies;
- elaborate on the three main parts of the framework: the annotation, design and strands, and commentary;
- make a case for how to classify MMR studies in terms of purpose and innovation.

Introduction

The third section of the book focuses on mixed methods research in action. The goal will be to analyze and review published MMR studies related to different topics on language teaching and learning. The published articles are selected from a variety of journals in the field of language teaching and learning. Hence, although not comprehensively, the chosen published articles represent the type of MMR studies readers are likely to encounter in their specific areas.

Analysis and review of the MMR studies needs to be done within a framework. Hence, a framework is presented and explained in this chapter. The framework consists of three main parts: annotation, design and strands, and commentary. The annotation part will provide an overview of the paper in question. The design and strands will present more details about how the quantitative and qualitative phases are dealt with in the MMR study. A critical review of the MMR study will then be presented in the commentary section, with a focus on the conceptual, methodological and inferential levels of each study. The three parts of the framework are explained in more detail in this chapter.

After the explanation of the framework in this chapter, the focus of the next four chapters will be on the analysis and review of MMR studies using the framework. Overall, eight published MMR studies will be reviewed, two in each chapter. Moreover, two additional MMR studies are suggested for review by readers in the learning task section at the end of each of the next four chapters. Readers will thus be exposed to 16 MMR studies overall, related to different aspects of language teaching and learning.

MMR studies to be reviewed

- In **Chapter 9** the two MMR studies are related to the teaching and learning of two language components, grammar and vocabulary.
- In **Chapter 10** the focus is on researching communication skills wherein two MMR articles related to two productive communication skills, speaking and writing, are reviewed
- In **Chapter 11**, motivation and attitudes in language teaching and learning will be the focus of review. The first MMR study in this chapter relates to Indian English language teachers' attitudes towards communicative language teaching. The second MMR study addresses language learning motivation in early adolescents in immersion programmes in the United States.
- Finally, in **Chapter 12**, the discussion of published MMR reports will focus on researching language testing and assessment. The first study relates to the predictive validity of an English as a second language (ESL) placement test, while the second is related to formative assessment or assessment for learning (AFL) and its usefulness in second language classrooms.

Obviously, the selected articles do not fully represent the range and variety of topics related to language teaching and learning. Given the space limitations, only some of these topics have been included. The purpose has thus been to present, review and discuss a sample of MMR studies with a language teaching and learning focus rather than to attempt to include and review all topics in this area. The MMR studies have, however, been selected to reflect a range of diverse contexts and research sites, involving a variety of participants. Collectively, the reviews and discussions of these MMR studies will hopefully help readers to improve their own analytical skills and, in turn, their understanding of how better to design their MMR studies when the time comes.

Each of the four chapters in this section will end with a learning task as mentioned above. In the learning task, two more MMR studies relating to the theme of each chapter are presented, each with an annotated bibliography. Readers are encouraged to pick one or both studies and review them using the framework presented in this chapter to further develop their understanding of the use of MMR in practice.

The FRAMMR framework

In this section a framework for analyzing MMR (FRAMMR) will be presented. The framework is designed to provide a consistent and coherent procedure for the review of the articles in the next chapters, and to support readers in better understanding and comparing the MMR studies in terms of their design and approach. The framework may also be used to review and analyze other MMR studies. Readers will find some hints from the review and analysis of these eight MMR studies that they can use when planning and designing their own MMR studies. The main goal is to unfold different aspects and nuances of the MMR designs as discussed and reported by the researchers in each paper so that the readers can read between the lines and get an insider view of the intricacies of the MMR designs. Importantly, each review and analysis will present both descriptive and critical information to assist readers to understand those methodological aspects the researchers themselves might not have directly and explicitly presented and discussed in their reports.

The framework includes three main parts, as shown in Figure 8.1. Each of the three parts will be explained briefly to better prepare readers for the subsequent chapters where the framework is applied.

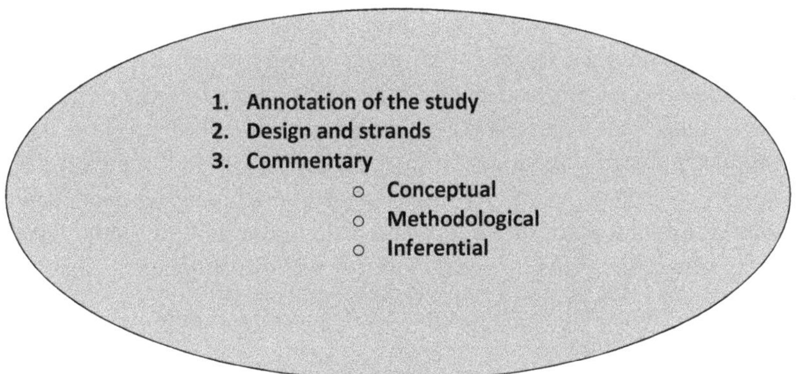

Figure 8.1 FRAMMR: a framework for the review and analysis of MMR studies

Annotation

According to the online Oxford Dictionary (https://en.oxforddictionaries.com), annotation means 'a note by way of explanation or comment added to a text or diagram'. Since full commentaries regarding each paper will be provided in the commentary section of the framework, the annotation section will be restricted to an overall summary of the study. The purpose of the annotation is to give readers a general understanding of the research problem addressed by the researchers, how they investigated the problem, and what findings they reported as a result of their research. The annotation will thus take the form of an extended abstract. Since the abstract of the papers is usually quite short (150–200 words) due to the limitations imposed by the journals, readers might not gain a full picture of the study from the original abstracts. Other pieces of information are therefore extracted from the articles and included in the annotation so that readers can develop a more complete picture of the study under review.

Each annotation includes the overall purpose and objectives, research questions, sample, data sources and main findings of the study. The overall purpose and objectives are explained, in particular, to introduce the topic as well as the specific content area. Since the broad purpose of the studies is usually stated at a general level, the research questions addressed in each study are exactly duplicated in the annotation section, with a page reference to the original paper. If there is any information stated in the article regarding the purpose for which the MMR approach was used, this will also be mentioned in the annotation.

The next pieces of information in each annotation relate to the sampling procedure, the data collection procedures and the findings of the study. The information about the sample of the study usually includes material about the participants (who, how many, from where and why) from whom the required data were collected. All the studies included in Part Three use an MMR design, so information about the quantitative and qualitative data sources of each study is provided in the annotation. Finally, each annotation ends with a summary of the overall and main findings of the study. The annotations therefore provide a snapshot of key information about each study and prepare the reader for the next steps in analysis.

Design and strands

Having presented a synopsis of the study under review in the annotation section, the FRAMMR then unpacks the design and strands used in each

MMR study. This section in each of the following chapters begins with a schematic diagram of the main stages involved in the study. The diagrammatic representation is in line with Creswell's (2015) recommendation and endorsement that such a 'diagram provides a useful overview of the procedures and helps readers understand complete features of the design' (p. 60). The graphs are produced in the Word program using shapes, text boxes and arrows. Figure 8.2 presents the shapes used in the graphs along with an explanation of each shape.

Another aspect of the design and strands is the representation of the design of the studies through the MMR notation system, as presented and discussed in Chapter 5. As explained in Chapter 5, Morse's (1991, 2003) notation system, as reproduced in Table 8.1, is used to represent the design of each of the MMR studies.

Following the schematic diagram of each of the MMR studies, an elaboration of the design and strands involved in the study provides additional details of the methods and procedures used in each strand. An attempt has been made to keep the explanations simple and clear and directly related to the methods employed in each phase of the study. In the original papers, usually information about the study's methodology is scattered in different parts of the article and incorporated with content materials, making it difficult for readers to gain a clear and concise idea of the design and procedures used by the researchers. Thus, the purpose in this section of the framework is to present a focused and clear explanation of the methodological issues with less, or no, emphasis on the topic and content aspects of the studies.

Table 8.1 Morse's notation system (1991, 2003)

Notation	Explanation	Example
Abbreviations	To present the abbreviations of quantitative and qualitative terms	quan and qual
Uppercase letters	To show the strand priority or emphasis	QUAL (more emphasis on the qualitative strand)
Lowercase letters	To show the strand with less priority or emphasis	quan (less emphasis on the quantitative strand)
Plus sign (+)	To show the simultaneity of the two strands	QUAL + QUAN or qual + QUAN
Arrow (→)	To show the sequence between the strands	QUAL → quan or qual → QUAN

Shape	Explanation
(oval)	The oval shape in each figure represents the target population of the study. A text box included in the shape provides a brief explanation of the target population.
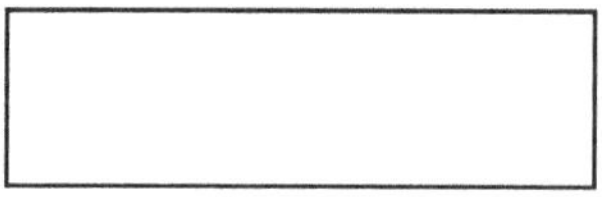 (single-line rectangle)	Single-line rectangles are used in the figures to denote the quantitative and qualitative strands in each MMR study.
(double-line rectangle)	Double-line rectangles are used in the figures to explain the data sources and/or data analysis in each of the strands of the MMR study.
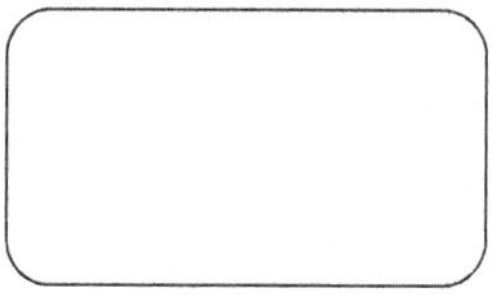 (curved rectangle)	Curved rectangles are used to represent the inferences made in the MMR studies.
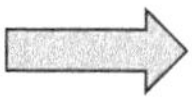 (arrow)	Arrows (regardless of their shape, length and thickness) are used to show links between different sections in the graphs.
 (dashed arrow)	A dashed arrow is used when the inferences are weakly integrated.

Figure 8.2 The shapes and their explanations as used in the graphical representation of the designs of the MMR studies

Readers should come to grips with the design and procedures of each study after reading this section and be well prepared for the next level of analysis and review, the commentary. The commentary section provides a more critical review of the design of the studies, focusing on the conceptual, methodological and inferential stages.

The initial two sections, the annotation and the design and strands, therefore help readers develop a mental representation of the MMR study and get ready for a critical discussion of the study in the final part of the FRAMMR, the commentary.

Commentary

Drawing on the preceding sections of the framework, the commentary section will provide a critical review offering a comment on each MMR study to illustrate how such studies could have been more improved in terms of their methodology and design. As such, the commentaries will draw on the three levels of analysis proposed by Riazi (2016): conceptual, methodological and inferential.

At the conceptual level, the focus will be mainly on how the researchers conceptualized and approached their study. Some researchers claim to follow a pragmatic approach and begin with research questions as the driving force in their studies (Creswell, 2003; Teddlie & Tashakkori, 2009). MMR studies driven by research questions usually prefer not to get involved directly in a theoretical discussion of the nature of the problem they are researching, which may require a sophisticated theoretical discussion of the **what** (ontology) of the research phenomenon. However, it appears that some MMR studies set out with a theoretical discussion of the research problem and try to frame a conceptualization of the phenomenon. Such a conceptualization of the research phenomenon will then lead the researchers to formulate their research questions. It is thus worthwhile and interesting to look for the point of departure in MMR studies. This step in the framework assesses whether the impetus for designing and conducting the MMR study was answering some particular research questions, or illuminating different aspects of a research phenomenon as conceptualized by the researchers in light of a theoretical discussion of the research problem and formulation of research questions accordingly.

Regardless of the approach, researchers generally attempt to find answers to some research questions. Nevertheless, such choices make a difference in terms of how an MMR study is designed and how the quantitative and qualitative strands serve the MMR study. As argued in Riazi (2016), question-oriented MMR studies consider mixing quantitative and qualitative data and analysis mainly as **methods** and are thus more concerned about design technicalities. Theoretically and conceptually oriented MMR researchers, meanwhile, attend to mixing quantitative and qualitative data and analysis as naturally corresponding to what can be known about different aspects of the research problem. They are thus mixing methods from the two approaches as a **methodology** in line with their conceptualization of the research problem (the ontology) and what can be known about (the epistemology) the research phenomenon through different methods. This discussion will be picked up further in the conceptual analysis of MMR studies.

Conceptual analysis of MMR studies

Two major issues to be analyzed and discussed at the conceptual level are (a) the purpose for which the MMR design is used by the researchers, and (b) the degree of innovation involved in using quantitative and qualitative methods to serve the MMR study.

As discussed in Chapter 3, Greene *et al.* (1989) identify five purposes for mixing methods from quantitative and qualitative approaches: triangulation, complementarity, initiation, development and expansion. Identifying the purpose for which the MMR researcher decided to mix certain quantitative and qualitative methods is a crucial stage in the analysis of the MMR studies. The identification of the purpose in each study will help the reader to evaluate the design and procedures for which the methods were mixed and, accordingly, the plausibility of the inferences made in each study. This process allows us to make judgements about the quality of the MMR study and the level of confidence we can have in its findings. Some researchers clearly state a purpose for mixing methods, while others do not refer explicitly to a particular purpose in their descriptions of the study. We can, however, infer from different parts in the published reports what purpose the researcher had in mind when they collected and analyzed both quantitative and qualitative data in a single MMR study.

How innovative is an MMR study?

In addition to identifying the purpose for which the researchers have mixed methods from the quantitative and qualitative approaches, we would be interested to evaluate the degree of the innovation used when choosing to do so. Drawing on the categorization presented by Riazi and Candlin (2014) and Riazi (2016), MMR studies may be classified as eclectic, principled or innovative. Figure 8.3 is designed to make a link between the researcher's orientation, MMR as **method** (question oriented) or MMR as **methodology**

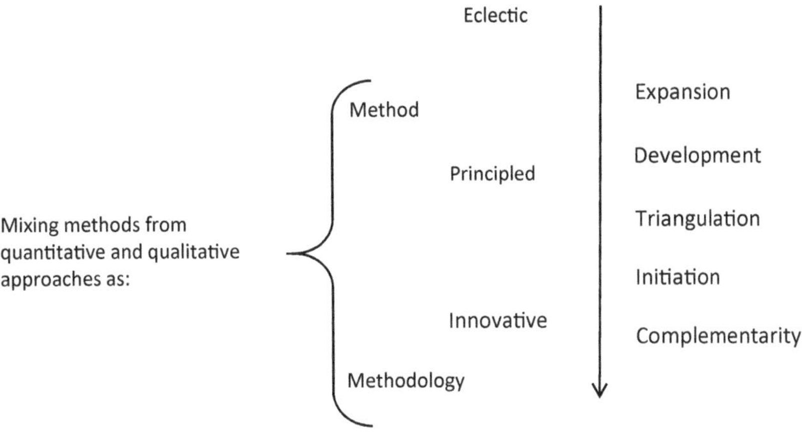

Figure 8.3 A suggestive model for the evaluation of MMR studies

(theoretically/conceptually oriented), the purpose for mixing methods, and thus the level of innovation in each of the MMR studies.

It should be made clear, however, that the classification of MMR studies into eclectic, principled and innovative is not meant to be a thorough, comprehensive and all-encompassing scheme with no exceptions. Rather, and like any other classification scheme, this categorization is suggested to help readers in their analysis and evaluation of MMR studies and the level of innovation they may be able to assign to each study. Each of the three categories of the classification scheme is discussed briefly here.

The eclectic category

As discussed in Riazi (2016), we can say that eclectic MMR studies are predominantly either quantitative-dominant or qualitative-dominant (Johnson, McGowan, & Turner, 2010). The other strand is usually used with a lower weight and in most cases for embellishment. Even in the best possible scenario where the methods are used with an equal weight and level of emphasis, eclectic MMR studies usually follow an 'expansion' purpose, which is considered to be the most flexible (Greene *et al.*, 1989) or even questionable (Bazeley, 2004) representation of the MMR. This is mainly because eclectic MMR studies, best represented by an expansion purpose, usually include two separately conducted and reported studies with the minimum, or no, integration of the two methods. The quantitative and the quantitative strands are presented in parallel in the MMR study, with almost no dynamic integration between the two.

Chronologically, eclectic studies preceded principled MMR studies since the current developments and resources were generally absent when researchers in the past tried to mix methods from the two approaches. However, some of the recent MMR studies may also be classified as eclectic because the researchers did not base their mixing of the methods on the basis of principles and designs presented in the MMR literature.

The principled category

The principled category of MMR studies includes those studies in which the researchers have drawn on the principles and design structures from the MMR literature in conducting and reporting their studies. MMR studies with 'triangulation' and 'development' purposes, and even some with 'expansion' purpose, can be potentially categorized as 'principled' MMR studies. This is based on the grounds that usually the researchers clarify at the outset the purpose for which they have chosen to mix methods and how they designed their study accordingly.

The principle nature of such MMR studies is also reflected in the researchers' familiarity with the principles of MMR design and how such principles have been followed and presented in practice. We can thus find enough reference to MMR literature in such studies as a representation of their researchers' familiarity with the principles of mixing methods. There might be some MMR studies with triangulation and development purposes that cross the borders of the principled category and enter into the innovative territory, but the author's anecdotal observation is that in general, triangulation and development MMR studies fit more within the principled category given the constraints they have, as discussed in Chapter 3.

The innovative category

The main criterion suggested by Riazi (2016) for considering an MMR study as innovative is that the mix of methods is, in fact, derived from and corresponds to the conceptualization of the research phenomenon. The researcher's conception of the research problem (the nature of the object of the study) would represent the type of understanding one could develop, or what could be known about the phenomenon (knowledge and inferences) and how (the methodology). From this perspective, the mixing of the methods is subsumed under a methodology in line with relevant ontological and epistemological conceptualizations of the research phenomenon.

With regard to the innovation criterion and the purpose for which methods are mixed, Riazi (2016) considers complementarity and initiation purposes as potentially being innovative. Rather than following a more pragmatic approach and beginning the study with some concrete research questions, researchers of MMR studies with complementarity and initiation purposes often begin with a discussion of how they conceptualized the research problem and how their conceptualization led them to formulate different research questions. The formulation of the research questions is done according to different aspects of the research phenomenon, each in need of certain types of data and analyses to be answered. In other words, the research questions are grounded in the theoretical/conceptual framework of the study. This process will call for a genuine and innovative mixing of the quantitative and qualitative methods so that the researcher can shed more light on different aspects of the conceptualized research phenomenon and make plausible inferences related to those aspects. When conducted rigorously, in MMR studies with complementarity and initiation purposes, researchers would integrate the inferences based on the quantitative and qualitative findings to produce meta-inferences and provide a more comprehensive understanding of the research problem.

The difference between principled and innovative MMR studies, as discussed in Riazi (2016), is thus whether the mixing was treated as another method corresponding to MMR design principles and technicalities, or the mixing was dealt with at higher levels and as a methodology. The eclectic category represents all other studies in which quantitative and qualitative methods are combined but not necessarily mixed within the principles and purposes of MMR.

Methodological analysis of MMR studies

At the methodological level, the focus will be on how each individual method is used in the MMR study and how different methods and strands are integrated in the representation of the MMR study. To this end, the underlying assumptions and principles for the use of each method will be checked and discussed. This covers a discussion of the quality of data collection and analysis in both strands, a brief note as to how this might look in quantitative and qualitative strands, and a summary statement about how these affect the credibility of findings and inferences.

Another key methodological concern is how different quantitative and qualitative strands are mixed to represent a coherent MMR design. This concern is mainly related to design typologies as proposed by such MMR researchers as Creswell (2003, 2015) and Creswell and Plano Clark (2011) and as were presented and discussed in Chapter 3. MMR researchers often identify the particular design of their MMR study by making reference to the relevant MMR literature. There might, however, be cases where this information is not clearly communicated in the research report. If that is the case, then an attempt has been made to disentangle the design of the study by using the information provided in different parts and especially the methods section of the articles. In light of the stated or implied information and evidence about the design of the MMR study, it would be possible to evaluate and make judgements about the plausibility of the design used in each particular study.

Inferential analysis of MMR studies

Finally, the third level of analysis and review in the commentary section of the framework relates to the inferences (quantitative, qualitative, and mixed or meta-inference) made by the MMR researchers in their studies. The studies will be analyzed and reviewed for the grounds on which the researchers made the inferences using the results of their data analyses and findings from different strands. As MMR studies, the expectation will be to see not only independent inferences made from the quantitative and qualitative data analysis outcomes, but also an integration of these inferences to generate higher-level or meta-inferences.

The methodological comments that preceded the inferential stage in the commentary section provide a context for the evaluation of the inferences made by the researchers. Both quantitative statistical inferences and qualitative interpretive inferences need to meet relevant underlying assumptions of the particular methods applied to be considered as plausible inferences. Each of the independent inferences will thus be evaluated against the underlying assumptions for that particular inference. Depending on the degree to which the underlying assumptions are fulfilled, the plausibility and credibility of the conclusions reached can be evaluated and judged. At a subsequent level, the focus will be on whether and how the researchers integrated the independent inferences in order to develop a more comprehensive meta-inference. Not all the MMR researchers may aspire to get to this level and/or achieve this element. The generation of a holistic meta-inference is thus one key focus in the analysis and discussion of the eight MMR studies in the next four chapters.

Concluding remarks

In this chapter, FRAMMR was presented and explained for the analysis and review of the MMR studies in the following chapters. The framework includes three parts: annotation, design and strands, and commentary. Each of the three parts in the framework presents one level of analysis; together, however, they assist readers to develop a coherent understanding of the MMR study. As explained above, the conceptual level of the framework embraces Greene *et al.* (1989) related to the purposes of MMR studies, and Riazi and Candlin (2014) and Riazi (2016) related to the categorization of the MMR studies. The aim has been to create a link between the purpose of the MMR studies and the degree of their innovativeness.

The eight MMR studies to be reviewed in light of the framework presented in this chapter are related to different issues pertaining to language teaching and learning. The analysis and review of the MMR studies complements the theoretical discussion of MMR as presented in the previous chapters with practical examples. It is hoped that the examples provide readers with necessary insights and procedures to be able to review other MMR studies related to their own areas.

To provide readers with an opportunity to review and analyze MMR studies independently, in the learning task section of each of the following four chapters two further MMR studies are included, each with an annotation. The annotations provide readers with an overall picture of the studies before they make a decision as to whether they would like to analyze and review them. However, the more MMR studies you as readers analyze, the more insights you will gain into how better to plan for and design MMR studies. This is based on the fact that the MMR studies reviewed in this book are either good examples of MMR studies or possibly demonstrate some methodological problems and weaknesses. The former will provide you with useful examples and models so that you can map your future MMR studies against them and make sure you are on the right track; you can learn from the shortcomings of the latter so as not to repeat the weaknesses in your future MMR studies.

References

Bazeley, P. (2004). Issues in mixing qualitative and quantitative approaches to research. In R. Buber, J. Gadner & L. Richards (Eds.), *Applying qualitative methods to marketing management research* (pp. 141–156). Basingstoke: Palgrave Macmillan.

Creswell, J.W. (2003). *Research design: Qualitative, quantitative, and mixed methods approaches* (2nd ed.). Thousand Oaks, CA: Sage.

Creswell, J.W. (2015). *A concise introduction to mixed methods research*. Thousand Oaks, CA: Sage.

Creswell, J.W. & Plano Clark, V.L. (2011). *Designing and conducting mixed methods research*. Thousand Oaks, CA: Sage.

Greene, J.C., Caracelli, V.J. & Graham, W.F. (1989). Toward a conceptual framework for mixed-method evaluation designs. *Educational Evaluation and Policy Analysis, 11*, 255–274.

Johnson, R.B., McGowan, M.W. & Turner, L.A. (2010). Grounded theory in practice: Is it inherently a mixed method? *Research in the Schools, 17*(2), 65–78.

Morse, J.M. (1991). Approaches to qualitative-quantitative methodological triangulation. *Nursing Research, 40*, 120–123.

Morse, J.M. (2003). Principles of mixed methods and multimethod research design. In A. Tashakkori & C. Teddlie (Eds.), *Handbook of mixed methods in social and behavioural research* (pp. 189–208). Thousand Oaks, CA: Sage.

Riazi, A.M. (2016). Innovative mixed-methods research (IMMR): Moving beyond design technicalities to epistemological and methodological realisations. *Applied Linguistics, 37*(1), 33–49.

Riazi, A.M. & Candlin, C.N. (2014). Mixed-methods research in language teaching and learning: Opportunities, issues and challenges. *Language Teaching, 47*, 135–173.

Teddlie, C. & Tashakkori, A. (2009). *Foundations of mixed methods research: Integrating quantitative and qualitative approaches in the social and behavioural sciences*. Thousand Oaks, CA: Sage.

9 Researching Language Components

This chapter will:

- briefly introduce the skills-components model of language proficiency;
- present an analysis and review of an MMR study that focuses on inductive and deductive approaches to teaching and learning grammar;
- present an analysis and review of learning vocabulary through technology among second-grade students;
- provide two further MMR studies in the learning task to be analyzed by readers.

Introduction

Carroll (1961, 1969) introduced a skills and components model of language proficiency. She conceived proficiency in a language as mastery of four skills – listening, reading, speaking and writing – and three components – sound system (phonology), grammar and vocabulary. This model of language proficiency has traditionally informed the language instruction curriculum in different parts of the world. The model has, however, been especially in use in teaching in English as a second or as a foreign language (ESL/EFL) contexts. The focus of this and the following chapter will thus be on language skills and components and how MMR researchers have planned to investigate them.

Traditionally, the three language components were taught, learned and assessed independently. Recently, however, with the emergence of communicative language teaching and learning approaches, the skills-components model of language proficiency has been questioned. This is based on the argument that the use of language in real-life communication events requires users of the language to engage in interactional and transactional discourse. Using language for communication and negotiation of ideas thus demands the language user to integrate language skills and components (Widdowson, 1983) in authentic and meaningful ways. Notwithstanding the communicative approach to language teaching and learning, there is still some emphasis on and different approaches to teaching language skills and components in educational settings.

In this chapter, two MMR studies, related to the teaching and learning of grammar and vocabulary, will be analyzed and reviewed. The first focuses on the teaching and learning of grammar in an intermediate-level college French classroom at a medium-sized, southern, private, liberal arts university in the United States. The study investigated the effectiveness of a guided inductive versus a deductive approach to the learning of French grammatical structures among intermediate-level college students. The second study investigated the effectiveness of integrating technology in second-grade students' vocabulary learning and development in a public elementary school in the south-eastern part of the United States. Both studies used experimental designs (Riazi, 2016) for the quantitative strand in the MMR study. The first study, however, used the same group of participants within a repeated-measures design (Riazi, 2016). The two studies also had a qualitative strand.

The two studies are referred to as Study 1 and Study 2, and will be analyzed and reviewed using the FRAMMR framework presented in Chapter 8. First, an annotation of the study will be provided, then design and strands are discussed, and finally each study will be commented on at the conceptual, methodological and inferential levels.

Study 1

Vogel, S., Herron, C., Cole, S.P. & Holly, Y. (2011). Effectiveness of a guided inductive versus a deductive approach on the learning of grammar in the intermediate-level college French classroom. *Foreign Language Annals, 44*(2), 353–380.

Annotation

Drawing on the importance of linguistic accuracy in proficiency oriented language instruction, Vogel *et al.* (2011) focused on grammar instruction in the intermediate-level college French classroom. The primary goal of the study was to compare two approaches to grammar instruction, a guided inductive approach and a deductive approach, and how these might affect student learning of grammar. The researchers were interested to find out whether the guided inductive approach would be more effective than that of a more traditional deductive approach with regard to student learning of grammar. The secondary goal was to determine participants' preference for grammar instruction and to find whether there was a relationship between students' preference and their performance on the grammar tests.

The researchers thus sought answers to the following five research questions.

1. What is the effect on the short-term learning of grammar by intermediate-level French students when grammatical structures are taught with a guided inductive approach versus a deductive presentational approach?
2. What is the effect on the long-term learning of grammar by intermediate-level French students when grammatical structures are taught with a guided inductive approach versus a deductive presentational approach?
3. Which instructional approach, guided inductive or deductive, do students prefer?
4. Is there a relationship between students' performance on immediate post-tests and their instructional preference?
5. Is there a relationship between students' performance on the grammar post-test and their instructional preference? (p. 357)

To answer the five questions, the researchers designed and conducted an MMR study with a quantitative and a qualitative strand. The quantitative strand included a within-subjects repeated-measures experiment featuring a pre-post test and immediate post-treatment tests. A learning preference questionnaire formed another part of the quantitative strand. The qualitative strand included the open-ended questions on the learning preference questionnaire and interviews with six participants.

Forty participants were selected from among 51 available students and provided the following data.

1. Pre-test and post-test grammar scores.
2. Immediate test scores for at least three treatment sessions in each condition (inductive vs. deductive).
3. A completed post-study learning preference questionnaire.
4. Post-intervention interview data (six participants).

The researchers used ten French grammatical structures for the instructional materials in their study. These ten structures were selected from the French curriculum and included '(1) use of c'est vs. il est, (2) use of the past tense with certain verbs that either use the auxiliary être or avoir (sortir, monter, descendre, rentrer), (3) order in placement of direct and indirect object pronouns, (4) superlative structures, (5) relative pronoun dont, (6) relative pronouns ce qui and ce que, (7) relative pronoun lequel, (8) use of causative expressions with faire, (9) gerundive, and (10) use of subjunctive vs. infinitive with expressions of desire and preference' (p. 359).

They used two approaches to teach these grammatical structures to intermediate-level college students. The first was an inductive approach and the second was a deductive approach. After the experiment was over, participants completed a learning preference questionnaire, which included both closed-ended and open-ended questions. Moreover, six participants took part in a post-study interview. Quantitative and qualitative data were analyzed and the results were used to answer the research questions.

Results of the quantitative data analysis showed a significantly greater effect of the guided inductive approach on students' short-term learning of the French grammatical structures. However, no significant results were found for the long-term learning of these structures, or for the relationship between student learning preferences and their performance scores on grammar tests. In fact, participants who preferred explanations of the rules (deductive approach) showed a better performance in the guided inductive approach.

Design and strands

Figure 9.1 shows a schematic diagram of the design and strands in Vogel *et al.*'s MMR study. As the figure illustrates, the study included a quantitative and a qualitative strand. The within-subjects repeated-measures experimental design in the quantitative strand enabled the researchers to compare the performances of each individual student in the two different treatment conditions (inductive vs. deductive), allowing each individual to serve as his or her own control.

The researchers referred to Creswell (2003) to describe their study as a sequential MMR design. They explained that the quantitative data were collected first within the course of a 14-week semester and that qualitative data were collected during the last week of the semester. The quantitative data and analysis did not, however, inform the qualitative strand. The main emphasis and priority were given to the quantitative data and, as the researchers explicitly stated, the 'qualitative data were used in a supporting fashion, to explain or elaborate on the quantitative results' (p. 357). The overall design of this MMR study, as described by the researchers, can thus

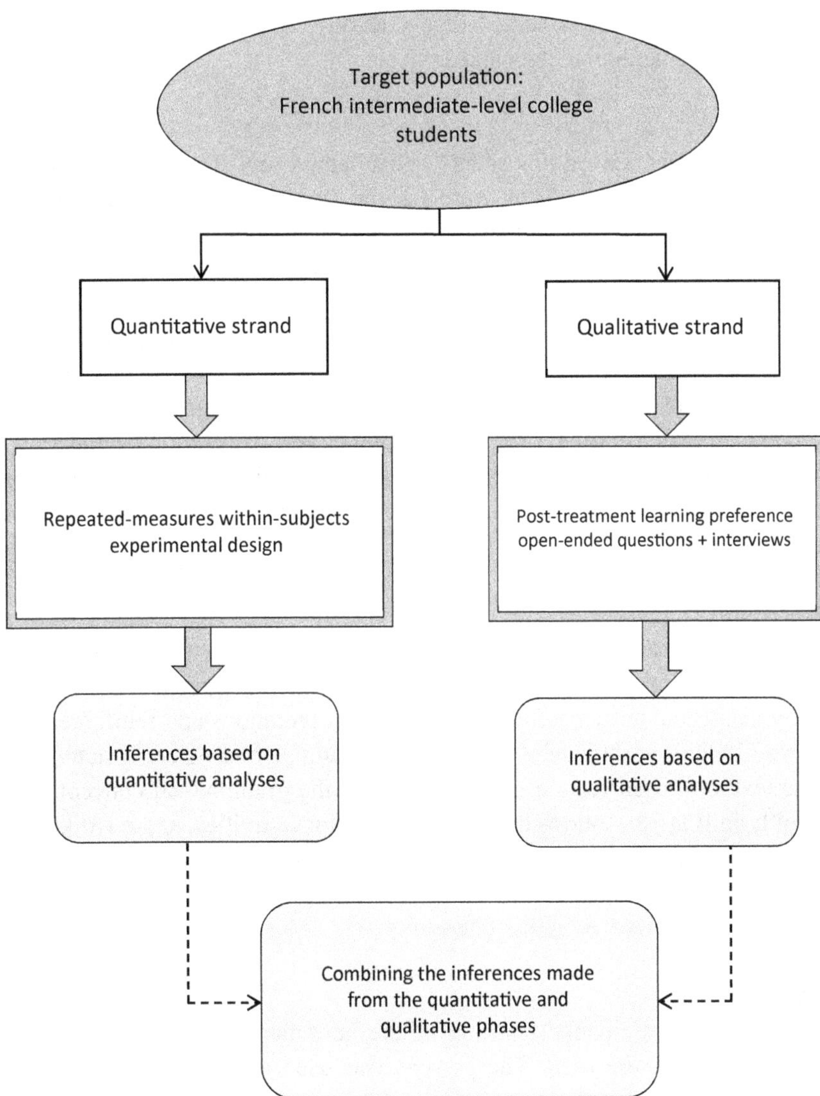

Figure 9.1 The design, strands and inferences made in Vogel *et al.'s* (2011) MMR study

be represented by QUAN → qual, with more emphasis on the quantitative strand. However, it can be argued, based on the explanations provided in the research report, that this study represents a QUAN + qual design. This is because the quantitative strand did not inform or help the researchers to develop the qualitative strand. In other words, the quantitative and the qualitative data were collected independently, with a major emphasis indeed on the quantitative data and analysis.

Methods

All 40 participants were exposed to both inductive and deductive approaches to grammar instruction. They were assigned to one of the three sections of the French intermediate course (A, B or C) through the university registrar system. The researchers randomly assigned sections A and B to Group 1 and section C to Group 2.

To counterbalance the order effect of the approach (inductive vs. deductive), the first group (sections A and B) received the first of the ten target grammatical structures with the guided inductive approach, while the second group (section C) received a deductive presentation of the same structure. For each of the subsequent grammatical structures, the groups switched conditions, alternating between a guided inductive and a deductive presentation.

Procedures

All research procedures and testing related to this study were incorporated in participants' regular class time and were entirely integrated into students' daily classroom activities, which included presentations and reinforcement of vocabulary, grammar lessons, cultural readings and listening activities. The textbook used for the course presented the grammatical concepts explicitly in English, followed by several learning activities, and a workbook provided additional grammatical practice in contextualized activities. Instructors could choose to introduce grammar points either deductively or inductively during the regular class time.

Data collection

To compare participants' learning of the grammar points, pre- and post-grammar tests were used. The pre-test was used to measure participants' baseline knowledge of the ten grammatical structures at the beginning of the study (semester), so that post-tests could be compared with it once the treatment was over. The test included 24 multiple-choice items, of which 20 focused on the targeted structures taught and evaluated during the treatment phase, with 2 items per structure taught. The remaining four items served as distracters and were later excluded from scoring and analysis. Possible scores for the grammar pre-test thus ranged from 0 to 20. The same grammar test was administered at the end of the study (semester) to assess students' learning of the ten structures over the course of instruction. The results of the post-test were used to compare the effect of the two instructional approaches (inductive vs. deductive). In addition to pre- and post-tests, an immediate test was administered to participants following the presentation of each grammatical structure. The immediate tests were meant to both ensure participants' understanding of the target structure and assess their ability to use it in a similar context. Each immediate test contained four open-ended items, with a possible total score ranging from 0 to 8.

The other instrument of data collection in Vogel *et al.*'s study was a learning preference questionnaire (LPQ). This consisted of both quantitative closed-ended items and qualitative open-ended questions. The questionnaire collected data on student participants' preferences for and experiences with the two instructional approaches and was administered at the end of the treatment (semester). The quantitative items were analyzed and included in the quantitative strand of the study. The qualitative questions asked students to state their preferences and opinions regarding each of the instructional approaches. These questions were analyzed and included in the qualitative strand of the study.

In addition to the qualitative open-ended questions in the questionnaire, and to further elicit student preferences, interviews were conducted with six students (four female and two male) after the quantitative data collection phase was completed. These short interviews were designed to elicit student preferences for the instructional approach to grammar instruction and their opinions regarding each of the two approaches used in the study. Each interview was audio-recorded and then transcribed verbatim for analysis.

Data analysis
Analysis of the quantitative data included descriptive and inferential statistical analyses. Descriptive statistics including mean and standard deviation were calculated and presented for the sample of the study. Means and standard deviations were calculated for immediate, pre- and post-tests. In addition, item analysis and internal consistency checks of the immediate tests as well as pre- and post-tests were conducted to ensure the appropriateness of the grammar tests in terms of the item difficulty and test reliability. Inferential statistical test of significance of analysis of variance (ANOVA) was also used to ensure that there was no significant difference between the participants' grammar knowledge in the three sections (A, B and C) at the pre-test stage.

- To answer the first research question, the researchers used paired-samples t-test (Riazi, 2016) to check for any significant difference in participants' short-term learning as represented by their scores on immediate tests for the guided inductive and deductive conditions.

- To answer the second research question, a two (pre-test, post-test) by two (deductive, guided inductive) repeated-measures ANOVA was conducted.
- To answer the third research question, frequency counts were calculated from the post-study LPQ along with the analysis of the qualitative data.
- To answer the fourth research question, the researchers used Pearson product-moment correlation (Riazi, 2016) to calculate the relationship between participants' immediate scores and their scores on the LPQ. Additionally, the researchers used paired-samples t-tests to check whether there were any significant differences between the scores on post-tests for the two approaches, with the participants' preferences as the categorical (independent) variable.
- To answer the fifth research question, the researchers used Pearson product-moment correlation to explore possible relationships between the participants' preference for a particular instructional approach and their score on the grammar post-test.

Analysis of the qualitative data included participants' responses to the open-ended items in the LPQ and the transcriptions of the six interviews. Each of these two qualitative data sources was examined and coded independently. The coded data were then re-examined to identify similarities, differences and contradictions existing across participants' experiences or within one participant's experience. As mentioned at the beginning of this section, the overall design of the study can be represented by QUAN + qual. The descriptions of the design and strands showed that the researchers put more emphasis and weight on the quantitative strand of the study. The qualitative data and analysis played a minor role compared with the quantitative data and analysis and were used to expand the breadth of the study and provide some supplementary explanations.

Commentary

Based on the FRAMMR framework presented in Chapter 8, the commentary will provide comments at the three levels of conceptual, methodological and inferential. In light of the comments, Vogel *et al.*'s study is evaluated to follow an 'expansion' purpose and is thus classified as 'eclectic' based on the FRAMMR framework.

Conceptual

The role of grammar in second language (L2) teaching and learning has been and continues to be controversial, especially with the rise of communicative language teaching in the late 1970s and early 1980s (see, for example, Burgess & Etherington, 2002; Nassaji & Fotos, 2004). While some researchers have argued that teaching grammar in isolation might not lead to student learning, other researchers have recently demonstrated that formal instruction of grammar can help L2 learners to achieve high levels of accuracy. Nassaji and Fotos (2004) provide a review of the literature on this controversy, and Burgess and Etherington (2002) investigate teacher attitudes to grammar instruction and its incorporation within an English for Academic Purpose (EAP) programme in British language centres.

There has been a distinction made between 'focus on form' and 'focus on forms', suggested by Long (1991) and Long and Robinson (1998). Whereas the former denotes a more structure-based grammar teaching, the latter is considered to have a focus on meaning. Focus on form and linguistic accuracy, however, remains one of the principles of the proficiency oriented approaches to language teaching and a component of communicative competence. Focus on forms, which draws students' attention to linguistic forms in real communication events, is considered more in line with the communicative approaches to language teaching and learning. From a pedagogical perspective, Long (2000, cited in Nassaji & Fotos, 2004) suggests that 'focus on forms' is learner-centred and, therefore, more effective for teaching grammar.

In light of the above discussion, Vogel *et al.*'s (2011) research problem was how grammatical structures should be taught to students. Their study investigated whether French language structures and grammatical rules are more efficiently taught explicitly in a deductive way and before students get the opportunity to practise, or whether the grammatical rules should be taught in an inductive manner and before an explicit focus on the rule. In particular, their concern was with comparing the effects of a deductive (explicit) and a guided inductive (implicit) approach in teaching French grammatical structures. They compared intermediate-level French college students' short- and long-term learning of the ten structures and their preferences for any particular approach.

Conceptually, Vogel *et al.* were driven by a debate in the literature about how language structures and grammatical rules should be presented to students and whether students express any preference for a particular approach. This debate led the researchers to investigate the short-term and long-term effect of a deductive and a guided inductive approach to teaching ten French grammatical structures to students and how students' learning of these structures might be related to their preference for approach. It can be implied from the elaborations in the annotation and design and strands that the researchers were driven by the five research questions they posed. The majority of these research questions required quantitative data to be answered.

Although Vogel *et al.* did not explicitly state a purpose for choosing and mixing methods from the quantitative and qualitative approaches, it can be implied that they followed an expansion purpose. This implication is based on their clear statement that '(P)riority was given to the quantitative data and qualitative data were used in a supporting fashion, to explain or elaborate on the quantitative results' (p. 357). Accordingly, Vogel *et al.*'s study can be described as an 'eclectic' example of an MMR study based on the explanations provided in Chapter 8.

Methodological

At the methodological level, the discussion is focused on whether the underlying assumptions and quality standards of each strand (qual/quan) are adequately applied. Vogel *et al.* adopted a sequential implementation strategy (Creswell, 2003) consisting of a major quantitative and a minor qualitative strand. Quantitative data were collected first, throughout the course of a 14-week semester, and qualitative data were collected during the last week of the semester. The purpose of the study was both to compare the effectiveness of two instructional approaches to teaching grammar and to provide a better insight into students' personal preference for a given teaching approach.

As the researchers themselves clarify, more emphasis and priority were given to the quantitative strand. According to Johnson *et al.* (2010), Vogel *et al.*'s study can be an example of a quantitative-dominant MMR study. The qualitative phase was used in a more supporting manner and to elaborate on the results obtained from the quantitative strand. Although the researchers followed a sequential approach (QUAN → qual), the qualitative phase was not built on the findings of the quantitative phase, suggesting that this could be classified as an MMR study with 'development' purpose. The researchers used the qualitative phase as a separate mini-project to elaborate on and provide supplementary explanations for the results achieved from the quantitative phase. For example, the open interview data were used to provide further information on the more structured questions of the learning preference questionnaire. Both the questionnaire items and the interviews were used to demonstrate further evidence about participants' preferred approach for learning grammar. The evidence provided in the report thus represents this study's design as QUAN + qual with an expansion purpose.

The higher priority on the quantitative strand is also evident in the data analysis. The statistical tests of significance used to answer research questions included a paired-samples t-test (to answer RQ1), repeated-measures analysis of variance (RMANOVA) (to answer RQ2) and Pearson product-moment correlation (to answer RQ4 and RQ5). Percentages of the participants' responses to closed-ended items on the LPQ were also used to answer RQ3. Furthermore, quantitative analyses were conducted on the test items and test reliability as well as the questionnaire's internal consistency.

Some comments about the quantitative data analyses are in order here. The researchers used parametric tests of statistical significance (t-test, RMANOVA and Pearson correlation) to answer four research questions. There is, however, no explanation about whether or to what extent the quantitative data met the requirements of the parametric tests they used. Furthermore, no effect sizes are presented for the results of the parametric tests, so the strength of the relationships found is not clear to the readers. Effect size is a statistical measure used to determine the strength of the observed relationship between the independent and dependent variables, and is different from statistical significance. Statistical significance shows only whether the observed relationship is due to sampling error or chance, while the effect size can indicate the strength of the observed relationships among variables.

When analyzing and reporting the closed-ended questions of the learning preference questionnaire to answer the third research question, the researchers did not report any inferential statistics, only reported percentages of the participants' responses to each question. In order to be able to generalize the findings obtained for the sample to the target population, appropriate inferential statistical test of significance should be used. In case of frequencies and percentages, usually a non-parametric test of significance such as Chi-square is used to show, for example, if participants' reported preferences for the deductive and inductive approaches are statistically significant or not and thus generalizable to the target population. MMR studies should apply the quality standards of quantitative methods when these are used in the study.

Regarding the qualitative data and analysis, which included the open-ended questions on the LPQ and interviews with the six participants, insufficient detail regarding analysis of these data is presented in the paper. The researchers stated only that:

Both the interview transcripts and the responses to the open-ended items of the learning preference questionnaires were examined and coded independently. The coded data were then reexamined to identify similarities, differences, and contradictions existing across participants' experiences or within one participant's experience. (p. 362)

This is the only explanation about the qualitative data and analysis that could be found in the report, perhaps because it constituted a minor part in the MMR study. More explanation about the procedures followed to analyze the qualitative data would add both to the credibility of the findings and more generally to the trustworthiness of the results reported.

Inferential

Not surprisingly, given the nature of Vogel *et al.*'s study as a quantitative-dominant eclectic MMR study, the main inferences made in this study were based on the quantitative data analysis results. Almost all the five researcher questions are predominantly answered on the basis of the quantitative data analysis results. The final conclusions and inferences followed the same pattern.

The inferences made were based on the outcomes of the statistical tests of significance. Based on the results of a paired-samples t-test, the researchers concluded that students performed better in the guided inductive condition compared with the deductive condition as related to their short-term learning. Using the results of the repeated-measures ANOVA, the researchers concluded an overall improvement in grammar knowledge over the course of the semester was achieved regardless of the approach used. Using the percentages of the participants' responses to the LPQ items, the researchers inferred that the majority of the participants ($n = 32$, 80%) preferred the deductive approach and being explicitly taught the grammatical rules, and only a minority ($n = 6$, 16%) preferred an inductive approach and discovering the rule with the guidance of the instructor. Moreover, based on the results of the Pearson correlation between the participants' preferred approach and their test performance, the researchers inferred that there was a significant relationship between a preference for the inductive approach and performance on immediate tests. However, the researchers concluded that there was no significant relationship between a preferred approach and participants' performance on the grammar post-test. However, based on a paired-samples t-test, the researchers concluded that those participants who preferred the deductive condition performed better in the inductive condition. This implies that there was a reversed relationship between language learners' preference for a deductive grammar instruction approach and their test performance, which turned out to be higher in the inductive mode.

It appears that the researchers made no independent inferences based on the results of the qualitative analysis of the LPQ open-ended questions or the interviews with the six participants. They seem only to have used the results of the qualitative data analysis to elaborate on their quantitative inferences about participants' preference for the deductive approach. The congruence between the results of the qualitative data and analysis led the researchers to make a triangulation inference about the two data sources and consider this as an index of the reliability of their analysis. Interestingly, though, the researchers noted a discrepancy between their quantitative results and students' preferred learning approach. The quantitative results showed a significant positive effect of the guided inductive approach on students' short-term learning of grammar. The qualitative results, in contrast, indicated students' preference for the deductive approach. The researchers could have followed this contradiction in the interviews and aimed for an 'initiation' purpose in their MMR study. The initiation purpose could then have resulted in more comprehensive inferences about the research problem. However, they did not do so, perhaps due to time constraints or not recognizing this opportunity, and maintained a primarily expansion purpose. Overall, therefore, this MMR study may be classified as eclectic within the categorization framework discussed in Chapter 8.

Study 2

Huang, S. (2015). Mixed-method research on learning vocabulary through technology reveals vocabulary growth in second-grade students. *Reading Psychology, 36*(1), 1–30.

Annotation

The second MMR study to be reviewed in this chapter is a mixed method embedded research project by Huang (2015). The study intended to investigate the effectiveness of the integration of technology for second-grade students' vocabulary development and learning in a public elementary school in the south-eastern part of the United States. MMR studies with an embedded design usually use experimental designs for the quantitative strand and either introspective or retrospective think-aloud protocols for the qualitative strand. In this instance, retrospective think-aloud protocols were collected from the participants after the intervention.

Two classes of second-grade students were randomly selected to participate in this MMR study for a semester. One class was treated as the experimental group ($n = 21$), while the other was considered as a control group ($n = 19$). Overall, the participants in this study included 40 second-grade students (21 boys and 19 girls) enrolled in the two classes. The treatment in the experimental group included using technology to enhance students' development of English words, and the purpose was to investigate how the treatment might affect students' reading motivation and engagement.

Both quantitative and qualitative data were collected and analyzed and then reported separately in the study. The quantitative data included participants' pre- and post-test scores on the Expressive Vocabulary Test-2 (EVT-2, Williams, 2007). The qualitative data included before and during intervention classroom observations as well as semi-structured interviews with 12 students (6 from each group). The interviews were conducted after the intervention. The before study classroom observation was conducted to discover the vocabulary teaching and learning activities so that the instructional materials could be prepared for the study. During treatment observations included weekly classroom observations on how students approached vocabulary learning and engaged in instructional activities. 'The interview protocol contained 17 questions related to students' general reading interests, strategies in vocabulary learning, other forms of literacy skills, and the use of intervention programs' (p. 7).

Two major research questions were addressed in this study.

1. How do new technologies and vocabulary–technology integration strategies support students' vocabulary development?
2. How effective are vocabulary–technology strategies in helping these second-grade students to develop vocabulary? (p. 5)

Results of the data analysis showed that the experimental group was generally more engaged in classroom activities. Results also showed significant improvement on the post-test for the experimental group, while the control group was found to show no change between the pre- and the post-test scores.

Design and strands

Figure 9.2 presents a schematic diagram of the design and strands in Huang's (2015) MMR study. As the figure shows, this study used an embedded or nested MMR design (Creswell & Plano-Clark, 2007; Riazi, 2016). The study included two strands involving both quantitative and qualitative methods. The quantitative strand included an experimental design with pre-post vocabulary performance measurements.

Method

To set up the experiment, the researcher randomly selected two second-grade classes from an elementary school and assigned one class to the experimental group ($n = 21$) and the other as the control group ($n = 19$). The experimental group received treatment, which included technology-integrated vocabulary instruction, while the control group practised the school's conventional vocabulary learning instruction. The qualitative strand included a pre-study classroom observation in order to design appropriate vocabulary teaching techniques to be used in the experimental and control groups. While the experiment was in progress, classroom observations were conducted to document students' approaches to vocabulary learning as well as their engagement in vocabulary learning activities. In addition to during-experiment observations, the researcher interviewed 12 participants (six from each of the two groups) after the experiment was completed to elicit students' reading interests and vocabulary learning strategies. The MMR study thus used an embedded design. In the embedded or nested designs, usually the core of the design is an experiment with an embedded qualitative strand including interviews or observations or both.

Data analysis

Analysis of the quantitative data was done on the participants' scores on the pre- and post-test regarding vocabulary learning to answer the first research question ('How do new technologies and vocabulary–technology integration strategies support students' vocabulary development?'). Both descriptive and inferential statistics were used to report the quantitative analysis of the scores. Descriptive statistics included the mean and standard deviation of participants' scores on both pre- and post-tests. Inferential statistics included a dependent or paired-samples t-test to determine whether a statistically significant change could be observed in test scores when comparing the pre- and post-test scores of the two groups.

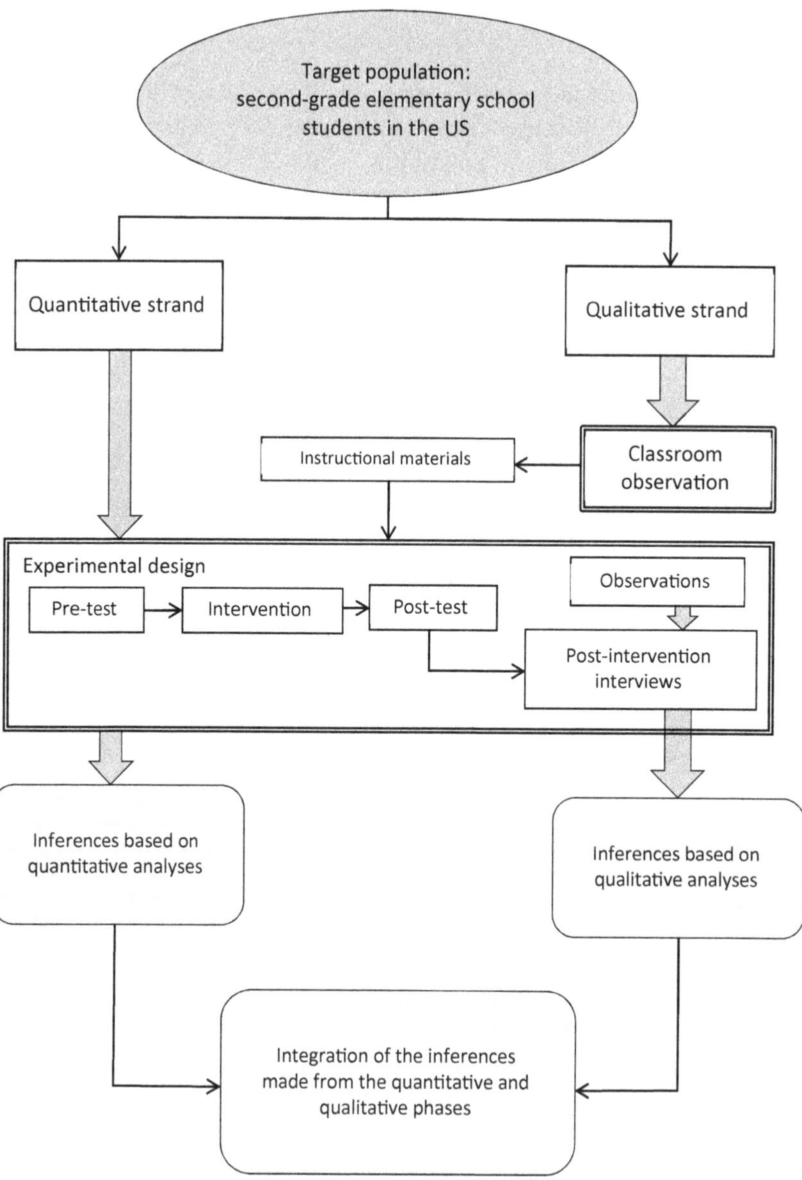

Figure 9.2 The design, strands and inferences made in Huang's (2015) MMR study

Analysis of the qualitative observations and post-intervention interviews was done through the constant comparative method (Glaser & Strauss, 1967; Riazi, 2016) to answer the second research question ('How effective are vocabulary–technology strategies in helping these second-grade students to develop vocabulary?').

Findings from the quantitative strand showed that the experimental group (exposed to vocabulary–technology activities) outperformed the control group on the post-test vocabulary test. Findings from the qualitative strand indicated that vocabulary–technology intervention effectively provided meaningful, goal-oriented vocabulary instruction and engagement in the learning environment. The teaching techniques in the experimental group also created more opportunities for students to engage in peer social interactions and collaborations.

Commentary

Conceptual

This MMR study draws on three theoretical perspectives and the researcher conceptualizes and contextualizes the research problem within these three theoretical frameworks. The first framework is the new literacies theory (Lankshear & Knobel, 2003; Leu *et al.*, 2004) presented and used to examine the opportunities that can enhance teaching practices by using and merging new technologies such as software, internet technologies, web pages and so on into the traditional literacy curriculum (Coiro *et al.*, 2008). Drawing on the new literacies theoretical framework, Huang (2015) focused on the impact of software programs on vocabulary learning for second-grade elementary students. The second theoretical perspective that informs Huang's study is the concept of literacy–technology integration (Watts-Taffe & Gwinn, 2005, 2007). Finally, Huang's study is grounded in the concept of scaffolding originally presented by Vygotsky (1978). Scaffolding provides a mechanism for children to interact with more experienced members of their learning community so that the control of cognitive activity can be transferred from the more experienced member (for example, the teacher) to the learner (Gauvain, 2006). Through scaffolding, learners would be able to gradually meet increasingly challenging tasks at different levels (Gambrell & Morrow, 1996). From this theoretical perspective, teachers can scaffold language learners, including struggling readers, in their vocabulary learning and also help them retain new vocabulary in meaningful ways and at all ages (Rupley & Nichols, 2005).

Merging these three theoretical perspectives, Huang (2015) presented a conceptualization for the integration of literacy with technology (p. 4) as adapted in Figure 9.3. This includes traditional literacy practices, new technologies and the integration of literacy–technology strategies in a vocabulary learning environment.

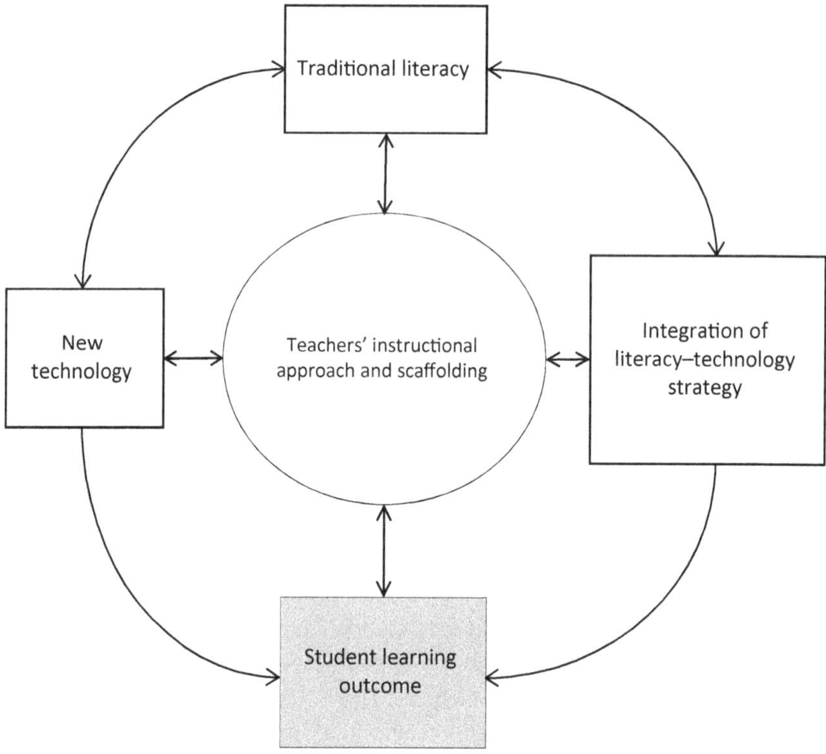

Figure 9.3 Huang's (2015) conceptualization of teachers' instructional approach and scaffolding

Huang proposed that the teacher's instructional approach and scaffolding are the core of the literacy curriculum, that the components related to it are interconnected, and that they directly affect student learning.

Based on the above conceptualization, this study had the potential of being an MMR study with a 'complementarity' purpose, and thus more innovative, to address the question of how the independent but interconnected components could have affected the teacher instructional approach and his or her scaffolding of student learning. Such a complementarity MMR study could have addressed different facets of the teacher instructional approach in a more comprehensive way. Nevertheless, the researcher decided to focus on one component, the integration of vocabulary learning with technology, and investigated how this integration might meet the needs of diverse learners' vocabulary development in second-grade students. The researcher was also interested in examining how technology and vocabulary–technology strategies affected this cohort of students' reading motivation and engagement. Huang's MMR study can thus be categorized as a principled MMR study with an embedded design, despite a relatively strong theoretical orientation.

Methodological

As discussed in the conceptual section, Huang decided to use an embedded MMR design to investigate how the integration of vocabulary learning with technology might fulfil the vocabulary development needs of diverse second-grade elementary students. MMR studies with a nested or embedded design usually use an experimental design for the quantitative strand and either introspective or retrospective think-aloud protocol procedures for the qualitative strand.

The difference between introspective and retrospective procedures relates to the time when they are collected. Introspective think-aloud protocols are collected from the participants as they are performing the language-related task. Retrospective think-aloud protocols are collected after the participants complete the task and usually turn into post-task performance interviews. Each of these two approaches has its advantages and disadvantages. For example, while introspective think-aloud protocols are considered to be more valid due to their immediacy to task performance, they have been judged to put extra cognitive load on the participants because they have to perform two tasks (the teaching/learning task itself and the think-aloud task) at the same time. Retrospective interviews, meanwhile, are less cognitively demanding but may not be as accurate and thus valid as the introspective think-aloud protocols. In Huang's study, retrospective post-intervention interviews were used to collect qualitative data from the participants and after the experimental intervention.

The quantitative strand

In the quantitative strand of the study, the researcher collected student pre- and post-test performance on the vocabulary test. The researcher then used paired-samples or dependent t-tests to compare the pre-post vocabulary test scores of the participants to answer the first research question ('How do new technologies and vocabulary–technology integration strategies support students' vocabulary development?'). However, and perhaps surprisingly, there is no report on the independent t-test in the results section to compare the post-test scores of the experimental group (exposed to technology for vocabulary learning) with those of the control group (exposed to traditional vocabulary learning). There is only a passing mention of the result of an independent test comparing the post-test of the experimental and control groups in the discussion section of the paper. Given the experimental nature of the quantitative strand, one would expect to see the results of the post-test scores of the two groups presented in the results section.

The qualitative strand

In the qualitative strand of the study, the researcher collected classroom observations (before treatment and during the experiment) as well as post-experiment interviews with 12 participants. Classroom observations before the experiment took one week and included the observation of the two participating classrooms. This observation was conducted to understand the context and then develop appropriate instructional procedures for the experimental and control groups. Analysis of the qualitative observations and post-intervention interviews was done through the constant comparative method (Glaser & Strauss, 1967; Riazi, 2016) to answer the second research question ('How effective are vocabulary–technology strategies in helping these second-grade students to develop vocabulary?').

There is little elaboration of the qualitative data analysis in the report. The researcher stated: '(T)o establish the validity and reliability of the qualitative data, the researcher used a triangulation strategy that involved interpreting meaning and moving back and forth between inductive and deductive reasoning, and also between description and interpretation' (p. 12). However, this seems too general for the readers to be able to understand (a) how exactly the researcher performed the qualitative data analysis, and (b) how the researcher used the 'triangulation strategy' to establish the validity and reliability of the qualitative data. Further elaboration on these two questions certainly could have helped the readers to better understand the procedures used to analyze the qualitative data.

Reflections

More details on the qualitative data analysis could have improved the dependability of the study. One of the indices of reliability of the research reports is the extent to which researchers provide details of the procedures used in data collection and analysis. Although the researcher made a cross-reference to Huang (2013) for the procedures of qualitative data analysis, this is insufficient detail of the analytical procedures in context and as relates to this study. The lack of details on the data analysis would also prevent readers from developing an understanding of how the data analysis results led the researcher to make plausible inferences. It should be emphasized here again that MMR requires the researcher to conform to the quality expectations and standards of both quantitative and qualitative approaches to data analysis.

Another methodological observation regarding Huang's (2015) study is the role and level of emphasis of each of the two strands (quantitative and qualitative) in the MMR design. The researcher made a reference to Creswell and Plano-Clark (2007) and stated that '(T)his study used a mixed-method embedded research design, which is a two-phase process involving both quantitative and qualitative methods, with the qualitative data taking a secondary role' (p. 5). However, this is by no means what we can see from the role of the qualitative strand in Huang's study as presented in the research report. If the qualitative strand is not more emphasized, it seems at least to have an equal weight with the quantitative strand. This is evident in the report, first, because there are only two research questions stated in the paper and each of the questions is answered by the findings from one strand. That is, the first research question has been answered by the results of the quantitative data and analysis and the second research question is answered by the results of the qualitative data and analysis. Accordingly, one might assign equal status to each of the two strands. Second, and as can be seen from the report, the results and discussion of the qualitative findings supersede those of the quantitative part, leading one to think that the qualitative strand was more dominant.

Based on the above observation, Huang's MMR study design can perhaps be represented as {qual → [QUAN (QUAL)] → QUAL}. The researcher observed the two classes for one week and, based on this phase of classroom observation, developed appropriate instructional procedures for the experimental and the control groups. A 'development' purpose is thus evident in both the approach and the processes of Huang's study. The researcher then used an embedded experimental design with a major focus on the experimentation (using a technology-enhanced procedure in the experimental group and traditional vocabulary learning in the control group), while observing the two groups and taking field notes. The researcher went on to interview 12 participants (six from the experimental and six from the control group) after the experiment and as a post-intervention qualitative data collection. The interviews were thus another source of qualitative data and analysis. It seems, therefore, that the qualitative strand played a significant role in Huang's MMR study, perhaps far beyond a secondary role as suggested by the researcher.

Inferential

Three types of inferences are made in Huang's MMR study, a quantitative inference, a qualitative inference and an integrated one. The quantitative inference is based on the results of the inferential statistics derived from the dependent and independent t-tests. This inference explains that while the treatment (technology-enhanced approach to vocabulary instruction) showed significant improvement in students' vocabulary test performance, the traditional game-based approach did not show any improvement in students' vocabulary development as represented by their test performance. Moreover, based on the independent t-test results, the researcher inferred that students in the experimental group significantly outperformed students in the control group on their post-tests.

The second inference made in Huang's MMR study is based on the outcomes of the qualitative data analysis, that the use of the technology-enhanced approach in the experimental group provided effective, meaningful and purpose-driven vocabulary instruction and resulted in students' engagement in the learning environment.

Huang also made an integrated inference based on a mixture of the quantitative and qualitative inferences. The final conclusion or inference presented in Huang's study is that using new technologies and technology-enhanced strategies created a digital learning environment that increased social interaction among students and teachers. The researcher used this integrated inference to support an earlier claim, made by Kamil *et al.* (2000), that social interactions and collaborations are central in an effective technology-enhanced learning environment. Overall, Huang's study can be evaluated as a 'principled' MMR study with a 'triangulation' purpose.

Learning task

Read the annotations below and analyze both or one of the articles using the FRAMMR framework outlined in this chapter. Start by preparing a schematic diagram for the design of the study and writing down details of each strand in each study. Then attempt to comment on the study at the conceptual, methodological and inferential levels.

- At the conceptual level, determine whether or not the researchers identified a particular purpose for mixing methods. If not, are you able to imply a purpose based on the information provided in each study? Use the explanations provided for the three categories of 'eclectic', 'principled' and 'innovative' in Chapter 8, and decide which of these categories each study falls into.
- At the methodological level, look for the details of the quantitative and qualitative data collection and analysis procedures and ascertain whether quality criteria and standards are observed in each strand.
- Finally, scan the reports, especially in the discussion and conclusions sections, to reveal what types of inferences are made based on which results, and whether the researcher has mixed the inferences in favour of a fuller meta-inference.

Isaacs, T. & Thomson, R.I. (2013). Rater experience, rating scale length, and judgments of L2 pronunciation: Revisiting research conventions. *Language Assessment Quarterly, 10*, 135–159.

The research problem addressed in Isaacs and Thomson's mixed methods research study concerns the effects of two variables (rating scale length and rater experience) on raters' judgements of L2 speech. The participants included 20 experienced and 20 novice raters, who were randomly assigned to judge speech samples of 38 newcomers to Canada using one of the two rating scales, one with a five-point and another with a nine-point rating scale. The quantitative data included numerical ratings for comprehensibility, accent and fluency of the L2 speakers. The qualitative data included think-aloud verbal protocols and post-task interviews with the raters. Results of the quantitative data analysis revealed high Cronbach's alpha coefficients and no group differences for rating scale length or rater experience. However, Rasch category probability plots revealed that raters had difficulty differentiating between scale steps, particularly in the mid-scale range – a challenge that was exacerbated in the nine-point scale condition. Results of the qualitative data analysis suggested that experienced and novice raters adopted strategies to either draw on or offset their perceived experience with L2 speech in conducting their ratings. The researchers provide some implications for L2 pronunciation research.

Martinez, I.A., Beck, S.C. & Panza, C.B. (2009). Academic vocabulary in agriculture research articles: A corpus-based study. *English for Specific Purposes, 28*, 183–198.

This study focuses on the development of discipline-specific academic word lists to meet the needs of ESL writers who must read and publish articles in English. Quantitative data included the identification of the academic words in a corpus of research articles of agriculture and comparing it with Coxhead's (2000) Academic Word List. Analysis of the quantitative data revealed a highly restricted list of words from the Academic Word List, including only 92 families. Qualitative data included the researchers' observations and analysis of the word families in the corpus. Analysis of the qualitative data indicated not only that some words had specific meanings and behaviours related to the genre, and also probably to the field, but also that some words from the Academic Word List had technical meaning in the corpus of research articles of agriculture. The researchers also observed that many words of general use had academic meaning in the corpus, and should probably be regarded as academic vocabulary. The researchers concluded, based on the findings, that there is a need to produce field-specific academic word lists, which, in their view, should incorporate all frequent academic lexical items necessary for the expression of the rhetoric of their specific research area.

References

Burgess, J. & Etherington, S. (2002). Focus on grammatical form: Explicit or implicit? *System, 30*, 433–458.

Carroll, J.B. (1961). Fundamental considerations in testing for English language proficiency of foreign students. In H.B. Allen (Ed.), *Teaching English as a second language* (pp. 364–372). New York: McGraw-Hill.

Carroll, J.B. (1969). What does the Pennsylvania foreign language study tell us? *Foreign Language Annals, 3*, 214–236.

Carroll, J.B. (1983). Psychometric theory and language testing. In J.W. Oller, Jr. (Ed.), *Issues in language testing research* (pp. 80–107). Rowley, MA: Newbury House.

Coiro, J., Knobel, M., Lankshear, C. & Leu, D.J. (Eds.) (2008). *Handbook of research in new literacies*. Mahwah, NJ: Lawrence Erlbaum.

Coxhead, A. (2000). A new academic word list. *TESOL Quarterly, 34*(2), 213–238.

Creswell, J.W. (2003). *Research design: Qualitative, quantitative and mixed methods approaches*. Thousand Oaks, CA: Sage Publications.

Creswell, J.W. & Plano-Clark, V.P. (2007). *Designing and conducting mixed methods research*. Thousand Oaks, CA: Sage.

Gambrell, L.B. & Morrow, L.M. (1996). Creating motivating contexts for literacy learning. In L. Baker, P. Afflervach, & D. Reinking (Eds.), *Developing engaged readers in school and home communities* (pp. 115–135). Mahwah, NJ: Erlbaum.

Gauvain, M. (2006). Sociocultural contexts of learning. In A.E. Maynard & M.I. Martini (Eds.), *Learning in cultural contexts* (pp. 11–40). New York: Kluwer Academic/Plenum.

Glaser, B.G. & Strauss, A.L. (1967). *The discovery of grounded theory: Strategies for qualitative research*. Chicago, IL: Aldine.

Huang, S.H. (2013). Factors affecting Chinese middle school students' reading motivation. *Reading Psychology, 34*(2), 148–181.

Johnson, R.B., McGowan, M.W. & Turner, L.A. (2010). Grounded theory in practice: Is it inherently a mixed method? *Research in the Schools, 17*(2), 65–78.

Kamil, M.L., Intrator, S.M. & Kim, H.S. (2000). The effects of other technologies on literacy and literacy learning. In M.L. Kamil, P.B. Mosenthal, P.D. Pearson & R. Barr (Eds.), *Handbook of reading research* (Vol. 3, pp. 771–788). Mahwah, NJ: Erlbaum.

Lankshear, C. & Knobel, M. (2003). *New literacies*. Maidenhead: Open University Press.

Leu, D.J., Jr., Kinzer, C.K., Coiro, J.L. & Cammack, D.W. (2004). Toward a theory of new literacies emerging from the internet and other information and communication technologies. In R.B. Ruddel & N.J. Unrau (Eds.), *Theoretical models and processes of reading* (5th ed., pp. 1570–1613). Newark, DE: International Reading Association.

Long, M. (1991). Focus on form: A design feature in language teaching methodology. In K. DeBot, R. Ginsberg & C. Kramsch (Eds.), *Foreign language research in cross-cultural perspective* (pp. 39–52). Amsterdam: Benjamins.

Long, M. (2000). Focus on form in task-based language teaching. In R.D. Lambert & E. Shohamy (Eds.), *Language policy and pedagogy: Essays in honor of A. Ronald Walton* (pp. 179–192). Philadelphia, PA: Benjamins.

Long, M. & Robinson, P. (1998). Focus on form: Theory, research and practice. In C. Doughty & J. Williams (Eds.), *Focus on form in classroom language acquisition* (pp. 15–41). Cambridge: Cambridge University Press.

Nassaji, H. & Fotos, S. (2004). Current developments in research on the teaching of grammar. *Annual Review of Applied Linguistics, 24*, 126–145.

Riazi, A.M. (2016). *The Routledge encyclopedia of research methods in applied linguistics: Quantitative, qualitative and mixed-methods research.* London: Routledge.

Riazi, A.M. & Candlin, C.N. (2014). Mixed-methods research in language teaching and learning: Opportunities, issues and challenges. *Language Teaching, 47*, 135–173.

Rupley, W.H. & Nichols, W.D. (2005). Vocabulary instruction for the struggling reader. *Reading & Writing Quarterly, 21*, 239–260.

Vygotsky, L.S. (1978). Interaction between learning and development. (M. Lopez-Morillas, Trans.) In M. Cole, V. John-Steiner, S. Scribner & E. Souberman (Eds.), *Mind in society: The development of higher psychological processes* (pp. 79–91). Cambridge, MA: Harvard University Press.

Watts-Taffe, S. & Gwinn, C.B. (2005). Viewing professional development through the lens of technology integration: How do beginning teachers navigate the use of technology and new literacies? In B. Maloch, J.V. Hoffman, D. Schallert, C.M. Fairbanks, & J. Worthy (Eds.), *The 54th Yearbook of the National Reading Conference* (pp. 443–454). Oak Creek, WI: National Reading Conference.

Watts-Taffe, S.W. & Gwinn, C.B. (2007). Integrating literacy and technology: Effective practice for grades 1–6. New York: Guilford Press.

Widdowson, H.G. (1983). *Learning purpose and language use.* Oxford: Oxford University Press.

Williams, K.T. (2007). *Expressive Vocabulary Test-2.* Minneapolis, MN: Pearson.

10 Researching Communication Skills

This chapter will:
- briefly explain oral and written proficiency;
- present an analysis and review of a longitudinal MMR study that focuses on English as a second language (ESL) learners' fluency and comprehensibility development;
- present an analysis and review of elementary students' engagement in authentic literacy activities;
- provide two further MMR studies in the learning task to be analyzed by readers.

Introduction

As discussed in Chapter 9, communication skills commonly refer to the four skills of listening, reading, speaking and writing. Listening and reading are usually called receptive skills, while speaking and writing are called productive skills. Listening and speaking together form oral proficiency, while reading and writing shape written proficiency. Language learners need to develop both oral and written proficiency if they are going to use the language functionally in different situations and contexts and for different purposes. As such, research on teaching, learning and assessing the four communication skills in both the first (L1) and second (L2) language has attracted many researchers in the field of applied linguistics for quite a long time.

The four communication skills have been taught and learned in classrooms with structured curricula and recently in more flexible ways beyond classrooms and in natural settings where language learners are exposed to naturally occurring communication events. As such, while some applied linguist researchers have been interested in – and conducted classroom-based research on – the teaching and learning of the four communication skills, others have been interested in researching how opportunities beyond the classrooms might improve language learners' communication skills. The latter approach especially has received more attention in recent years, given the mobility of language learners across the globe as well as access to language learning resources beyond classrooms, particularly through information technology facilities.

The two MMR studies to be reviewed and analyzed in this chapter are related to oral and written proficiency. The first is a longitudinal mixed methods study that compared the oral fluency of well-educated adult immigrants from two language backgrounds, Mandarin (Chinese) and Slavic (Russian). These adult immigrants were enrolled in an English as a second language (ESL) course in Canada. The study was conducted over a two-year period, during which improvement in participants' fluency and comprehensibility in English beyond the classroom was investigated through a mixed methods approach. The second study addressed written proficiency and involved students in grades 3–5 as they were reading books, exchanging letters about the books with an adult pen pal, and participating in small-group discussions about the content of the books.

The two studies are referred to as Study 3 and Study 4, and will be analyzed and reviewed using the FRAMMR framework presented in Chapter 8. First, an annotation of the study will be provided, then design and strands are discussed, and finally each study will be commented on at the conceptual, methodological and inferential levels.

Study 3

Derwing, T., Munro, M.J. & Thomson, R.I. (2007). A longitudinal study of ESL learners' fluency and comprehensibility development. *Applied Linguistics, 29*(3), 359–380.

Annotation

Derwing *et al.* (2007) were responding to a call (Ortega & Iberri-Shea, 2005) for further research on L2 development that emerged from Ortega and Iberri-Shea's review of the literature on second language acquisition (SLA). In their review, Ortega and Iberri-Shea identified a lack of well-designed longitudinal investigations of L2 development. Derwing *et al.* investigated the developmental aspects of adult immigrant ESL learners' oral productive skills by taking into account the learners' exposure to English language outside the classroom. The researchers compared the oral fluency of well-educated adult immigrants from Mandarin (Chinese) and Slavic

(Russian and Ukrainian) language backgrounds using a longitudinal mixed methods approach. Their study addressed three research questions.

1. How do comprehensibility and fluency in the English productions of beginner Mandarin language speakers (MAS) and Russian and Ukrainian (Slavic) language speakers (SLS) develop over a period of two years?
2. How are judgments of comprehensibility and fluency related to learners' exposure to English outside the ESL classroom?
3. What are English L2 learners' reactions to their English learning experiences in terms of difficulties, L2 use, and utility of their classes? (pp. 362–363)

The researchers were interested to determine whether these two groups of adult immigrants were able to develop their oral fluency as they were enrolled in an introductory ESL course in Canada over a two-year period and as they were exposed to the language outside the classroom. Participants of the study included two groups of Mandarin ($n = 16$) and Slavic ($n = 16$) speaking ESL learners. Data collection from the two groups included speech samples at three points over the two-year period, together with estimates of weekly exposure to and use of English language as reported by participants. The researchers also conducted interviews with the participants in the last data collection session in the ESL class. The interviews were used 'as an adjunct to the quantitative analyses' (p. 369) in which participants described their daily opportunities to communicate in English. Both groups of language learners started at the same level of oral proficiency in English.

Analysis of the data included 33 native English speakers' evaluation of the participants' fluency and comprehensibility of their speech samples at the three points. The language learners' progress in terms of their fluency and comprehensibility was examined in light of their exposure to English language outside of their ESL class.

Results of the quantitative data analysis showed that English language learners with a Slavic background had a small but significant improvement in both their English fluency and comprehensibility, whereas the language learners with a Mandarin background did not show any changes in their English fluency and comprehensibility over the two years. Results of the qualitative data analysis indicated that while neither of the two groups of learners had extensive exposure to English language outside their classes, mostly due to their employment and family responsibilities, the Slavic-language speakers reported slightly more opportunities and exposure. Results of both quantitative and qualitative data analysis were integrated and interpreted by the researchers using the 'willingness to communicate' (WTC) (MacIntyre *et al.*, 1998) framework.

Design and strands

Figure 10.1 presents the schematic diagram of Derwing *et al.*'s MMR study. As it shows, the study's target population was immigrant adult ESL learners.

The sample of the study was two groups of Mandarin ($n = 16$) and Slavic ($n = 15$ Russian and 1 Ukrainian) language backgrounds. When the participants arrived in Canada, their English language proficiency was initially assessed using the Canadian Language Benchmarks assessment tool (Centre for Canadian Language Benchmarks, 2006). All 32 participants were found to be at Stage 1 of the Canadian Language Benchmarks and they were all enrolled in full-time beginner ESL classes at the outset of the study.

Data collection

The required data for the study were collected seven times over the course of two years. The first six data collection points were at approximately two-month intervals and the final data collection was 12 months after the sixth one.

The researchers, however, chose to use and report in this study the data collected at Time 2 (T2, after four months), Time 6 (T6, eight months later after twelve months) and Time 7 (T7, a year after T6). Picture narratives were used to assess participants' oral fluency and comprehensibility at these three data collection points. The picture narratives were identical and the same as the one used at Time 1, so the participants were familiar with the assessment task. At each data collection point, participants were given the same set of pictures to narrate a story in English. The narratives were recorded in a quiet room using high-quality digital recorders. At each data collection session, the participants also reported their exposure to and use of English language outside the classroom using a five-point scale: 'less than one hour', 'one hour', 'two hours', 'three hours' and 'more than three hours'. The participants used this scale to estimate their exposure to English radio and television programmes.

A second scale was used to estimate how often the participants interacted with both native speakers (NS) and non-native speakers (NNS) in English for more than ten minutes. The ten-minute criterion was used to rule out the brief or passing interactions such as greetings. This scale ranged from 'never' to 'one to three times a week', 'four to six times a week', 'once a

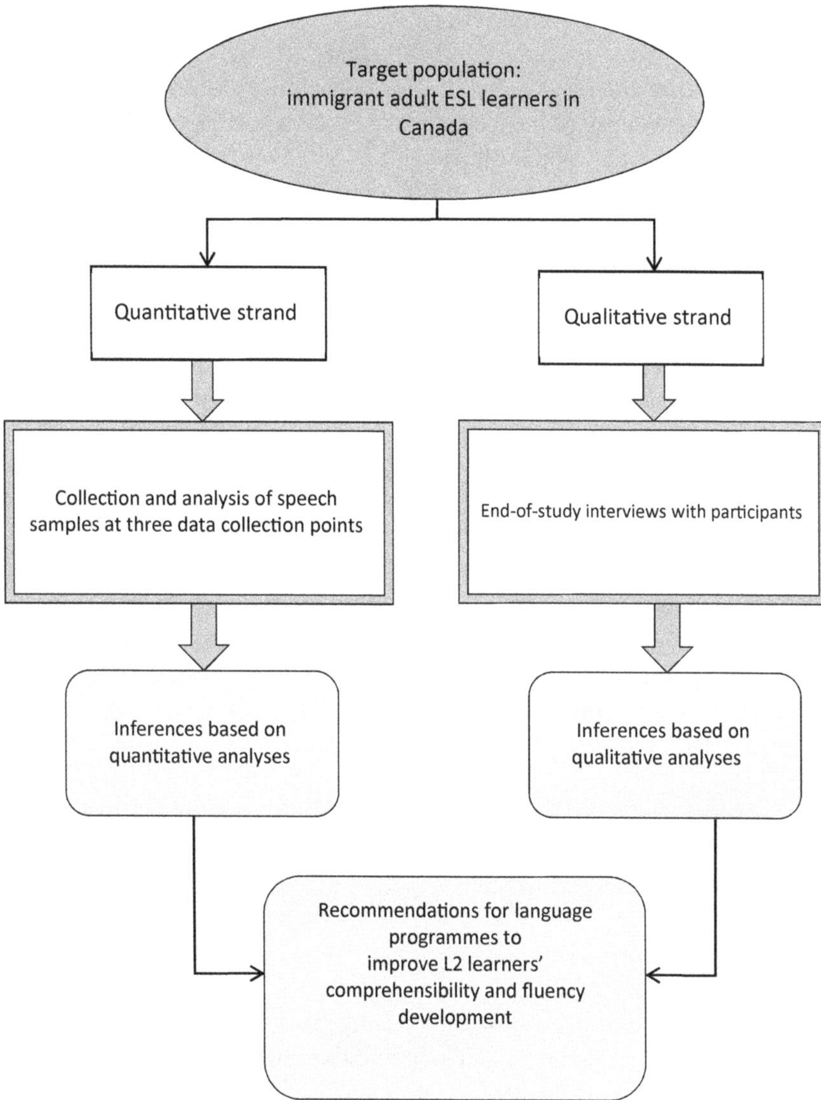

Figure 10.1 The design, strands and inferences made in Derwing *et al.'s* (2007) MMR study

day' and 'several times a day'. Finally, at Time 7, the participants took part in individual interviews and responded to a series of prepared questions in an open-ended manner. Each interview lasted 30–60 minutes. The researchers recorded the interviews for subsequent transcription and analysis.

Rating of participants' oral proficiency

A total of 33 native-speaking English listeners (6 males and 27 females) rated the speech samples. These raters evaluated and assessed the fluency and comprehensibility of the participants' English language using two seven-point Likert scales, one for fluency (1 = extremely fluent, 7 = extremely dysfluent) and one for comprehensibility (1 = very easy to understand, 7 = extremely difficult to understand). To avoid the confusion of 'fluency' with 'proficiency', the researchers asked raters not to take into consideration grammar and vocabulary in their ratings.

To check the consistency among the raters (inter-rater reliability), intra-class correlation coefficients were calculated for the raters. The intra-class correction coefficient is a measure of the reliability of ratings when two or preferably more raters rate a number of participants, as was the case in Derwing *et al.*'s study. Each participant may be rated by a different and random selection of a pool of raters, or by the same raters (see McGraw & Wong, 1996; Shrout & Fleiss, 1979). The inter-rater reliability was obtained to be 0.97 for fluency and 0.95 for the comprehensibility ratings. This means that the raters agreed on 97% and 95% of their ratings of participants' fluency and comprehensibility, respectively. Accordingly, the researchers used the mean scores of comprehensibility and fluency ratings across all raters to calculate each participant's scores as well as the mean for each of the two groups of participants.

Data analysis

In order to analyze the quantitative data, the researchers used the following statistical tests of significance:

- analysis of variance (ANOVA);
- Pearson correlation;
- non-parametric test of significance, Mann-Whitney U-test (see Riazi, 2016 for an explanation of these statistical tests).

To compare changes in participants' fluency and comprehensibility as represented by their mean scores over the three data collection points (T2, T6 and T7), two separate mixed-design (between-within group) ANOVAs were used. As reported by the researchers, the participants' first language (Mandarin vs. Slavic) was used as the between-groups factor, and the three points of data collection (T2, T6 and T7) were used as the within-groups factor. Moreover, Pearson correlation was used to investigate the relationship between participants' scores of fluency and comprehensibility. Finally, the non-parametric Mann-Whitney U-test was used to compare the participants' reports of time spent listening to English talk radio and watching English television, and the frequency of interactions in English of ten minutes or more with both native and non-native speakers at each of the three reporting periods.

The qualitative data analysis in Derwing *et al.*'s study included analysis of the open-ended interviews conducted with participants at the final session of data collection about their perceptions of the opportunities to communicate in English. The researchers applied MacIntyre *et al.*'s (1998) WTC framework to their analysis. However, they focused on the lower three levels of the model, which represent relatively stable aspects of the learners' motivational propensities: social/individual, affective/cognitive contexts and motivational propensities. Results of the qualitative data analysis indicated that despite some variation across participants, there were commonalities in the Slavic background group attitudes and motivational tendencies. Similarly, members of the Mandarin group showed many commonalities in this regard.

Commentary

Using the FRAMMR framework presented in Chapter 8, this section offers comments on Derwing *et al.*'s study at conceptual, methodological and inferential levels. Based on the three level commentaries, this study is classified as an MMR study striving to achieve a 'triangulation' purpose and thus classified as 'principled' using the FRAMMR framework.

Conceptual level

Derwing *et al.*'s study is an example of an MMR study driven by research questions and thus following a more pragmatic approach, as discussed in Chapter 8. The researchers were concerned with two groups of immigrant ESL adult language learners and how their English language might develop as a result of being exposed to the language outside the classroom and using English language to communicate with others. The researchers were interested in investigating how the fluency and comprehensibility of the two groups of participants developed over a period of two years (RQ1). They were also interested in determining whether the participants' improvement in their fluency and comprehensibility might be related to their exposure to English language outside the ESL classroom (RQ2) and the participants' reactions to their English learning experiences in terms of difficulties, L2 use and utility of their classes (RQ3).

Research goal

The researchers stated at the beginning of their report that the study intended to fill a gap in the literature. This gap was identified by Ortega and Iberri-Shea (2005) in their review paper on second language acquisition. The authors noted that there was a lack of longitudinal studies in general in the field of SLA and called for better designed long-term investigations of L2 development. Responding to this call, Derwing *et al.* designed a longitudinal study (collecting data over a period of two years) of adult immigrants' development of their oral fluency and comprehensibility in an ESL environment. The choice of the topic and the formulation of the research questions are thus based on an identified gap in the literature and a call for further longitudinal studies in the field of SLA. The researchers appreciated the value and utility of the cross-sectional studies in SLA in which data are collected at a particular point in time; however, they contended that 'following a cohort of learners over time can lead to a greater understanding of their progress' (p. 359). The researchers focused on two important aspects of oral proficiency, fluency and comprehensibility, and collected and analyzed both quantitative and qualitative data from the two groups of L2 learners over a period of two years.

Theoretical considerations

Theoretically, this study is informed by second language acquisition theory in a broad sense as related to particular groups of L2 learners' development of fluency and comprehensibility in English. This broad theoretical framework informed the first two research questions. More specifically, the third research question was informed by the willingness to communicate model, which was conceptualized by MacIntyre *et al.* (1998) for the use of English as a first language. WTC is considered an essential prerequisite for successful interactions, particularly in the case of people who live and work in the L2 environment (MacIntyre *et al.*, 1998). It refers to how probable it might be for users of the language to engage in communication when they are free to choose.

WTC is a multilevel heuristic model, as suggested by MacIntyre *et al.*, that incorporates six levels and can be used quite rigorously as a theoretical/ conceptual framework leading to more innovative MMR studies with 'complementarity' purposes, as discussed in Chapter 8. However, as Derwing *et al.* indicated, due to the intricacies of the model, they adopted only three levels of the model, with an emphasis on exposure to English outside the ESL classroom. These three levels included social/individual, affective/ cognitive contexts and motivational propensities.

Conceptually, therefore, this study could be categorized as a pragmatic 'principled' MMR study in which the two strands of the study were presented in parallel to answer the three research questions posed by the researchers, leading to recommendations for second language pedagogy. Alternatively, it could have been possible to reconceptualize the construct of WTC pertaining to the Canadian ESL context and relating to the L2 learners in that context. This reconceptualization could lead to a multi-layered construct of willingness to communicate and thus to higher-order research questions in need of both quantitative and qualitative data and analysis and a more comprehensive understanding of the construct. The researchers, in this case, utilized the WTC model only partially, without involving themselves in more sophisticated conceptualization of the construct of WTC, perhaps missing an opportunity for a more innovative MMR study.

Methodological level
As discussed above, this mixed methods longitudinal study represents a 'principled' MMR study and comprises a quantitative evaluation of the L2 learners' fluency and comprehensibility, and a qualitative investigation of the two groups' English language learning experiences. The design of the study can be represented by QUAN + qual and is mainly driven by three research questions. The first two questions were answered by the quantitative data and analysis and the third was answered by the qualitative interview data and analysis.

The sampling procedure
The first methodological observation is that there is no explanation about the sampling procedure and why these two groups of ESL learners were chosen to participate in the study. The researchers stated that '(T)he learners in this study are a subset of participants in Derwing *et al.* (2006)' (p. 364). They further explained that of the original 20 Mandarin speakers in the Derwing *et al.* study, only 16 participants took part in the seventh round of the data collection, and to equalize the sample sizes they chose 16 Slavic participants from among the 19 available. Researchers decided to remove three Slavic participants from the sample after they matched the participants of the two groups in terms of the time they had spent in Canada. This was done to make the two groups as similar as possible as related to the initial range of data collection. Since there is no explanation about the sampling procedure in the report, it can be implied that the researchers used a 'convenience' sampling procedure (Riazi, 2016). Convenience sampling procedure simply means selecting participants on the basis of their availability.

The research design

The second methodological observation is related to the overall design and aims of the study. Since the participants were apparently not selected randomly to represent the target population of ESL learners in Canada, making generalizations from the sample findings to the target population is not warranted. There is no statement regarding the intention of the researchers to generalize their findings either. If the generalization of the findings is ruled out due to sampling procedure restrictions, the question arises as to the intended goal of the study. An alternative may have been to frame it as a case study (Riazi, 2016). In case studies, researchers concentrate on a particular case of an individual or a group of language learners to investigate how the individual or the group acts in terms of language learning in a particular context. It is also possible to make within- and cross-case comparisons in terms of the participants' experiences. Although it is not explicitly stated by the researchers, Derwing *et al.*'s study corresponds to a quantitative-dominant MMR case study. Each of the two groups of language learners forms a case, and the researchers made cross-case but not within-case comparisons.

The statistical analysis

The other methodological observation about this study regards the statistical analysis of the quantitative data. The data of the ratings of the participants' sample speech and their exposure to English language outside the classroom were analyzed using two sets of ANOVA. The ANOVAs seem to be two-way, with participants' L1 (Mandarin vs. Slavic) and time (Time 2, Time 6 and Time 7) as the categorical independent variables, and the fluency and comprehensibility ratings as the dependent variables. Since there have been two dependent variables (fluency and comprehensibility), it is not clear why the researchers did not consider using multivariate analysis of variance (MANOVA) instead of two separate sets of ANOVAs. Undertaking several ANOVAs could have increased the likelihood of a Type I error (rejecting a null hypothesis when it is true). In contrast, MANOVA combines all the measures into a single analysis and controls for the Type I error. Running multivariate analysis when more than one dependent variable is included in the analysis tests all the dependent variables simultaneously and keeps the Type I error rate equal to the designated alpha level. MMR studies should apply the quality standards of quantitative methods when these are used, therefore a clear justification of statistical tests applied, compared with alternative approaches, would be expected.

Inferential level

Following a 'principled' approach to MMR, the researchers posed three questions to be answered by quantitative data and analysis (the first two research questions) and qualitative data and analysis (the third question). The quantitative inferences made by the researchers were based on the quantitative data and analysis, which included the ratings of participants' oral fluency and comprehensibility and the analysis of variance of these data. In summary, 'there was no indication of improvement over time for the MAS [Mandarin Speaking] in either comprehensibility or fluency' (p. 367), while the Slavic group improved somewhat on both dimensions. Given that separate ANOVAs were used to check the participants' fluency and comprehensibility across the two groups over the three time periods, as discussed at the methodological level, the researchers needed to be cautious about this inference.

The researchers made qualitative inferences based on their qualitative analysis of the interviews conducted with participants regarding their daily opportunities to listen to English radio programmes and watch English TV, and to communicate in English. Using the lower three levels of MacIntyre *et al.*'s (1998) model of variables influencing WTC, the researchers focused on the relatively stable aspects of the social/individual, affective/cognitive contexts and motivational propensities. They concluded that despite some variation across participants, they observed shared elements in the attitudes expressed within the Slavic group and similarly, members of the Mandarin group exhibited many commonalities.

The two types of inferences (quantitative and qualitative) were presented separately in the study, and based on them some recommendations were made for language programmes to improve L2 learners' comprehensibility and fluency development. The researchers did not attempt integration except in the conclusions/recommendations section. The integration of the quantitative and qualitative inferences had, in fact, a feed forward rather than a feedback function. That is, rather than integrating the two types of inferences to provide a more comprehensive understanding of the problem, the researchers generated separate inferences to make suggestions for language programmes. This makes more sense when we understand that this MMR study was more pragmatically oriented, dealing with L2 learners' English language development.

Study 4

Gambrell, L.B., Hughes, E.M., Calvert, L., Malloy, J.A. & Igo, B. (2011). Authentic reading, writing, and discussion: An exploratory study of a pen pal project. *Elementary School Journal, 112*(2), 234–258.

Annotation

Gambrell *et al.*'s mixed methods study was an exploratory study investigating reading, writing and discussion within the context of a pen pal programme. Exploratory studies are usually used when the knowledge and understanding of the phenomenon, whether a group, a process, an activity or a situation, are limited. The goal is thus to explore and then present an overall picture of the research problem and to formulate more precise questions that could be addressed by subsequent explanatory studies (Riazi, 2016).

The researchers were interested to explore how students were involved in authentic literacy tasks in a social context. The study was based on the assumption that deep and thoughtful reading, effective and purposeful writing, and critical thinking are essential to high-quality literacy instruction. It was thus assumed that authentic literacy tasks in social contexts could support students in being motivated to learn what they needed to know in order to become engaged and accomplished literacy learners. Three research questions guided this study.

1. Does engagement in a pen pal intervention that focuses on authentic reading, writing and discussion tasks influence the literacy motivation (self-concept and value of reading) of grade 3–5 students, and are there differential effects for gender?
2. Does engagement in a pen pal intervention that focuses on authentic reading, writing and discussion tasks provide a context for small-group interactions that reflect dimensions of accountable talk (community, content and critical thinking)?
3. What do students report regarding their participation in a pen pal intervention that focuses on authentic reading, writing and discussion tasks? (p. 239)

The study involved grade 3–5 elementary students ($n = 180$) as they were reading books, exchanging letters about the books with an adult pen pal and participating in small-group (6–8 students) discussions about the content. The study adopted a mixed methods design with a triangulation-convergence design (Creswell, 2003; Creswell & Plano Clark, 2006) and intended to explore the relationship between authentic literacy tasks and the literacy motivation of elementary students. The researchers also sought to document accountability to community, content and critical thinking during small-group discussions as demonstrated by the students. The instruments for data collection included the Literacy Motivation Survey (LMS) questionnaire, which was administered at pre- and post-stages of the study, small-group discussions and interviews with 28 key student informants. The quantitative strand included analysis of students' scores on the LMS questionnaire (to answer RQ1). The qualitative strand included data and analysis of the transcriptions of the small-group discussions (to answer RQ2) and interviews with key student informants (to provide insights about students' literacy motivation in RQ1 and to answer RQ3).

Results of the study, drawn from an integration of the quantitative and qualitative data sources, suggested that authentic literacy tasks had the potential to support and sustain students' literacy motivation. In addition, analysis of the small-group peer-led discussions revealed that students demonstrated accountability to community, content and critical thinking.

Overall, the researchers concluded that results of the study 'provide support for the social constructivists' view, which holds that students appropriate the tools for understanding through the socially embedded connections provided by discussions and letter exchanges (Vygotsky, 1978/1934; Wells, 1994)' (p. 251).

Design and strands

Figure 10.2 presents the schematic diagram of this MMR study. The target population of the study was elementary students in grades 3–5 in the United States. The sample of the study comprised 180 students from different racial backgrounds. Both quantitative and qualitative data were collected to answer the three research questions addressed. Quantitative data were collected as pre- and post-intervention scores with a seven-month separation using the Literacy Motivation Profile (LMP). The LMP questionnaire was adapted from the Motivation to Read Profile (MRP) (Gambrell *et al.*, 1996) and two items related to writing were added to the Reading Survey portion for the purpose of this study. The quantitative analysis of this survey questionnaire focused on the constructs of self-concept and value and possible gender differences, and was used to answer the first research question.

Qualitative data were collected from students' small-group discussions of text, with the transcriptions of these being analyzed to answer the second research question, which pertained to accountability to community,

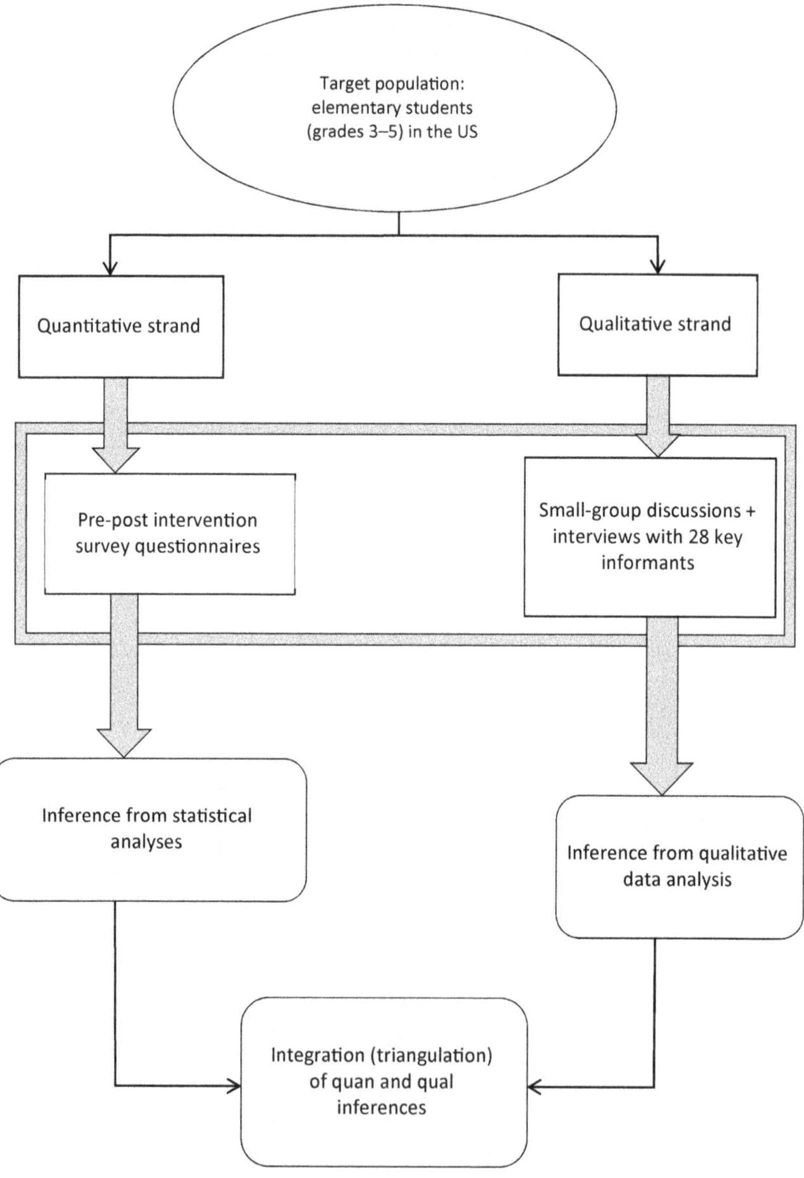

Figure 10.2 The design, strands and inferences made in Gambrell *et al.*'s (2011) MMR study

content and critical thinking. Further qualitative data were collected through semi-structured interviews with 28 key student informants to provide insights about students' literacy motivation and further insights for the first research question, as well as to answer the third research question.

Method and procedures

The pen pal project described in this study was carried out in the participating schools over a seven-month period and was implemented during the reading/language arts period of the day in addition to the core reading programme. The time period, approximately 30 minutes each day, was primarily devoted to language arts instruction. Students in the participating classrooms were matched with selected adult pen pals who volunteered to participate as part of a community service commitment. The adult pen pals were provided with access to an online tutorial to guide them in writing letters to elementary students in a manner that would support literacy development. The intervention in this study included involving student and adult pen pals in authentic literacy tasks, reading common books and exchanging letters about the books.

Students also engaged in purposefully selected small-group discussions about important ideas in the books, and a further purposeful sample of 28 student key informants selected from the quantitative sample of 180 participated in the post-intervention semi-structured interviews. The interviews provided opportunities for the students to comment on their perceptions of the pen pal experience and the reading, writing and discussion tasks they engaged in as a part of the study.

Data analysis
The pre- and post-intervention survey questionnaires were analyzed quantitatively using a paired-samples t-test to test any differences in the students' pre and post responses to questionnaire items. In addition to the t-test, a series of one-way ANOVAs was conducted to identify any significant differences in students' pre-post responses by gender. The quantitative analyses were used to answer the first research question. The recordings of 15 small-group discussions were transcribed and then analyzed using a deductive coding scheme for features of accountable talk to answer the second research question. Also, semi-structured interviews with 28 key informants were transcribed and then analyzed to provide insights about students' literacy motivation (RQ1) and to explore students' responses to participation in authentic literacy tasks (RQ3).

As can be seen from both Figure 10.2 and the above discussion, the researchers made quantitative and qualitative inferences based on the quantitative and qualitative data and analyses about the elementary students' literacy motivation as they engaged in authentic literacy tasks. The researchers also integrated the two types of inferences through triangulation processes.

Commentary

Conceptual level

Two theoretical frameworks informed Gambrell *et al.*'s study: the social cognitive theoretical perspective (Bandura, 1997; Schunk, 2008) and the social constructionism framework as presented by Vygotsky (1978/1934) and further elaborated on by Bruning *et al.* (2004) and Wells (1994). From a sociocognitive perspective, language is essentially a dialogic or reciprocal tool, and literacy events are instances of the social uses of language wherein the social purposes of language are mediated by individual cognitions (Halliday & Hasan, 1976). From a sociocognitive perspective, then, the development of the four communication skills – listening, reading, speaking and writing – is seen to involve both social practices and cognitive processes. From the second social constructionism perspective, the cognitive interpretations available to individuals for appropriation of language use in the social context are a valued learning resource. Based on the above theoretical perspectives, and especially from a sociocognitive perspective, learning is an outcome of purposeful observation or modelling (Bandura, 1997) on the part of learners.

Gambrell *et al.* (2011), following the work of Purcell-Gates (2002) and her colleagues (Purcell-Gates *et al.*, 2004; Purcell-Gates *et al.*, 2007) on authentic literacy tasks and practices, focused on pen pal learning activity. They considered student learning as they observed the ways in which an adult partner discussed a shared text and as they attempted to respond to the adult partner in a similar way. The study is thus grounded in relevant theoretical and conceptual frameworks as discussed above. This level of theorization and conceptualization had the potential for designing an MMR study with a 'complementarity' purpose in that the construct of authentic literacy could be conceptualized as a multi-layered and multi-faceted construct. The research questions corresponding to different layers and facets in the construct could then have been answered using different methods of data collection and analysis, resulting in a more innovative MMR study. The researchers, however, chose to use MMR with a 'triangulation-convergence' (p. 239) purpose and explored what happened in a pen pal authentic literacy activity in terms of student literacy motivation and learning.

The researchers used Edelsky's (1991) and Purcell-Gates's (2002) definitions and characteristics of authentic literacy tasks. Gambrell *et al.* thus considered reading, writing and discussion tasks that encouraged purposeful literacy activities to be more authentic than those too general to be useful tasks that simply required extraction and recall of information. It was assumed that authentic literacy tasks would lead students to the construction of new meanings. The reading, writing and discussion tasks were also perceived to provide some personal relevance for students and hence require some ownership or control on the part of the participants. This, in turn, presumed participants' knowledge and awareness of what society valued in terms of literacy events. Drawing on this conceptualization, the researchers' problem was then to find out whether such authentic literacy tasks and activities would develop elementary students' literacy motivation, accountable talk regarding community, content and critical thinking, and how students would perceive the overall pen pal experience and the reading, writing and discussion tasks they engaged in.

The researchers found MMR appropriate and useful in conducting their research and answering questions. Specifically, they used MMR to corroborate findings from one strand (quantitative) with findings from the other (qualitative). The integration of the results made through triangulation of the findings allowed the researchers to draw conclusions about how a group of elementary students participated in an authentic literacy activity and how their participation and activities could enhance their literacy motivation and learning.

Methodological level

Gambrell *et al.* used the MMR design with a triangulation-convergence purpose. Their design comprised a pre-post intervention quantitative strand and a qualitative peer-group discussion and interview-based strand. The pre-post intervention survey, with a seven-month time interval, involved the administration of the LMS at the beginning and end of the study with all the 180 participants. In between, participants reflected on and responded to the books they had read by writing letters to their adult pen pals and then talking about the books and letters they received from their adult pen pals in small-group discussions. The researchers also randomly selected 28 key student informants from the pool of the participants to participate in semi-structured post-intervention interviews at the end of the study, and to reflect on their experiences of being involved in authentic literacy tasks and activities. As such, they used the quantitative data and analysis from the survey questionnaire to answer the first research question, and the qualitative data and analysis from the small-group discussions to answer the second question. They then used the qualitative interviews with the key student informants to obtain further insights and corroborate findings related to the first question as well as to answer the third research question.

Methodological reflections

There are several methodological points to be discussed in regard to Gambrell *et al.*'s MMR study. First, there seems to be a mismatch between the researchers' conception of the study as 'exploratory' and the actual 'interventionist' nature of the study, which is usually the characteristic feature of experimental (pre-post) designs and 'explanatory' research. Exploratory or descriptive research studies are used when the knowledge and understanding of the phenomenon, be it a group, a process, an activity or a situation, are limited. The goal in exploratory research is, therefore, to discover and then present a picture of the social phenomenon and to formulate more precise questions that could be addressed by subsequent explanatory studies (Riazi, 2016). As such, the purpose in exploratory studies is mostly to answer 'what' questions ('what is going on?') and to provide more details of the hitherto unknown or limited known phenomena. Gambrell *et al.* used a pre-post design in their research, although they intended to explore what might happen in a pen pal authentic literacy activity and what elementary students might gain from engaging in such activity in terms of literacy motivation and learning. The pre-post experimental design is mostly used to investigate the effect of an intervention and to explain the impact of the intervention on the outcome variables, so Gambrell *et al.*'s study might more probably be considered to be an 'explanatory' study, especially in light of the strong theoretical background provided by the researchers.

However, the study cannot be considered as a true experiment with an explanatory objective. In true experimental designs, participants are randomly selected and assigned to experimental and control groups. In the experimental group, a treatment, which can be a new instructional activity such as authentic literacy practice, is introduced, while in the control group, the conventional methods are used. After the experiment, the performances of the experimental and control groups are compared to make inferences about the causal relationships between the independent and dependent variables. In Gambrell *et al.*'s study, there exists pre- and post-survey questionnaire administration with an intervention in between (writing letters to an adult pen pal about the books read and discussing the books and the pen pals' responses in small groups). There was, however, no control group to be used as a reference group and for comparison of performance. This confusion may explain why the researchers suggested '(F)uture studies using experimental and quasi-experimental designs are needed to determine the causal effects of authentic tasks on literacy motivation and critical thinking skills' (p. 251). The situation thus leaves the reader in limbo as to whether the study follows an exploratory or explanatory mandate, although the researchers aimed for the former.

Reflection on the quantitative data analysis

The third methodological issue regards the use of statistical tests of significance (Riazi, 2016). Two tests of statistical significance are used in Gambrell *et al.*'s MMR study. The first is a paired-samples t-test used to compare students' pre and post scores on the LMS to find out whether there is any significant difference due to the intervention, participation in pen pal activity. The paired-samples t-test seems to be an appropriate statistical test of significance here because the same students were measured at two points and the resulting scores were compared with each other. Similarly, the researchers explained that they conducted a series of one-way ANOVAs to investigate whether any significant differences could be found between male and female students in terms of different scales or categories of the post-intervention LMS questionnaire. There are no explanations in the report of whether the quantitative data met the requirements of the parametric tests, the t-test and the ANOVA; it is left to the readers to assume they did.

Once more it should be emphasized that MMR researchers are required to provide details about the quality standards for quantitative analyses if they are applied in the study.

Reflection on the qualitative data analysis

The first observation, based on the researchers' accounts of the qualitative data and analysis, is that qualitative data were predominantly quantified in the form of frequencies and percentages, with occasional quotes from the participants to support the quantitized data. Using a deductive approach and a prepared coding scheme with three primary coding categories (community, content and critical thinking), the researchers tallied the students' responses in terms of the coding categories. In other words, the researchers did not make full use of their qualitative data using an inductive approach and exploring the whole data.

Although the researchers cited Merriam (1998) and referred to constant comparative analysis (Riazi, 2016), there is no elaboration in the report about the application of a constant comparative method and how it helped the researchers in their analysis of the qualitative data. The same observation holds true in regard to the analysis of the interview transcriptions. The researchers explained that 'two of the researchers read the responses to each question and identified meaning statements and meaning clusters that emerged using constant comparative analysis' (p. 244), but again there is no explanation about what explicit procedures were undertaken to perform a constant comparative analysis as regarded their qualitative interview analysis.

As explained in Riazi (2016), the constant comparison method is an inductive procedure in qualitative data analysis and is usually used in the grounded theory method to make connections between data and the researcher's emerging theoretical explanations about the phenomenon. A fully fledged constant comparative method requires an iterative data collection and analysis procedure in which the researcher constantly moves back and forth between the developed theoretical elaborations and the new data until the new data do not contribute to the refinement of the theoretical explanation any further. There are no explanations in the report about how this robust qualitative data analysis procedure was implemented. This lack of explanation jeopardizes the rigour and credibility of the study. As emphasized above, MMR researchers should report how the expectations and quality standards for different types of data analysis have been observed. This may prove difficult given the limited space and word limits in journal articles, but should be addressed to ensure the credibility of analyses and findings.

Inferential level

The first type of inferences made in Gambrell *et al.*'s study related to the quantitative results, as is usually the case in most quantitatively oriented MMR studies. The LMS questionnaire included three parts, and so four scores were calculated from each participant's pre- and post-intervention survey questionnaires: a score for the self-concept as a reader, value of reading, motivation to write, as well as a total score for the LMS as a whole. Two types of quantitative inferences were made in this study. The first reported the effect of the intervention on students' literacy motivation as represented in the first research question. Based on the results of the t-tests and Cohen's effect size (*d*) (Riazi, 2016), the researchers inferred that the intervention yielded a small to moderate magnitude of effect (0.39). Similarly, they reported that the students' mean responses to the additional two items on the post survey regarding writing were significantly higher than the same two items on the pre survey, with a moderate to large magnitude of Cohen's effect size (0.65). With respect to self-concept and value scores, the inference was, however, that students' responses did not differ from pre to post for this construct.

It is indeed encouraging to see that the researchers reported effect size with their inferences from the statistical data analysis outcomes. Effect size is a statistical measure used to determine the strength of the observed relationship between the independent and dependent variables, and is different from statistical significance, which shows only whether the observed relationship is due to sampling error or chance or a meaningful one, while the effect size can indicate the strength of the observed relationships among variables. Cohen (1992) was among the first researchers to provide a scale for the interpretation of this statistical measure. Conventionally, the effect size measure ranges between 0.1 and 0.5, with effect sizes between 0.1–0.2 showing a 'small effect size', 0.3–0.5 a 'medium effect size' and larger than 0.5 showing a 'large effect size'. Gambrell *et al.* made further quantitative inferences in regard to the significant differences observed between male and female students' scores based on the pre- and post-intervention questionnaire measurements.

As discussed in the methodological section, although qualitative data were collected from small-group discussions, these data were quantitized in terms of the frequency of occurrence of predominant deductive coding categories. The researchers thus made further quantitative inferences from the qualitative discussion data about students' accountability to demonstrate community, content and critical thinking. It can therefore be argued that the researchers did not exploit, or at least did not report, the full capacity of their qualitative data to generate more robust qualitative inferences. Qualitative inferences were mainly based on the analysis of the interviews with key student informants, but with the limitations discussed above. These inferences were related to student perceptions of their experiences of the pen pal intervention in general, as well as the reading, writing and discussion experiences in particular as related to the third research question. At a higher level, the researchers were able to relate their qualitative inferences to the social constructivists' view, which holds that students appropriate their tools and processes of understanding through the socially embedded connections. In this study, the socially embedded connections were letter exchanges with adult pen pals and discussion of the books read and letter responses in small groups. Overall, therefore, Gambrell *et al.*'s study can be classified as a 'principled' MMR study with a 'triangulation' purpose.

Learning task

Read the annotations below and choose the one closest to your research interest. Read the full article and analyze it using the FRAMMR framework used in this chapter. Start by preparing a schematic diagram for the design of the study and writing down details of each strand in each study. Then attempt to comment on the study at the conceptual, methodological and inferential levels.

- At the conceptual level, determine whether the researchers identified a particular purpose for mixing methods or not. If not, are you able to imply a purpose based on the annotation provided for each study? Use the explanations provided for the three categories of 'eclectic', 'principled' or 'innovative' in Chapter 8 and decide which of the three categories each study can be grouped under.
- At the methodological level, look for the details of the quantitative and qualitative data collection and analysis procedures and ascertain whether quality criteria and standards are observed in each strand.
- Finally, scan the reports, especially in the discussion and conclusions sections, to reveal what type of inferences are made based on which results, and whether the researcher has mixed the inferences in favour of a fuller meta-inference.

Plakans, L. & Gebril, A. (2012). A close investigation into source use in integrated second language writing tasks. *Assessing Writing, 17*(1), 18–34.

This mixed methods research investigated the input sources used in integrated second language writing tasks. Integrated writing tasks require writers to integrate two or three skills (reading and writing, listening and writing or reading, listening and writing) to synthesize information and create a coherent piece of writing. The integration of reading and writing in such tasks has raised a number of questions with regard to writers' use of input sources in their writing, the functions these sources serve and how writers' language proficiency might affect their synthesis of the information.

To answer these questions, the researchers of the current study recruited a group of 145 undergraduate students in a Middle Eastern university to work on a reading-to-write task and completed a questionnaire. In addition, nine students provided think-aloud protocols in writing sessions and participated in follow-up interviews. Analysis of the qualitative data yielded initial patterns, which were then explored further by quantitative analysis of relevant questionnaire items using descriptive statistics and a non-parametric test of significance, Chi-square. Results of the data analyses indicated that source use serves several functions for L2 writers, including generating ideas about the topic and serving as a language resource. The participants' language proficiency level affected text comprehension, especially at lower levels, but was not found to relate to the source used by participants.

> O'Bryan, A. & Hegelheimer, V. (2009). Using a mixed methods approach to explore strategies, metacognitive awareness and the effects of task design on listening development. *Canadian Journal of Applied Linguistics, 12*(1), 9–38.

This mixed methods research study intended to identify the patterns of awareness and use of listening strategies of four low-intermediate to high-intermediate level male students enrolled in an ESL listening course at a large Midwestern research university. The researchers used a concurrent nested design (Creswell, 2003) with predominantly qualitative data collection and analysis. Think-aloud verbal protocols, interviews and student notes were collected from the participants and then quantitized in order to allow for a comparison of quantitative results (strategy frequencies) with qualitative (verbal protocol) data. Meanwhile, the researchers employed a sequential explanatory design (Creswell, 2003), where the interpretation of quantitative, Likert scale questionnaire data was supported by qualitative data, to explore students' metacognitive awareness of strategies used while listening to oral texts.

The researchers intended to answer the following three research questions. (1) What are the differences in students' reported listening strategies and processes, by level of language proficiency, when listening to an academic text? (2) What impact does repetition have on listening strategies used while listening to academic texts? (3) How does the metacognitive awareness of these students' listening strategies develop over the course of the semester?

References

Bandura, A. (1997). *Self-efficacy: The exercise of control*. New York: Freeman.

Bruning, R.H., Schraw, G.J., Norby, M.M. & Ronning, R.R. (2004). *Cognitive psychology and instruction* (4th ed.). Upper Saddle River, NJ: Merrill/ Prentice-Hall.

Centre for Canadian Language Benchmarks (2006). www.language.ca/index.cfm?V oir=sections&Id=18700&M=4032

Cohen, J. (1992). A power primer. *Psychological Bulletin, 112*, 155–159.

Creswell, J.W. (2003). Research design: *Qualitative, quantitative, and mixed methods approaches* (2nd ed.). Thousand Oaks, CA: Sage.

Creswell, J.W. & Plano Clark, V.L. (2006). *Designing and conducting mixed methods research*. Thousand Oaks, CA: Sage.

Edelsky, C. (1991). *With literacy and justice for all: Rethinking the social in language and education: Critical perspectives on literacy and education*. London: Falmer.

Gambrell, L.B., Palmer, B.M., Codling, R.M. & Mazzoni, S.A. (1996). Assessing motivation to read. *Reading Teacher, 49*(7), 518–533.

Halliday, M.A.K. & Hasan, R. (1976). *Cohesion in English*. London: Longman.

MacIntyre, P.D., Clement, R., Dornyei, Z. & Noels, K.A. (1998). Conceptualizing willingness to communicate in a L2: A situational model of L2 confidence and affiliation. *The Modern Language Journal, 82*(4), 545–562.

McGraw, K.O. & Wong, S.P. (1996). Forming inferences about some intraclass correlation coefficients. *Psychological Methods, 1*, 30–46.

Merriam, S.B. (1998). *Qualitative research and case study applications in education*. San Francisco, LA: Jossey-Bass.

Ortega, L. & Iberri-Shea, G. (2005). Longitudinal research in second language acquisition: Recent trends and future directions. *Annual Review of Applied Linguistics, 25*, 26–45.

Purcell-Gates, V. (2002). Authentic literacy in class yields increase in literacy practices. *Literacy Update, 11*, 7.

Purcell-Gates, V., Duke, N.K. & Martineau, J.A. (2007). Learning to read and write genre-specific text: Roles of authentic experience and explicit teaching. *Reading Research Quarterly, 42*(1), 8–45.

Purcell-Gates, V., Jacobson, E. & Degener, S. (2004). *Print literacy development: Uniting cognitive and social practice theories*. Cambridge, MA: Harvard University Press.

Riazi, A.M. (2016). *Routledge encyclopedia of research methods in applied linguistics: Quantitative, qualitative and mixed-methods research*. London: Routledge.

Schunk, D.H. (2008). *Learning theories: An educational perspective* (5th ed.). Upper Saddle River, NJ: Pearson/Merrill/Prentice-Hall.

Shrout, P.E. & Fleiss, J.L. (1979). Intraclass correlations: Uses in assessing rater reliability. *Psychological Bulletin, 86*(2), 420–428.

Vygotsky, L.S. (1978). *Mind in society: The development of higher psychological processes* (M. Cole, V. John-Steiner, S. Scribner & E. Souberman, Eds. & Trans.). Cambridge, MA: Harvard University Press. (Original work published 1934.)

Wells, G. (1994). The complementary contributions of Halliday and Vygotsky to a 'language-based theory of learning'. *Linguistics and Education, 6*, 41–90.

11 Researching Motivation and Attitude

This chapter will:

- present an analysis and review of an explanatory MMR study that investigated early adolescent students' motivation and attrition in immersion language programmes;
- present an analysis and review of an embedded MMR study that investigated the attitudes of Indian English language teachers towards communicative language teaching;
- provide two further MMR studies in the learning task to be analyzed by readers.

Introduction

The two MMR studies to be reviewed in this chapter are related to motivation and attitudes towards language learning and teaching. The first study is an explanatory MMR study that investigated early adolescent students' motivation and how it was related to the students' attrition from language immersion programmes. The students, 131 graduates of five public elementary immersion schools, completed a survey questionnaire, and 33 of them participated in interviews to provide both quantitative and qualitative data for the study. The second study is an embedded MMR study that investigated the attitudes towards and practices of 31 Indian English language teachers of communicative language teaching in India. The researchers used an attitude questionnaire for the quantitative strand, and classroom observations and interviews with six teachers for the qualitative strand. The first study will be referred to as Study 5 and the second one as Study 6.

These two MMR studies will be analyzed and reviewed using the FRAMMR framework presented in Chapter 8. First, an annotation of the study will be provided, then design and strands are discussed, and finally, each study will be commented on at the conceptual, methodological and inferential levels.

> ## Study 5
>
> Wesely, P.M. (2010). Language learning motivation in early adolescents: Using mixed methods research to explore contradiction. *Journal of Mixed Methods Research*, 4(4), 295–312.

Annotation

Drawing on theoretical frameworks of motivation, Wesely (2010) conceptualized 'motivation' as a social psychological construct with both contextual (social) and individual (psychological) components. Wesely referred to McInerney (1998), who argued that the construct of motivation has posed an 'emic–etic dilemma'. This has resulted in researchers approaching and investigating motivation using either a positivist or a constructivist orientation (see Chapter 1 for an explanation of these orientations to research in language teaching and learning). Wesely considered this either–or approach as a puzzle that has prevented researchers from developing a fuller understanding of the issues related to this construct. Consequently, Wesely decided to conduct an MMR study through which the researcher could integrate both approaches to produce a more comprehensive understanding of students' motivational problems. She described the design of her study as a modified 'explanatory design' (Creswell & Plano Clark, 2007) with an 'initiation' purpose (Greene, Caracelli & Graham, 1989; Riazi, 2016a) to shed more light on previous contradictory findings about why students left immersion programmes. The researcher believed that through an initiation MMR study, she could also address any paradox and contradiction found in her own data sources, a feature of the initiation purpose. She aimed to investigate second language learners' motivation to participate in L2 immersion programmes and the reasons for their discontinuation of the programme.

The two research questions that guided the data collection and analysis in Wesely's study were as follows.

1. What does an examination of the second language (L2) learning motivation of early adolescent immersion graduates reveal about important issues in immersion education?
2. How do the data collected through student interviews compare with the data generated by the results of the Attitude/Motivation Test Battery (AMTB)? (p. 299)

The sample of the quantitative strand comprised 131 graduates of five public elementary immersion schools, and the sample of the qualitative strand, which was a sub-sample of the quantitative strand, was 33 students interviewed by the researcher with parental consent. The required data were thus collected through survey questionnaires and interviews with a sub-sample of participants. The quantitative and qualitative data were analyzed using both statistical and thematic analysis. Inferences were made from the quantitative and qualitative data analysis results and these inferences were integrated to produce a more comprehensive meta-inference to explain possible causes for students' attrition from the language immersion programme.

Design and strands

Figure 11.1 presents the schematic diagram of the design and strands of Wesely's study. As the figure shows, the target population was 358 sixth- and seventh-grade graduates (11–13 years old) and continuing students of French and Spanish immersion programmes.

Data collection

The study consisted of two main strands, a quantitative and a qualitative one. In the quantitative strand, a survey questionnaire was used to elicit motivational data from a sample of 133 of both continuing and non-continuing graduates of the immersion programmes.

An adapted version of Gardner's motivation questionnaire (1985a, 1985b, 2001a, 2001b) was sent to the whole target population (358 sixth- and seventh-grade graduates and their parents) of graduates and continuing students of French and Spanish immersion programmes. Of the whole population, 133 participants (a response rate of 36%) completed and returned questionnaires. In addition, parents of 33 participants provided consent for the researcher to interview their students.

The questionnaire used in the quantitative strand included 40 Likert-type questions using a five-point scale of 'strongly agree', 'agree' 'neutral', 'disagree' and 'strongly disagree'. The scale was used to produce interval-like (Turner, 1993) data to allow the use of parametric statistical tests of significance (Riazi, 2016a). The interviews followed a semi-structured procedure in which the researcher used some core questions and asked the participants to reflect on their language learning experiences and their motivational factors. The semi-structured procedure allowed the researcher to look for further elaboration from the participants' responses when and where necessary. Each interview took 15–35 minutes and all the interviews were completed

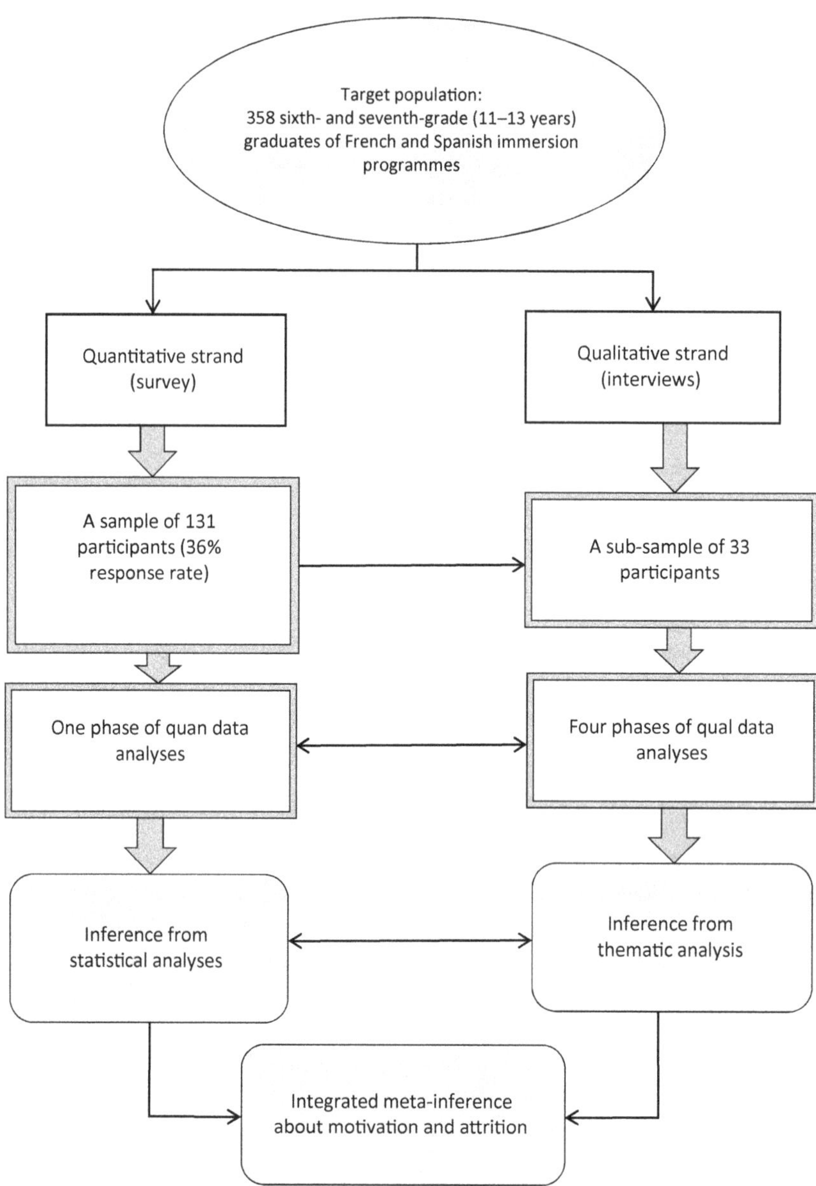

Figure 11.1 The design, strands and inferences made in Wesely's (2010) MMR study

over three months. During each interview the researcher took some notes of the relevant and interesting themes related to the participants' language learning experiences and their motivation.

Data analysis

The analysis of the qualitative and the quantitative data was completed in six phases. Although the researcher collected the quantitative data first through questionnaires, she preferred to postpone the analysis so that her qualitative data analysis would not be influenced by the findings of the former. Analysis of the qualitative data was conducted first using the 'constant comparative method' (Heigham & Croker, 2009; Riazi, 2016a; Richards, 2003), which allowed the researcher to move back and forth between data collection and analysis in an iterative way. Once an individual interview was completed and preliminary data analysis was conducted, further questions and gaps in the emerging explanation of students' motivational factors instigated subsequent interviews with other participants. The completion of the interviews hence took three months.

The first phase of the qualitative data analysis was done on each individual interview once the interview was completed. Further questions and information gaps observed in the analysis of each individual interview were followed up in subsequent interviews. This helped the researcher to use constant comparison analysis. Once all the individual interviews were completed using constant comparative analysis, the second phase of the qualitative data analysis was an initial analysis of the whole set of interviews. To analyze the whole set, the researcher developed a coding scheme from two sources: interviews and Gardner's (1985a, 1985b, 2001a, 2001b) socio-educational model of motivation. The interviews, the notes that were taken during each interview and the memos written while transcribing the interviews all helped the researcher to develop initial codes and categories that were then refined and finalized using the concepts and categories in Gardner's model of motivation.

In the quantitative phase (the third phase) of the data analysis, the researcher analyzed the completed questionnaires through statistical procedures. In particular, the researcher used t-test and ANOVA to identify relationships and group differences of those who continued the immersion programmes and those who decided not to continue as related to the type of immersion programme they attended. Rather than following and using Gardner's (2001a) approach to aggregate scores to provide assessments of constructs in the motivation model, the researcher focused primarily on an examination of the individual sub-scales in the questionnaire. She believed this would allow her to use the qualitative data and analysis to provide insights into the quantitative data and analysis because she could use sub-scales such as 'attitude towards language learning' from the motivation questionnaire. This decision allowed her to create an interaction and integration between the qualitative and the quantitative strands.

In the fourth phase of the data analysis, the researcher performed a second iteration of qualitative thematic analysis of the interview data. At this phase she went beyond the initial content analysis to develop a theoretical explanation using the emerging themes from the first and second phases of the qualitative data analysis. This phase of data analysis was also used to check and enhance the dependability, a qualitative term similar to reliability, of the qualitative data analysis. The researcher recoded some of the previously coded segments to ensure that she had been consistent. In addition, she checked the codes and themes against the actual data to ascertain that they corresponded to what participants discussed and reported.

The fifth phase comprised the comparison of the results of the quantitative and qualitative data analysis. The researcher compared the results and looked for not only the areas of convergence in the two data sources, but also where findings from one data set were not revealed in another data set. The qualitative and quantitative results, as well as the literature in the fields of language learning motivation and immersion education, helped the researcher to refine, combine and organize the presentation of her findings.

The sixth and final level included analysis of data from mini case studies conducted with some participants, which due to space limitation were not reported in the article.

Commentary

Conceptual level

Wesely's MMR study has several strengths. The first, and perhaps the foremost, is the researcher's conceptualization of the research problem, the construct of language learning motivation. While Gardner's socio-educational model, generally recognized as the most influential model of language learning motivation in L2 research, provided the primary theoretical framework for Wesely's study, she considered other theoretical frameworks. This was done in the belief that a single theoretical framework may have been loaded with either a positivist (quantitative) or constructivist (qualitative) view, as is the case with Gardner's socio-educational model that has driven quantitative approaches to language learning motivation.

Wesely therefore exploited and incorporated three other theoretical frameworks of language learning motivation: the attribution theory (Covington, 1984), which considers students' past successes and failures and their perceived causes of those successes and failures as related to their own capabilities; the investment motivational framework (Norton, 2000), which recognizes the multiple and changing desires of a language learner; and the L2 motivational self system (Dornyei, 2005, 2009), which examines consequences of the L2 learning in learner identity formation. Wesely thus drew on different theoretical frameworks and conceptualized the construct of L2 motivation in a way that allowed the generation of new insights by researching different aspects of the construct using both quantitative and qualitative data and so avoiding the either–or dilemma in researching language learning motivation.

Another strength of Wesely's MMR study relates to the purpose for which she used mixed methods research, that is, 'initiation'. As discussed in Chapter 3 and Chapter 8, MMR studies with complementarity and initiation purposes potentially represent innovative approaches to research. This is chiefly because these purposes require a more robust conceptualization of the research problem that subsequently allows the researcher to integrate the two research approaches (quantitative and qualitative) at different stages in the research process. The initiation purpose allowed Wesely to identify and address issues and paradoxes in the literature and data sets about L2 learning motivation, and to seek new perspectives, thus contributing to the knowledge base on the topic.

Through quantitative analysis of the survey questionnaire, Wesely observed some unexpected attitudes and revealing trends reported by the participants. She noticed that, surprisingly, those participants who left the immersion programmes developed slightly more positive attitudes towards learning the language than those who remained. More surprisingly, partic-ipants from the programmes with the highest attrition rates indicated more positive attitudes towards learning the language in the sub-scales of the attitudes questionnaire. These rather unexpected and paradoxical findings extended the scope of Wesely's initiation purpose.

Methodological level

Wesely's conceptualization of the research problem (motivation for learn-ing a second language in immersion programmes) went beyond an either–or conceptualization. This conceptualization has considered motivation as either a personal and psychological trait or a contextual and social issue. This either–or approach has split researchers of language learning motiva-tion. Some have investigated issues related to this construct from a positiv-ist quantitative perspective, mostly testing hypotheses related to a relevant theory, predominantly that of Gardner's socio-educational one. Another group of researchers has investigated L2 motivation from a constructivist qualitative viewpoint, with the intention of generating hypotheses related to L2 motivation in particular contexts.

Methodologically, the former approach is usually referred to as an 'etic' approach, while the latter is usually referred to as an 'emic' approach. As discussed in Chapter 1, from an etic perspective, the researcher is detached from the researchee (object of the study) and so the researcher can provide an objective understanding and explanation of the research phenomenon. From an emic perspective, however, the researcher is entangled with the object of the study and thus any understanding and explanation of the research phenomenon are subjectively co-constructed from the researcher's and participants' lenses.

As indicated in the 'annotation' section, Wesely critiques the 'etic–emic' dilemma and opts for a more coherent and comprehensive conceptualization of the construct of the L2 motivation that could embrace both perspectives. This orientation helped Wesely to design her MMR in an innovative way and to conceive language learning motivation and attrition as a complex research issue in need of a more rigorous methodology for its investigation. As discussed in Chapter 8, innovative MMR studies are those that use and integrate both quantitative and qualitative data and analysis to answer research questions derived from a sound and more comprehensive theorization and conceptualization of the research problem. Wesely's study demonstrates this approach.

Another methodological strength of Wesely's MMR study is its constant comparative method in the analysis of the qualitative interview data. Through constant comparative analysis, researchers are able to move back and forth between data and analysis on the one hand, and between data and theory on the other. The method includes analysis of the partial data collected (for example, one or two interviews) and the development of some preliminary hypothetical explanations. However, at this stage, due to the limited data, there might be too many gaps in the emerging themes and theoretical explanation. These gaps lead the researcher to seek further information from the participants in subsequent interviews. Being aware of the gaps in the explanation of the research phenomenon, the researcher could probe the participants for further elaborations on the gaps found in the preliminary analyses. By using constant comparative analysis on the one hand, and integrating qualitative findings with those obtained from the survey questionnaires on the other, the researcher 'illustrates how an Explanatory Design mixed methods study can be used to investigate contradiction and paradox in the data' (Wesely, 2010, p. 309).

Inferential level

As can be seen from Figure 11.1, Wesely integrates inferences made from the quantitative and qualitative strands of her MMR study. This is another strength of her study because a majority of MMR studies fall short of integrating inferences made from different strands of the study in favour of more comprehensive and meta-inferences. The inferential stage in the process of MMR study is where researchers could show how the outcomes of the study could be looped back into the conceptualization stage, and how the integration of the inferences made from the quantitative and qualitative strands could provide a fuller explanation of students' motivation for language learning and their attrition from immersion programmes.

Wesely achieved this by undertaking six phases of data analysis and linking the inferences made at each phase with her conceptualization of the research problem. The first research question ('What does an examination of the L2 learning motivation of early adolescent immersion graduates reveal about important issues in immersion education?') was answered by inferences made from the thematic analysis of the interviews at phases 1, 2 and 4; the calculation of effect sizes of groupings on AMTB sub-scales at phase 3, and an integration of both quantitative and qualitative inferences at phase 5. The second research question ('In what ways do the data collected through student interviews provide insight into the data generated by the results of the AMTB?') was answered by integrating qualitative (interviews) and quantitative (survey questionnaire) results achieved in phase 5 and the relevant inferences made from those results. There is therefore an organic link between the three stages of the conceptual, methodological and inferential levels in Wesely's study, making it a strong exemplar of an innovative MMR study.

Study 6

Christ, T.W. & Makarani, S.A. (2009). Teachers' attitudes about teaching English in India: An embedded mixed methods study. *International Journal of Multiple Research Approaches, 3*(1), 73–87.

Annotation

Christ and Makarani (2009) focused on the importance of communicative language teaching (CLT) in developing students' communication skills in

India. The researchers considered the fact that CLT, as an approach rather than a single teaching methodology (Nunan, 1988), has caused some misunderstanding about CLT in the English language teaching profession. Relying on two definitions of CLT, one from Matthews (1997) and another from Brown (1994), Christ and Makarani investigated the Indian English language teachers' attitudes towards and practices of CLT. The sample of the study included teachers who completed a survey questionnaire, and a sub-sample of six teachers who participated in interviews and allowed their classes to be observed. Data were collected from these teachers regarding their attitudes towards CLT and how they implemented CLT in their teaching of English in two schools in India. The researchers used an embedded sequential exploratory MMR design (Christ, 2007; Teddlie & Taskakkori, 2009), with a 'triangulation' purpose (Greene, Caracelli & Graham, 1989; Riazi, 2016a) so that the attitudinal data and analysis derived from the survey questionnaire could be cross-validated and corroborated with the interviews and classroom observations data and analysis.

The term 'embedded' means that one strand of the MMR study (usually with less emphasis) is embedded within a more dominant strand (Creswell *et al.*, 2003; Greene & Caracelli, 1997). In the case of Christ and Makarani's study, the qualitative strand, including the qualitative interviews and classroom observations, constituted the dominant strand and the quantitative survey data and analysis constituted the less dominant strand embedded within the dominant qualitative strand.

Christ and Makarani's study posed four research questions.

1. What are EFL teachers' attitudes towards CLT?
2. What are EFL teachers' philosophies about using CLT to teach English?
3. To what degree are EFL teachers incorporating CLT strategies to teach English in their classrooms?
4. What challenges do EFL teachers face while implementing CLT? (p. 76)

To answer the first question, the researchers used both the quantitative and the qualitative data and analysis, while to answer the subsequent three questions they used only the qualitative data and analysis. It is thus easy to note the dominance of the qualitative strand.

Design and strands

Figure 11.2 presents the schematic diagram of the design and strands of Christ and Makarani's MMR study. As the figure shows, the target population was Indian English language teachers. However, the focus of this study was two schools in Gujarat, India. The study therefore can be rather considered as a case study of English language teachers in those two schools in India. The embedded MMR design of the study consisted of two strands (quan → QUAL), including a dominant qualitative strand and an embedded quantitative one.

Data collection

First, in the quantitative strand, a survey questionnaire was used to elicit attitudinal data from a sample of 31 English language teachers from the two schools in Gujarat. The Karavas-Doukas (1996) CLT questionnaire was used to investigate these teachers' knowledge and attitudes towards CLT. The questionnaire consisted of 24 items representing five constructs of (1) group and pair work; (2) quality and quantity of error correction; (3) the role and contribution of learners in the learning process; (4) the role of teacher in the classroom; and (5) the place and importance of grammar. The questionnaire items were based on a five-point Likert scale ranging from 'strongly agree' to 'strongly disagree'.

Second, in the qualitative strand, semi-structured interviews were conducted with six teachers. The interview questions asked the teachers about their attitudes, implementation techniques and problems they faced when using CLT strategies. Finally, a one-hour classroom session with each participant teaching an English lesson using CLT was video recorded.

Commentary

Conceptual level

Christ and Makarani's (2009) study can be considered a 'principled' MMR study using the criteria discussed in Chapter 8. The two strands of the quantitative and qualitative data and analyses were used for the triangulation purpose as stated by the researchers and illustrated in Figure 11.2. This principled MMR study aligns with what Johnson *et al.* (2010) call qualitative-dominant because the main focus of the study was on a qualitative case study of six English language teachers in two schools in Gujarat. As a qualitative-dominant MMR case study, the core and the main focus of Christ and Makarani's study was to discover what were six teachers'

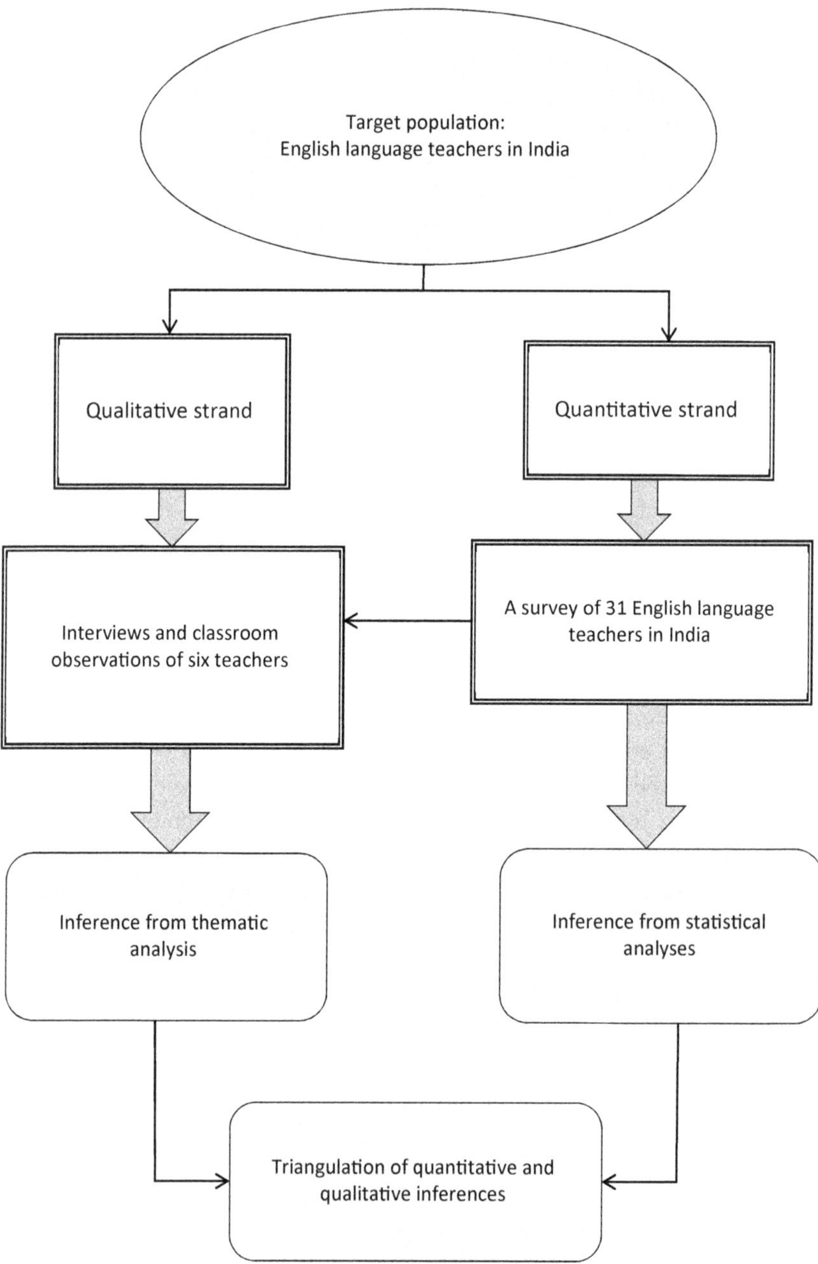

Figure 11.2 The design, strands and inferences used in Christ and Makarani's (2009) MMR study

knowledge and attitudes about communicative language teaching, how they implemented CLT in their classes and which challenges they faced when they used CLT as their teaching method.

To achieve the goals of the study, Christ and Makarani used a purposive sampling procedure (Riazi, 2016a) to collect and analyze qualitative data from six teachers familiar with CLT. The researchers were informed by and followed all the steps required in qualitative research in general, and the case study method in particular. Drawing on Maxwell's (2005) interactive model of research design, the researchers built and illustrated the interrelationship among the five components of goals, conceptual framework, methods, validity and the research questions.

The researchers clearly stated that they subscribed to a constructivist worldview that influenced their focus, design, research questions, data collection, analysis and interpretation. Drawing on Lincoln and Guba (2005), '(T)he members of the research team shared ontological and epistemological assumptions that reality and knowledge is socially constructed and co-constructed between researcher and participants' (p. 77). Based on the researchers' explicit assertion and the evidence provided in the article, this MMR case study can be clearly considered a qual-dominant MMR case study, as stated above.

The quantitative strand seems to have played two roles in Christ and Makarani's study. First, it was used as a basis on which the qualitative strand was built. As such, it can be described as an MMR study with a 'development' purpose (Greene *et al.*, 1989; Riazi, 2016a). This is because the researchers stated that they selected the six teachers purposefully after they analyzed the survey questionnaires in the first strand and identified those participants who showed more knowledge and positive attitudes towards CLT. The second role of the quantitative strand seems to have been to extend the scope of the qualitative case study and provide further evidence for the representation and generalization of the case study findings. This role has been fulfilled through triangulation of findings from the classroom observations and interviews with the attitudinal findings from the questionnaire survey, and with an aim to present 'a more complete and credible representation of the participants' attitudes and behaviors' (p. 76).

Another conceptual observation regarding Christ and Makarani's study is that despite their explicit subscription to a constructivist worldview and a qualitatively dominant approach, the study is heavily influenced by Karavas-Doukas' (1996) theoretical framework on CLT. This is based on the evidence provided in the paper at the stages of data collection and data analysis. The researchers stated that the three core interview questions were based on

Karavas-Doukas' original categories of teachers' perspectives on CLT, their teaching philosophy and the challenges they faced when using CLT in their classes. At the level of qualitative data analysis of the interviews, although a hermeneutic grounded process was used to code and analyze the data, the researchers clarified that the 26 descriptors or codes that emerged during the coding process were classified into the three categories suggested originally by Karavas-Doukas. There seems, therefore, to exist a discrepancy between how the researchers described their constructivist inductive approach and worldview (developing a theoretical explanation about teachers' CLT approach) and how they actually conducted the research (more of applying a particular theoretical deductive framework of CLT to their data). The researchers, however, justified their use of the Karavas-Doukas categories in their analysis as a way to provide consistency in their 'interpretation of data obtained from the CLT attitude questionnaire, the coded interviews, and the classroom observations' (p. 80). In other words, the researchers based their conceptualization of the research problem on an existing theoretical framework and did not take the opportunity to extract theoretical explanations from the qualitative data.

Methodological level

Christ and Makarani labelled their study an embedded sequential exploratory mixed methods design. They considered this design to be the most appropriate for their study, which intended to investigate Indian English language teachers' attitudes and practices of CLT in two schools in Gujarat. The sample of the study included six high school English language teachers who were teaching in grades 8–12. They were non-native speakers of English who had completed a Bachelor of Arts (BA) or a Master of Arts (MA) degree in Education and who had access to communicative language teaching training and professional development.

The researchers elaborated on the term 'embedded' as used in their design clarification and explained that in an embedded MMR design, one strand receives more emphasis than the other. In their study, it was the qualitative strand which received the main emphasis, and included a case study through which interview and classroom observation data were collected from the English language teachers. The qualitative strand received the main emphasis, with findings from this data used to answer three out of four research questions.

Sequential aspect of the design

The study was also sequential, meaning that the outcomes of one strand of the study (in this case the quantitative) were used to build on and design the second strand (the qualitative), represented as quan $\rightarrow$ QUAL.

Sequential MMR studies like this one are also frequently categorized as 'development' in terms of purpose. However, Chris and Makarani did not refer to 'development' as a purpose for their study; rather, they considered 'triangulation' as the main purpose and claimed their study corresponded to the four methods of triangulation as suggested by Creswell (2008), Maxwell (2005), Patton (1999) and Tashakkori and Teddlie (2003). These four methods were data triangulation, researcher triangulation, theory triangulation and expert audit. (See also Chapter 3 for a discussion of triangulation in MMR.) However, there is not much elaboration in the paper to explain how each and/or all of these four methods of triangulation were tackled in the study. Perhaps data and method triangulation were the main type of triangulation one could trace in this study because the results of the qualitative data analysis were corroborated by the results of the quantitative data analysis.

Exploratory aspect of the design

Finally, Christ and Makarani used 'exploratory' as another definitional term for their MMR design. They explained that the term exploratory was used because both strands in their study were used to explore teachers' knowledge and attitudes towards CLT, their implementation of CLT and the challenges they faced when they implemented CLT in their classes. The term exploratory is generally applied when little is known about the object of the study or the research problem. As Creswell and Plano Clark (2011) also stated, 'an exploration is needed for one of several reasons: (1) measures or instruments are not available, (2) the variables are unknown, or (3) there is no guiding framework or theory' (p. 86). However, there are significant studies on CLT in different contexts and a variety of instruments developed for the investigation of CLT. This rich existing literature on the topic of CLT could have provided the researchers with necessary theoretical frameworks and instruments to design and approach their study more rigorously and with greater explanatory power. Creswell and Plano Clark (2011) also contended that explanatory designs are used to explain initial quantitative results with a qualitative strand.

Data analysis observations

Related to the quantitative data analysis, only descriptive statistics, including the mean and standard deviation of the five categories of the CLT questionnaire, were presented in the report. No inferential test of significance was used to judge whether or not there were any significant differences among the teachers' reported answers to the questions in each section. The use of a statistical test of significance would have enabled the researchers to make inferences about the target population based on the findings of the sample statistics. Since there were no reported inferential statistics in the article, it would be hard to make quantitative inferences, as will be discussed in the inferential level.

Considering the researchers' approach towards qualitative data analysis, they referred to their analysis as a reiterative and hermeneutic grounded process and explained the five-step sequence they went through: (1) writing idea memos on the margins of the transcripts, which were then used to develop a set of 26 initial codes; (2) coding the transcription of the interviews; (3) checking the coded data for fit and relevance; (4) developing categories from the coded data; and (5) looking for the relationship among the categories to present a theoretical explanation of the phenomenon. However, they clearly stated that the 26 descriptors or codes that emerged during the coding process were then classified into the three categories suggested originally by Karavas-Doukas (1996): perspectives on CLT, teachers' teaching philosophy and the challenges they faced when using CLT in their classes. These three categories were also those used as the core interview questions.

Karavas-Doukas' theoretical framework on CLT has thus had a major impact on the conceptual and methodological levels of this study, despite the fact that the researchers started off with a constructivist worldview to discover participant teachers' attitudes towards and practices of CLT. There seems to be a mismatch between the researchers' conceptual constructivist worldview and their methodological handling of data collection and analysis. The relatively severe adherence to a particular theoretical framework at the levels of data collection and analysis in a qualitatively oriented case study could have constrained the potentialities of a grounded approach to the data collection and analysis.

Overall, therefore, Christ and Makarani's (2009) study can be categorized as a 'principled' MMR study with both a 'development' and a 'triangulation' purpose. The reason for labelling this study as 'development' is the sequential nature of the study in which the qualitative strand was built on the outcomes of the quantitative strand. However, the researchers preferred to consider and focus on 'triangulation' as the main purpose for their study, mainly because they could achieve their research goal through data and method triangulation.

Inferential level

Christ and Makarani made three inferences based on the results of their quantitative and qualitative data analysis. The first regarded participants' attitudes towards CLT as represented by the five categories or constructs in the questionnaire. As mentioned in the methodological discussion, descriptive statistics including the mean and standard deviation were calculated for each of the five categories: group work, error correction, role of learner, role of teacher and place of grammar in teachers' teaching of English language. Since the mean for all the five categories was above 3 on a 0–5 scale, the researchers inferred that participants in their study were generally knowledgeable about and expressed positive attitudes towards CLT. There were, however, no inferential statistics reported in the article, making it difficult to infer whether there were any significant differences among the five categories or whether the sample findings could be generalized to the target population of English language teachers in India.

The second type of inference made by the researchers pertained to the outcomes of the qualitative analysis of the interviews and classroom observations. The researchers inferred from the analysis of the interviews that teachers varied in their opinions regarding the usefulness of learning English as an additional language, that the majority of teachers believed that CLT decreased teachers' habit of lecture style instruction, and that all teachers identified a list of barriers facing them when they wanted to implement CLT as their teaching method.

Finally, the researchers stated that they integrated the conclusions drawn from the quantitative and qualitative strands to make more comprehensive inferences. Despite this claim, there was little evidence in the report of how the integration of the inferences was made and how results of the quantitative and qualitative data analysis were triangulated.

Learning task

Read the annotations provided below and choose the one closest to your research interest. Read the full article and analyze it using the FRAMMR framework used in this chapter. Start by preparing a schematic diagram for the design of the study and writing down details of each strand. Then comment on the study at the conceptual, methodological and inferential levels where sufficient details permit.

- At the conceptual level, determine whether or not the researchers identified a particular purpose for mixing methods. If not, is it possible to imply a purpose based on the annotation provided for each study? Use the explanations provided for the three categories of 'eclectic', 'principled' or 'innovative' in Chapter 8 in order to allocate the study to one category.
- At the methodological level, look for the details of the quantitative and qualitative data collection and analysis procedures, and ascertain whether quality criteria and standards are observed in each strand.
- Finally, scan the reports, especially the discussion and conclusions sections, to reveal what type of inferences are made based on which results and whether the researcher has mixed the inferences in favour of a fuller meta-inference.

Busse, V. & Walter, C. (2013). Foreign language learning motivation in higher education: A longitudinal study of motivational changes and their causes. *The Modern Language Journal, 97*(2), 435–456.

This paper reported a study which explored the experiences of first-year modern foreign languages students from a motivational perspective. The participants were students enrolled in a degree of German language at two major universities in the United Kingdom. The study used a longitudinal MMR approach to investigate the time- and context-sensitive nature of motivational attributes. Both quantitative and qualitative data were gathered and analyzed. Quantitative data were collected using a questionnaire developed on the basis of the relevant literature and a pilot study. Qualitative data were gathered from interviews with five participants and followed a semi-structured procedure. Results suggested that participants' efforts to engage with language learning decreased over the course of the year, despite their increasing wish to become proficient in German. This change coincided with participants' decreasing levels of intrinsic motivation and self-efficacy beliefs.

The researchers discussed the relationships between motivational changes and contextual factors in higher education against the backdrop of students' transition experience from school to university. The authors suggested pedagogical implications for dealing with first-year students' declining motivation for learning modern foreign languages.

Hamid, M., Sussex, R. & Khan, A. (2009) Private tutoring in English for secondary school students in Bangladesh. *TESOL Quarterly, 43*, 281–308.

This article reported a mixed methods study that investigated the nature and practice of private tutoring in English (PT-E) in a disadvantaged rural area of Bangladesh. The researchers related PT-E to scholastic achievement in English and investigated student attitudes and motivations in PT-E. They created a core profile of PT-E in relation to the school system, parent and student expectations, attitudes and motivations, and students' habits. Quantitative data were collected through an English language proficiency test, a student-background survey questionnaire and students' grades obtained from school records. Qualitative data were collected by one-on-one interviews with selected students.

Results of the quantitative data analysis showed some positive links between PT-E and English achievement. This finding was elaborated through a broader qualitative analysis of the interviews. Through further analysis, a set of social, psychological and institutional factors was identified that contributed to the popularity of PT-E in a less affluent society like rural Bangladesh. The authors discussed the implications of the results for policy makers and curriculum developers.

References

Brown, H. (1994). *Teaching by principles: An interactive approach to language pedagogy*. Englewood Cliffs, NJ: Prentice Hall Regents.

Christ, T. (2007). A recursive approach to mixed methods research in a longitudinal study of postsecondary education disability support services. *Journal of Mixed Methods Research, 1*(3), 226–241.

Covington, M.V. (1984). The motive for self-worth. In R. Ames & C. Ames (Eds.), *Research on motivation in education* (Vol. I, pp. 77–113). New York: Academic Press.

Creswell, J. (2008). *Educational research: Planning, conducting, and evaluating quantitative and qualitative research*. Upper Saddle River, NJ: Merrill Prentice Hall.

Creswell, J.W. & Plano Clark, V.L. (2007). *Designing and conducting mixed methods research*. Thousand Oaks, CA: Sage.

Creswell, J.W. & Plano Clark, V.L. (2011). *Designing and conducting mixed methods research* (2nd ed.). Thousand Oaks, CA: Sage.

Creswell, J.W., Plano Clark, V.L., Gutmann, M. & Hanson, W. (2003). Advanced mixed methods research designs. In A. Tashakkori & C. Teddlie C (Eds.), *Handbook of mixed methods in social and behavioral research* (pp. 209–240). Thousand Oaks, CA: Sage.

Dornyei, Z. (2005). *The psychology of the language learner: Individual differences in second language acquisition*. Mahwah, NJ: Lawrence Erlbaum.

Dornyei, Z. (2009). The L2 motivational self system. In Z. Dornyei & E. Ushioda (Eds.), *Motivation, language identity, and the L2 self* (pp. 9–42). Clevedon: Multilingual Matters.

Gardner, R.C. (1985a). *Social psychology and second language learning: The role of attitudes and motivation*. Baltimore, MD: Edward Arnold.

Gardner, R.C. (1985b). The attitude/motivation test battery: Technical report. University of Western Ontario. Retrieved from: http://publish.uwo.ca/~gardner/docs/AMTBmanual.pdf

Gardner, R.C. (2001a). Integrative motivation and second language acquisition. In Z. Dornyei & R. Schmidt (Eds.), *Motivation and second language acquisition* (Vol. 23, pp. 1–19). Honolulu, HI: University of Hawaii, Second Language Teaching & Curriculum Center.

Gardner, R.C. (2001b). Language learning motivation: The student, the teacher, and the researcher. *Texas Papers in Foreign Language Education, 6*, 1–18.

Greene, J.C. & Caracelli, V.J. (1997). *Advances in mixed-method evaluation: The challenges and benefits of integrating diverse paradigms. New directions for evaluation: Number 74*. San Francisco, CA: Jossey-Bass.

Greene, J.C., Caracelli, V.J. & Graham, W.F. (1989). Toward a conceptual framework for mixed-method evaluation designs. *Educational Evaluation and Policy Analysis*, 11, 255–274.

Heigham, J. & Croker, R. (Eds.) (2009). *Qualitative research in applied linguistics: A practical introduction*. London: Palgrave.

Johnson, R.B., McGowan, M.W. & Turner, L.A. (2010). Grounded theory in practice: Is it inherently a mixed method? *Research in the Schools, 17*(2), 65–78.

Karavas-Doukas, E. (1996). Using attitude scales to investigate teachers' attitudes to the communicative approach. *ELT Journal, 50*(3), 187–198.

Lincoln, Y.S. & Guba, E. (2005). Paradigmatic controversies, contradictions, and emerging confluences. In N.K. Denzin & Y.S. Lincoln (Eds.), *The Sage handbook of qualitative research* (pp. 191–214). Thousand Oaks, CA: Sage.

Matthews, P.H. (1997). *The concise Oxford dictionary of linguistics*. New York: Oxford University Press.

Maxwell, J.A. (2005). *Qualitative research design: An interactive approach* (2nd ed.). Thousand Oaks, CA: Sage.

McInerney, D.M. (1998, April). Multidimensional aspects of motivation in cross-cultural settings and ways of researching this. Paper presented at the American Educational Research Association Annual Meeting, San Diego, CA.

Norton, B. (2000). *Identity and language learning: Gender, ethnicity and educational change*. New York: Pearson Education.

Nunan, D. (1988). *The learner-centered curriculum: A study in second language teaching*. Cambridge: Cambridge University Press.

Patton, M. (1999). Enhancing the quality and credibility of qualitative analysis. *Health Services Research, 35*(5), 1189–1208.

Riazi, A.M. (2016a). *The Routledge encyclopedia of research methods in applied linguistics: Quantitative, qualitative and mixed-methods research*. London: Routledge.

Riazi, A.M. (2016b). Innovative mixed-methods research (IMMR): Moving beyond design technicalities to epistemological and methodological realisations. *Applied Linguistics, 37*(1), 33–49. DOI: 10.1093/applin/amv064.

Riazi, A.M. & Candlin, C.N. (2014). Mixed-methods research in language teaching and learning: Opportunities, issues and challenges. *Language Teaching, 47*, 135–173.

Richards, K. (2003). *Qualitative inquiry in TESOL*. London: Palgrave Macmillan.

Tashakkori, A. & Teddlie, C. (2003). *Handbook of mixed methods in social and behavioral research*. Thousand Oaks, CA: Sage.

Teddlie, C. & Tashakkori, A. (2009). *Foundations of mixed method research: Integrating qualitative and quantitative approaches in the social and behavioural sciences*. Thousand Oaks, CA: Sage.

Turner, J. (1993). Another researcher comments . . . *TESOL Quarterly, 27*, 736–739.

12 Researching Language Testing and Assessment

This chapter will:

- present an analysis and review of a complementarity MMR study that investigated the predictive validity of an English as a second language (ESL) placement test;
- present an analysis and review of an MMR study that examined the usefulness of formative assessment in second language (L2) classrooms;
- provide two further MMR studies in the learning task to be analyzed by the readers.

Introduction

As discussed in Chapter 1, language testing and assessment is a field that is heavily influenced by a quantitative research approach, mainly due to the nature of the topics related to this field. This trend is reflected in some of the review papers of the published articles in major language testing and assessment journals, as presented in Chapter 1. To refresh readers' minds, Chalhoub-Deville and Deville's (2008) review of published articles in the two major language assessment journals, *Language Assessment* and *Language Assessment Quarterly*, from their commencement up to 2005, is referred to again here. Based on their analysis of the methodology section of the articles published in these two journals, Chalhoub-Deville and Deville concluded that the predominant research methodology used in the studies reported was quantitative.

Turner (2013) followed up Chalhoub-Deville and Deville's review by examining the methodological trends in published articles in the three major journals of the field, *Assessing Writing, Language Testing* and *Language Assessment Quarterly*. Turner's analysis of the methodology section of the published articles showed that up to approximately the year 2003, researchers used predominantly quantitative methods in their investigation of issues related to language assessment. This trend of heavy reliance on quantitative methods seems to be gradually changing, however, and being complemented by qualitative and mixed methods research. Cheng and Fox (2013), for instance, reviewed recent doctoral dissertations in the field of language assessment in Canada and concluded that the use of multiple methods approaches is increasing in doctoral dissertations compared with those using single research methods. It is interesting, therefore, to review MMR studies conducted on issues related to language testing and assessment and to find out how language assessment researchers have mixed methods in their studies.

The two MMR studies reviewed in this chapter are related to (1) the predictive validity of a university placement test and (2) the usefulness of formative assessment or assessment for learning in second language classrooms. The first MMR study followed a 'complementarity' purpose and investigated the relationships between graduate students' test scores on an English as a second language placement test and the measures of their academic performance in a United States university.

The second study examined the assessment practices in a Canadian continuing education programme specializing in pre-university English for Academic Purposes (EAP) classes. Nine teachers and forty-two students participated in the study and provided the required data, including curriculum documents, completed questionnaires, interviews and classroom observations.

These two articles are referred to as Study 7 and Study 8, and will be reviewed and discussed using the FRAMMR framework to clarify how researchers employed MMR to investigate topics of their concern.

First, an annotation of the study will be provided, then design and strands are discussed, and finally, each study will be commented on at the conceptual, methodological and inferential levels.

Study 7

Lee, Y. & Greene, J. (2007). The predictive validity of an ESL placement test: A mixed methods approach. *Journal of Mixed Methods Research, 1,* 366–389.

Annotation

Lee and Greene (2007) investigated the predictive validity of an institutional ESL placement test, the Computerized Enhanced ESL Placement Test

(CEEPT), in a large public university in the United States. They examined the relationships between graduate students' test scores on the CEEPT and the measures of academic performance of graduate students. This performance was conceptualized and operationalized by three related facets: students' grade point average (GPA), faculty members' evaluation of student performance and student self-assessments. Data were collected from 100 students and 55 faculty members and included students' scores and student and staff questionnaires and interviews.

Two research questions were addressed in Lee and Greene's (2007, p. 369) study.

1. To what extent do scores on an institutional ESL placement test (the Computerized Enhanced ESL Placement Test [CEEPT]) predict international graduate students' academic performance and their language difficulties in content courses during the first semester of their graduate education?
2. To what extent and in what ways do qualitative interviews with students and faculty members serve to contribute to a more comprehensive and nuanced understanding of this predictive relationship between CEEPT scores and student academic performance, via integrative mixed methods analyses?

The participants of the study included 100 international graduate students from 'a range of graduate fields – business ($n = 43$), humanities ($n = 20$), science ($n = 9$) and technology ($n = 28$) – and various first-language backgrounds – Chinese ($n = 32$), Korean ($n = 31$), Spanish ($n = 10$) and other ($n = 27$)' (Lee & Greene, 2007, p. 370). These participants formed 91% of graduate students in a public university in the United States who took the university's English placement test.

In addition to participants' scores on the placement test and their GPA, a self-assessment questionnaire was sent to all 100 participants to elicit information about their assessment of their language proficiency and academic performance at mid-semester – 55 students completed the questionnaires and returned them, resulting in a response rate of 55%.

The researchers also approached 55 faculty members, whose contact information was provided in response to one of the questions on the student questionnaires, for further data collection. The researchers sent an evaluation questionnaire to these faculty members to inquire about their assessment of their students' language proficiency and academic performance. Faculty members completed and returned 34 questionnaires (a response rate of 62%). Of the 34 returned questionnaires, seven faculty members sent blank questionnaires and e-mail messages explaining why they were not able to complete the questionnaire. The actual response rate of the completed questionnaires was therefore 49%, corresponding to the 27 completed questionnaires.

The researchers conducted both quantitative and qualitative data analysis to answer the two research questions. Inferences were made from the quantitative and qualitative data analysis results and these inferences were integrated to produce a more comprehensive meta-inference to explain the predictive validity of the CEEPT placement test and students' academic success.

Design and strands

Figure 12.1 presents the schematic diagram of the design and strands of Lee and Greene's study. As the figure shows, the target population was the international graduate students who took the university's English language placement test. The MMR design of the study consisted of two main strands, a quantitative and a qualitative one. The two strands received equal weight in the research process, so the design of the study can be represented as QUAN + QUAL. The data of the quantitative strand included the 100 students' placement test scores and their GPA. Additional quantitative data included a self-assessment survey that was sent to all the 100 participants to elicit how they assessed their own language proficiency and academic performance – 55 students completed and returned the self-assessment questionnaire, resulting in a response rate of 55%.

Student self-assessment and faculty evaluation questionnaires

The self-assessment questionnaire included both closed-ended five-point Likert scale items and open-ended questions. The Likert scale items were used to tap various dimensions of the students' performance in relevant courses, while the open-ended questions were used to elicit additional information about students' broader definitions of academic success and their perception of factors affecting their academic performance. The open-ended questions therefore enabled the researchers to consider students' definitions and perspectives as an integrative aspect of the construct of academic performance and success.

In addition to the quantitative data collected from the student participants, an evaluation questionnaire was sent to the 55 faculty members whose names were provided by the student participants. Of those 55 faculty members,

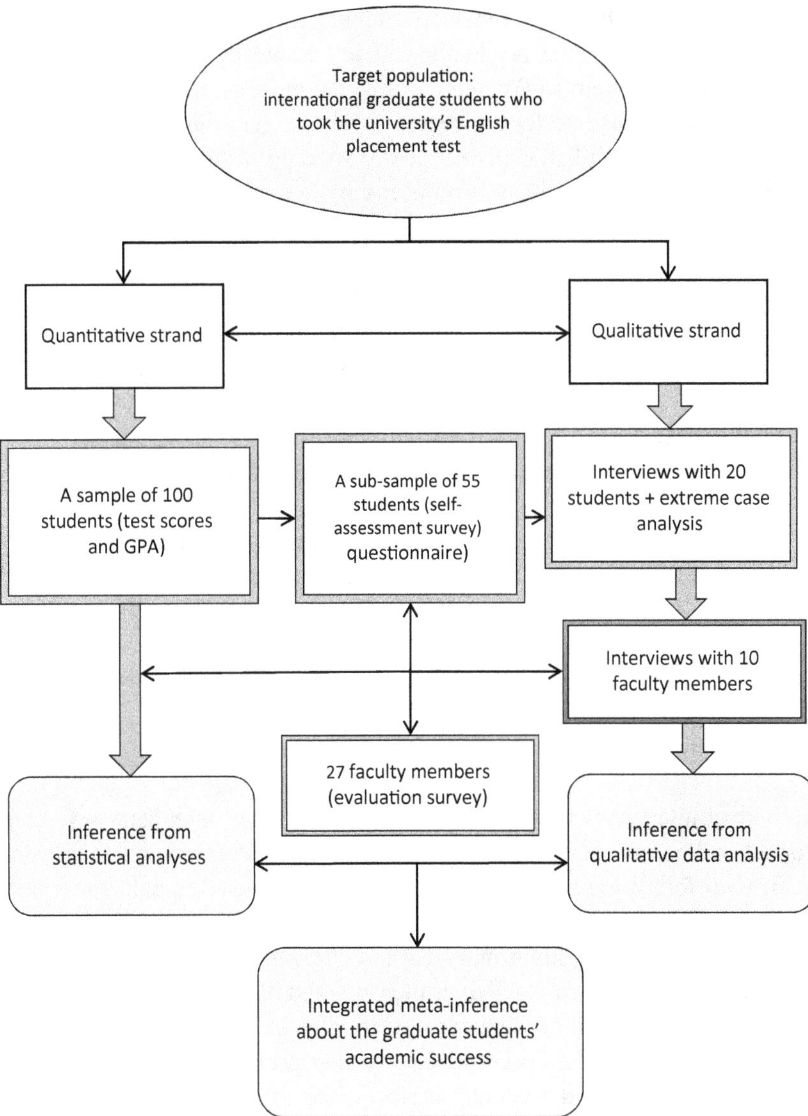

Figure 12.1 The design, strands and inferences made in Lee and Greene's (2007) MMR study

27 completed and returned the questionnaires, indicating a response rate of 49%. The faculty questionnaire presented two types of items, closed-ended Likert-type and open-ended explanatory ones. The questions asked faculty members to evaluate 'students' English proficiency, academic performance

in the course, and the extent to which students' level of proficiency hindered their performance in the academic course'. Some of the questions 'also asked for faculty members' perceptions of the most essential English skills for successful course performance and to what extent the targeted students had the requisite English skills needed to succeed in the courses' (p. 371). Faculty members were given the opportunity to answer the questions using a five-point rating scale as well as elaborating on their answers through specific examples. The combination of the quantitative closed-ended and qualitative open-ended questions on the student and faculty questionnaires enabled researchers to collect further quantitative and qualitative data and therefore gave them the opportunity to draw on a variety of data sources.

Qualitative data
The data collected for the qualitative strand originated from four sources:

- responses to open-ended questions on the questionnaires;
- interviews with 20 student participants who had expressed willingness in response to a final question on the self-assessment questionnaire;
- interviews with ten faculty members who had expressed their willingness to participate in a follow-up interview;
- critical case analysis (Riazi, 2016a) of outliers.

Individual interviews with 20 students and 10 faculty members were conducted in Lee and Greene's study. Each student interview lasted for one hour, with follow-up interviews when needed, and each faculty interview took about 30 minutes, with follow-up emails where needed. The student interviews created an opportunity for the students to further elaborate on their perceptions of their English proficiency and of their substantive preparation for the courses they were enrolled in. The faculty interviews provided the researchers with the opportunity to further probe the faculty members' perceptions of targeted students' performance in their courses, including their perceptions of students' English language proficiency and content performance, as well as the relationship between the two. They were also asked to discuss their justifications for the grades they assigned to the students, the relative ranking of the students and, if applicable, the quality of term papers submitted by students. Both sets of interviews thus provided the researchers with rich qualitative data on other aspects related to students' academic performance and success usually not accessible when considering GPA as the only representation of this construct.

Turning to critical case analysis, three student participants were found to have scores much lower (two standard deviations) than the means of the student participants' placement test and GPA scores. These three students were thus considered outliers and were interviewed to provide further information and perceptions about students' academic success or failure.

Data analysis

Both descriptive and inferential statistics (Riazi, 2016a) were used to analyze the quantitative data. Descriptive statistics included mean and standard deviation for the placement test scores, students' GPA, and quantitative items of the student and faculty questionnaires. Inferential statistics included the use of Pearson product-moment correlation (Riazi, 2016a) to investigate the relationship between the students' CEEPT scores and their first-semester GPA. Pearson correlation was also used to investigate the relationship between the students' CEEPT scores and the student self-assessment on the one hand, and the faculty evaluation questionnaire measures on the other.

Qualitative data analysis included coding of the transcribed interviews with student participants and faculty members and thematic analysis (Riazi, 2016a) of these interviews. Moreover, a critical case analysis was conducted on the three students whose placement test performance and GPA were significantly (two standard deviations) lower than those of other student participants. The outcome of the critical case analysis gave the researchers further information about student perceptions of academic performance. As Figure 12.1 illustrates, the outcomes of the quantitative and qualitative analyses were integrated to make meta-inferences about student academic success.

Commentary

Conceptual level

Based on the FRAMMR framework presented in Chapter 8, Lee and Greene's study followed a 'complementarity' purpose and can thus be classified as an 'innovative' MMR study. As discussed in Chapter 8, MMR studies with a complementarity purpose usually conceptualize the research problem as multi-layered and multi-faceted, in need of a mixed methods approach for investigating different layers and shedding more light on different facets of the research problem. In line with this criterion, Lee and Greene's study met the innovative criteria, which resulted in the use of MMR as a methodology corresponding to the multi-layered conception of the nature of academic success (ontology) and what the researchers could know about it (epistemology).

Conceptualization of the research problem

At the ontological level (the nature of the research problem), the researchers used students' academic performance represented by their GPA as merely one of the facets of 'academic success'. They extended their conceptualization of the construct of 'academic success' to include other facets such as students' self-assessment as well as faculty members' evaluation of the students' academic performance. Such a multi-faceted conceptualization of the research problem enabled the researchers to genuinely use and mix methods from the two research approaches (quantitative and qualitative).

The conceptualization stage in the research process is very important because it reflects the researcher's ontological perspective (the nature of the research phenomenon), which, in turn, leads to the methodological choices and the use of specific and appropriate procedures for collecting and analyzing data. The first, and perhaps the foremost, point of departure in Lee and Greene's study was, therefore, their conceptualization of the construct of academic performance and success as a multi-layered and multi-faceted concept. Ordinarily, academic performance and success are conceived as a cognitive 'trait', usually represented by students' GPA and measured through objective procedures. Lee and Greene not only attended to this aspect of the academic performance by including students' GPA in their analysis, they also considered two other contextual and more subjective definitions or representations of the construct. The researchers' conceptualization of the research problem as multi-faceted resulted in a complementarity MMR study that enabled the researchers to produce a more comprehensive understanding of different aspects of a complex phenomenon such as academic performance and success.

Based on the FRAMMR framework presented in Chapter 8, one of the features of innovative MMR studies is the theoretical/conceptual orientation, in which researchers draw on different theoretical orientations, allowing them to investigate various aspects of the perceived problem. MMR studies with complementarity and initiation purposes are usually good candidates for fulfilling the innovative criterion in the FRAMMR framework. The mixing of various methods from different research paradigms in such studies would be a response to the investigation of different aspects of the research phenomenon as reflected in the conceptualization of the research problem. As such, research questions in innovative MMR studies stem from and are grounded in the conceptualization of the research problem.

Methodological level

Methodologically, Lee and Greene's study was classified as innovative because researchers investigating the predictive validity of language tests conventionally follow a quantitative approach and mostly use correlational designs. Lee and Greene used a combination of data collection and analysis procedures, including student test and academic performance scores, and perspectives of faculty members and students on academic performance to build a more comprehensive understanding of the construct of academic performance and success.

Another methodological innovation of the study was that the researchers used 'extreme case analysis' (Caracelli & Greene, 1993; Riazi, 2016a) and a 'joint display' table within a mixed methods framework to shed more light on different facets across various data sets. Extreme case analysis is commonly used in qualitative research to fine-tune the emerging theoretical explanation of the phenomenon from the data sources. Contrary to quantitative research in which outliers are excluded from analysis, in qualitative research, negative or extreme cases can shed more light on the emerging patterns from the data. Outliers can be identified through different methods, such as using scatter-plots or box plots. Including 'extreme case analysis' within an MMR study, as Lee and Greene did, enabled the researchers to shed more light on the 'inconsistencies and even contradictions across various data sets' (p. 369). In addition, through a joint display matrix, the researchers displayed both qualitative and quantitative data and outcomes alongside each other. This helped the researchers to identify analytical relationships between quantitative and qualitative data sets and enabled them to integrate both sources of data and provide a more complete understanding of the research problem.

The researchers' success in integrating different data and analyses contributed to the methodological innovation of the study.

Inferential level

Quantitative inference

Lee and Greene made three types of inferences. The first was related to the relationship between students' scores on the CEEPT, their first-semester GPA scores, and the quantitative items on the student self-assessment and faculty evaluation of students' performance questionnaires. At this level, the researchers were able to make inferences about the magnitude, the direction and the significance of the relationships. Lee and Greene used Pearson product-moment correlation, which is a parametric test of significance, to make inferences about the significance, magnitude and direction of relationships.

Qualitative inference

The second type of inference was qualitative. This was based on the out-comes of the qualitative data analysis conducted on the open-ended questions on the student and faculty questionnaires as well as student and faculty interviews augmented by extreme case analysis. The thematic analysis of the qualitative data sources enabled the researchers to make inferences about different aspects of the construct of students' academic performance and success as perceived by students and faculty members. For example, the four major themes extracted from the interviews with faculty members included the importance of English language skills for successful course performance, the importance of research skills for graduate studies, students' relationships with instructors and their peers, and the challenges of adapting to a new academic environment. Such thematic analysis unfolded aspects and factors related to academic performance and success that could not have been inferred merely from the correlation between students' CEEPT scores and their GPA.

Meta-inference

An important stage in the process of making inferences in MMR studies is the ability of the researchers to integrate quantitative and qualitative inferences in the form of meta-inferences that can provide a more complete understanding of the research problem. Such an understanding responds to and is in line with different aspects of the conceptualized research problem. Although the researchers believed that the 'separate analyses of students' and faculty members' views of academic performance in a content course, and of the relationships between these varied assessments of academic performance and English proficiency as measured by the CEEPT, did not neatly interconnect to form a coherent portrait or pattern, as was hoped for in this complementarity mixed methods study' (p. 379), the process of making meta-inferences was convincingly executed in this study. The integration was achieved through the 'joint display' matrix on pages 383–385. By linking quantitative placement and GPA scores with qualitative quotes in an effective way and through display techniques, the researchers presented data and outcomes from different strands of their MMR study. Although it is now a common belief that language proficiency alone, as measured by a predictor such as a proficiency or placement test, is no guarantee of academic success, Lee and Greene were able to generate inferences about other important factors and their likely mediating roles in a predictor–achievement relationship and construct. These inferences were based on extreme case analysis and were built to account for the factors that caused the observed discrepancy between the students' CEEPT scores and their GPA.

Overall, therefore, the separate as well as integrated analyses and their related inferences presented in this study contribute to a more comprehensive understanding of the construct of academic performance and success in graduate programmes. This construct was defined as a multi-faceted and multi-layered construct far beyond a simple relationship between English language proficiency and students' academic performance usually measured and represented by students' GPA.

Study 8

Colby-Kelly, C. & Turner, C.E. (2007). AFL research in the L2 classroom and evidence of usefulness: Taking formative assessment to the next level. *The Canadian Modern Language Review, 64*, 9–38.

Annotation

Recently, there has been a focus on formative assessment, or assessment for learning (AFL), in educational settings to enhance student engagement in the learning and learning processes. Drawing on this background, Colby-Kelly and Turner (2007) used a mixed methods research design to investigate the usefulness of AFL in a second language classroom in a Canadian continuing education programme specializing in pre-university EAP. Using the Bachman and Palmer (1996) 'test usefulness' framework, and Bachman's (2005) assessment use argument (AUA), the researchers collected data and presented preliminary results and evidence for the usefulness of AFL in pre-university EAP classes.

Three research questions were addressed in this study.

1. What are teacher and student perceptions of formative assessment in a second language classroom setting?
2. What is the nature of formative assessment in a second language classroom setting?
3. What evidence can be found that formative assessment benefits learning? (p. 18)

The researchers collected data from nine teachers and forty-two students in four classes, including curriculum documents, teacher questionnaires, student interviews and classroom observations. Curriculum document analysis comprised the analysis of the speaking section of the school's curriculum guide to determine the kinds of assessment practices used. The teacher questionnaire included both closed-ended items regarding 'course assessment needs' and open-ended questions asking teachers to report on the assessment tasks they preferred to use and those they preferred not to use. The student interviews generally followed the open-ended questions on the teacher questionnaire and asked students about their perceptions and preferences for assessment tasks. Twelve students from the four classes were also interviewed at a post-study stage and were asked about whether or not the teacher–student conferencing assessment worked for them to enhance their learning.

The closed-ended teacher questionnaire items, the curriculum document analysis and the classroom observations data were analyzed quantitatively using frequency counts to answer the first research question. The classroom observations, field notes and student interviews were analyzed qualitatively to answer the other two research questions.

Design and strands

Figure 12.2 presents the schematic diagram of Colby-Kelly and Turner's (2007) study. The two strands of the study received equal weight and so the study's design can be represented as QUAN + QUAL.

The target population in Colby-Kelly and Turner's study was students and teachers in EAP programmes in Canada. The sample of the study comprised 9 EAP teachers and 42 students recruited from four classes in an EAP programme. The teachers, one male and eight females, were described as experienced EAP teachers and were all native English speakers. The student sample included only international students with different first-language backgrounds. There was no explanation about the sampling procedure in the report. The reader can thus assume that the researchers used a convenience sampling procedure (Riazi, 2016a). This type of sampling procedure is used when researchers do not randomly select participants; rather, they usually use available participants from intact classes in schools or other research sites.

Data collection

Data were collected over eight weeks of an intensive EAP course and included pre-, during- and post-session data collection.

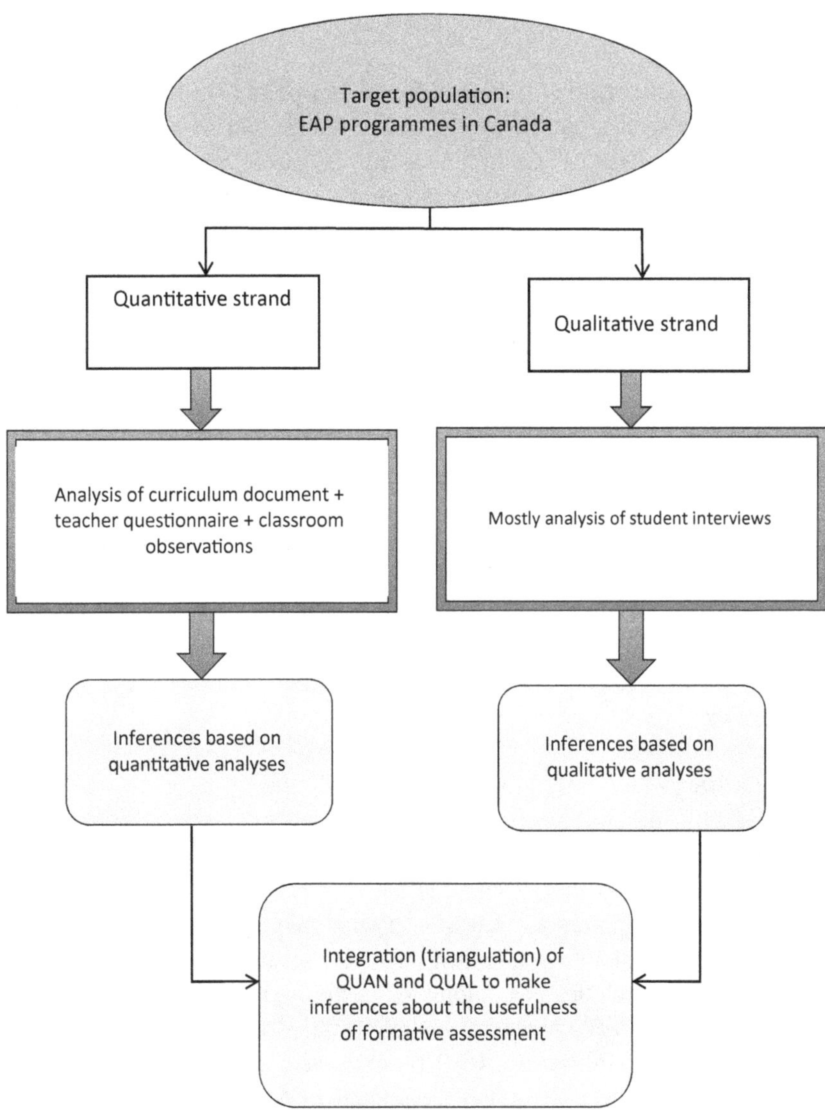

Figure 12.2 The design, strands and inferences made in Colby-Kelly and Turner's (2007) MMR study

At the pre-session stage, questionnaires were administered to nine EAP teachers. The questionnaire was based on a review of the literature, particularly Harlen and Winter's (2004) work. It comprised 51 items classified into four categories of assessment and students, assessment and teachers, assessment and learning, and course assessment needs. The questionnaire was used to elicit teachers' perceptions about classroom-based formative assessment practices.

The questionnaire items were based on a four-point Likert scale: 'strongly disagree', 'disagree', 'agree' and 'strongly agree'. No neutral or undecided option was used to exclude indecisive responses from the participants. During the session and as classes were running, two advanced-level classes, each made up of 17 students, were observed. These classes were observed 16 times over three months and were audio-recorded while the observers also took field notes. Finally, at the post-session stage in the process of data collection, interviews were conducted with 12 students from the four classes. The student interviews were also audio-recorded while field notes were taken.

Data analysis

Quantitative analysis of the teacher questionnaire, curriculum document and classroom observations was used to determine the frequency counts of the formative assessment tasks employed in the EAP classes. The open-ended teacher questionnaire, the classroom observation field notes and student interviews were analyzed qualitatively to make inferences about the teachers' and students' perceptions and assessment task preferences. Quantitative and qualitative data analysis results were then scrutinized for possible similarities.

Commentary

Conceptual level

Though it was not explicitly stated in the research report, Colby-Kelly and Turner's study appeared to follow a 'triangulation' purpose based on the researchers' statement that 'all of the data were scrutinized and triangulated' (p. 20). The research problem addressed in the study related to teacher and student perceptions of and usefulness of formative assessment or AFL in an advanced level pre-university EAP programme in Canada. The construct under investigation was formative assessment or AFL. Based on a literature review of classroom-based formative assessment and AFL, the researchers found Leung and Mohan's (2004) theoretical discussion of classroom-based formative assessment practices informative and useful and thus used it as their working definition for the analysis of assessment tasks in the advanced-level EAP curriculum documents.

The other theoretical frameworks used in the study were the 'test usefulness' framework (Bachman & Palmer, 1996) and the 'assessment use argument' (Bachman, 2005). The researchers used these to help with the design of analytical procedures and to seek evidence for and investigate the representation and substantiation of formative assessment in the EAP programme. The study thus represented an exploratory mixed methods evaluation research in which the researchers intended to examine the types of assessment tasks used in an EAP programme and whether AFL was useful in L2 classrooms. Based on the above analysis and the criteria discussed in the FRAMMR framework in Chapter 8, this study can be categorized as a 'principled' MMR study with a 'triangulation' purpose.

One of the requirements of the MMR studies with triangulation purpose, as discussed in Chapter 3, is that the same and a single definition of the construct informs different data collection instruments and data analysis procedures. The unitary definition of the construct would enable MMR researchers to cross-validate the findings from the quantitative strand with those from the qualitative strand. This is how MMR studies with triangulation purpose are differentiated from MMR studies with complementarity purpose in which the construct of the study is usually perceived to be multi-faceted, requiring different definitions and operationalization leading to different instruments for data collection. Perhaps having been aware of this requirement, Colby-Kelly and Turner used and held the definition of 'formative assessment' suggested by Leung and Mohan throughout their study, including the conceptual, methodological and inferential stages.

Conceptual reflections

The first reflection regarding this MMR study is the multi-dimensionality nature of the construct of formative assessment as represented by the theoretical definitions in the study. The researchers, however, used one of the definitions of 'formative assessment' suggested by Leung and Mohan to inform their study at different stages in the research process. A more sophisticated conceptualization of formative assessment based on different theoretical frameworks could have resulted in a more comprehensive study. The second reflection is that the multi-dimensionality of the construct was also represented in the curriculum document, and in the teachers' and students' perceptions of the construct. Interestingly, the researchers stated that while there was a great deal of formative assessment recommended in the curriculum document, none of these was actually used in practice, as the classroom observations showed.

The third reflection is that the researchers reported that they encountered many examples of the teachers' hesitancy regarding the use of formative assessment in their classes. The discrepancies in teacher and student perceptions, and the teachers' hesitancy over the usefulness of formative assessment in their classes, were worthy observations in need of further investigations and through more carefully designed stages of data collection and analysis. This could have resulted in an MMR study with complementarity or initiation purposes looking for more comprehensive understanding and presentation of the construct of formative assessment in L2 classrooms. It should be pointed out, however, that researchers bring certain views to their investigation of research problems and conduct their study within contextual constraints, as also noted by these researchers.

Methodological level

The design of Colby-Kelly and Turner's study, as discussed and presented earlier and especially in Figure 12.2, can be notationally represented as QUAN + QUAL. Since the perceived purpose of the study was triangulation, it can therefore be inferred that the two strands of the study had equal weights. The quantitative strand included quantitative data and analysis derived from the curriculum document, quantitative items of the teacher questionnaire, and the classroom observations. The qualitative strand, meanwhile, included classroom observation notes and student interviews. The two types of data sources were analyzed and reported separately and were finally scrutinized for possible similarities and thus triangulation of findings from the quantitative and qualitative strands.

Methodological observations

As Figure 12.2 shows, the two strands of the MMR study were conducted in parallel. Results of the two strands were also presented separately in the research report. First, the nine teachers' perceptions of classroom-based assessment were presented. Teachers' perceptions were related to four aspects of classroom-based assessment: learners and assessment, teachers and assessment, learning and assessment, and course assessment needs. The frequency (number) of teachers' responses for any of the four-point agreement scales as related to the four categories in the questionnaire was also presented in four tables. The researchers, however, did not report any inferential statistics, perhaps because of the small number of participants and, in turn, the small number of responses in each of the four scale categories for each question. Nonetheless, it might have been possible to use some non-parametric tests of significance (Riazi, 2016a), especially because the researchers have made inferences about the teachers' preferences for certain categories of classroom-based assessment.

The second level of quantitative analysis in this study was that of the curriculum document for the type of assessment tasks included in the curriculum. These assessment tasks, including teacher feedback ($n = 11$), peer assessment ($n = 11$) and self-assessment ($n = 4$), were presented in two tables in terms of the frequency and percentage of each assessment task. Subsequently, quantitative results of two classroom observations over five weeks in terms of the use of formative assessment in teaching and learning activities were presented in another table. These included four kinds of assessment incidents: self-assessments, peer assessments, and two types of teacher feedback (teacher–student conferencing and teacher–group feedback). Again, no inferential statistics are reported for the quantitative results presented in different tables and it may therefore be difficult to make any generalizations about the target population of EAP programmes in Canada. Indeed, this makes sense because the sample of the study was not selected randomly and so making generalizations may not be warranted here. Since the focus was on one EAP programme and the sample featured a convenience sampling procedure, the MMR study may be treated simply as a case study of formative assessment in an EAP programme. It is also noteworthy to remember that the document analysis was restricted to only frequency counts of the type of assessment tasks and not subjected to further qualitative analysis, such as thematic analysis.

Qualitative data analysis included in the report covered the classroom observation notes and student interviews. There is a brief explanation of the interviews conducted with 12 students from the four classes. The interviews were conducted near the end of the school's academic session when other data had already been collected. These students were asked to explain how useful they found the teacher–student conferencing assessment task in the school and in their learning. The section related to the qualitative data and analysis is brief, with minimum explanation about the analysis procedures: 'Qualitative analyses consisted of the examination and reporting of the classroom observation field notes and student interview content' (p. 20). Overall, therefore, the qualitative analysis reported in this study looks very weak.

Following the presentation of the results, an assessment use argument figure is presented in the research report. The figure has two columns, one with evidence from the data and analysis that supported the usefulness of formative assessment and the other with evidence that rejected the usefulness of formative assessment, or rebuttals.

Inferential level

At the inferential level, and given the purpose of the study, which was perceived to be triangulation, it was expected that three types of inferences were presented: first, the quantitative inferences based on the quantitative data analysis results; second, the qualitative inferences based on the qualitative analysis results; and finally, an integration of these inferences in favour of a more meta-inference or triangulation. The quantitative inferences were more explicitly presented and took more prominence in the paper. However, all quantitative inferences were made based on only descriptive statistics, that is, the frequency and percentages derived from the quantitized teacher questionnaire and curriculum document analysis. Since there was no report of any inferential statistics in the report, it would be hard to make legitimate and generalizable inferences about the target population. Perhaps the researchers did not intend to make any generalizations either.

Some examples of the researchers' conclusions were: 'These responses in the teacher questionnaires answer our first research question, and their stated preferences in assessment choices reflect a solid formative assessment component in their classrooms' (Colby-Kelly & Turner, 2007, p. 26). Or, based on a frequency and percentage analysis of the classroom-based assessment incidents in the curriculum document, '(T)he results of the curriculum analysis partially answer our second research question', which was about the nature of formative assessment in a second language classroom setting. The quantitative conclusions and inferences were thus mostly based on the sample characteristics, which, as discussed earlier, may be considered more as a case with no potential for any generalizations.

As discussed in the methodological section, there was not adequate explanation about the qualitative data analysis in the research report. Accordingly, it would be difficult for the reader to develop an understanding of how the qualitative inferences were made from the outcomes of the qualitative data analysis. The researchers presented an AUA figure as a way of triangulating the findings of the two strands, and to make conclusions about the usefulness of formative assessment in this particular context, which was indeed useful. However, as indicated in the methodological reflections, since the qualitative analysis was weak, the integrated inferences could not provide strong conclusions.

Learning task

Read the annotations below and choose the one closest to your research interest. Read the full article and analyze it using the FRAMMR framework used in this chapter. Start by preparing a schematic diagram for the design of the study and writing down details of each strand. Then comment on the study at the conceptual, methodological and inferential levels where sufficient details permit.

- At the conceptual level, determine whether or not the researchers identified a particular purpose for mixing methods. If not, is it possible to imply a purpose based on the annotation provided for each study? Use the explanations provided for the three categories of 'eclectic', 'principled' or 'innovative' in Chapter 8, in order to allocate the study to one category.
- At the methodological level, look for the details of the quantitative and qualitative data collection and analysis procedures, and ascertain whether quality criteria and standards are observed in each strand.
- Finally, scan the reports, especially the discussion and conclusions sections, to reveal what type of inferences are made based on which results, and whether the researcher has mixed the inferences in favour of a fuller meta-inference.

Barkaoui, K. (2010). Do ESL essay raters' evaluation criteria change with experience? A mixed method, cross-sectional study. *TESOL Quarterly 44*(1), 31–58.

The problem addressed by this study was the relationship between the essay raters' holistic and analytical evaluation of essays written by learners of English as a second language and their level of experience. Two groups of raters, experienced ($n = 31$) and novice ($n = 29$), participated in this study and rated a sample of 180 ESL essays using holistic and analytical evaluation criteria and provided written explanations for their holistic scores on each essay. The quantitative data included essay scores as well as raters' experience, and the qualitative data included raters' explanations of their holistic scoring, with 1,069 score explanations provided by experienced and novice raters. Both quantitative statistical analysis and qualitative analysis of the data were conducted to identify the criteria that the raters used to rate the essays holistically.

Results of the data analysis showed that both groups of raters assigned more importance to the communicative quality of the essays than to other aspects of student writing. Novice raters were found to be more lenient, however, and to give more importance to argumentation than the experienced raters did. Meanwhile, the experienced raters tended to be more severe, to consider linguistic accuracy more important, and to make reference to evaluation criteria not listed in the rating scale more frequently than the novice raters did. The researcher concluded the article by inviting other researchers to conduct longitudinal research to investigate the extent to which rater evaluation criteria might change over time and across contexts.

> Fisher, R., Cavanagh, J. & Bowles, A. (2011). Assisting transition to university: Using assessment as a formative learning tool. *Assessment & Evaluation in Higher Education, 36*(2), 225–237.

The focus of this study was on formative assessment and its use in assisting students' transition to university. The researchers intended to explore the effectiveness of an intervention as pertaining to formative assessment in a first-year core business course. The purpose of the study was to explore whether there was a significant difference between students submitting drafts of their first assessment and those who did not in terms of their academic achievement.

Of the 539 students who completed all assessment tasks, 106 were invited to submit a draft of their first assessment in Week 5 and receive feedback, while 433 did not. Students who received feedback were invited to provide feedback to the researchers on the effectiveness or otherwise of the intervention. Four students participated in face-to-face conversations, while fifteen more responded by email. Both quantitative and qualitative analyses were conducted and results of the data analysis showed that the intervention not only assisted students' overall learning but significantly facilitated higher marks in assessments.

References

Bachman, L. (2005). Building and supporting a case for test use. *Language Assessment Quarterly, 2*(1), 1–34.

Bachman, L. & Palmer, A. (1996). *Language testing in practice: Designing and developing useful language tests.* Oxford: Oxford University Press.

Caracelli, V. & Greene, J. (1993). Data analysis strategies for mixed method evaluation designs. *Educational Evaluation and Policy Analysis, 15*, 195–207.

Chalhoub-Deville, M. & Deville, C. (2008). Utilizing psychometric methods in assessment. In E. Shohamy & N.H. Hornberger (Eds.), *Encyclopedia of language and education* (2nd ed., Vol. 7, pp. 211–224). New York: Springer Science+Business Media LLC.

Cheng, L. & Fox, J. (2013). Review of doctoral research in language assessment in Canada (2006–2011). *Language Teaching, 46*, 518–544.

Creswell, J.W. & Plano Clark, V.L. (2007). *Designing and conducting mixed methods research*. Thousand Oaks, CA: Sage.

Creswell, J.W. & Plano Clark, V.L. (2011). *Designing and conducting mixed methods research* (2nd ed.). Thousand Oaks, CA: Sage.

Harlen, W. & Winter, J. (2004). The development of assessment for learning: Learning from the case of science and mathematics. *Language Testing, 21*(3), 390–408.

Leung, C. & Mohan, B. (2004). Teacher formative assessment and talk in classroom contexts: Assessment as discourse and assessment of discourse. *Language Testing, 21*(3), 336–359.

Riazi, A.M. (2016a). *Routledge encyclopedia of research methods in applied linguistics: Quantitative, qualitative and mixed-methods research*. London: Routledge.

Riazi, A.M. (2016b). Innovative mixed-methods research (IMMR): Moving beyond design technicalities to epistemological and methodological realisations. *Applied Linguistics, 37*(1), 33–49.

Riazi, A.M. & Candlin, C.N. (2014). Mixed-methods research in language teaching and learning: Opportunities, issues and challenges. *Language Teaching, 47*, 135–173.

Turner, C.E. (2013). Mixed methods research. In A.J. Kunnan (Ed.), *The companion to language assessment* (pp. 1403–1417). Hoboken, NJ: Wiley-Blackwell.

13 Conclusion: Round-up of the Book

This chapter will:
- present an overview of the whole book;
- discuss major steps in planning and conducting MMR;
- discuss challenges facing MMR researchers;
- round up with a brief concluding remark.

Introduction

This final chapter of the book will present an overview of different chapters. It will then discuss the major steps in planning and conducting MMR studies, and continues with the challenges facing mixed methods researchers. The chapter will start with a synopsis of the book, followed by the steps taken when conducting MMR projects. Next, the main challenges facing mixed methods researchers will be discussed. Finally, the chapter offers a brief concluding remark.

A synopsis of the book

The book started off by introducing three methodological approaches.

1. Quantitatively oriented research practices rooted in a (post)-positivist paradigm.
2. Qualitatively oriented research practices rooted in a constructivist and interpretivist paradigm.
3. Mixed methods research practices rooted in the different worldviews of pragmatism, transformative, dialectical pluralism and critical realism.

It was discussed in various chapters that a major advantage of mixed methods research is that it enables researchers to simultaneously draw on and employ the first two methodological approaches in a single study. Such integration will allow researchers to address both explanatory/confirmatory (quantitatively oriented) and exploratory (qualitatively oriented) research questions. This, however, requires MMR researchers to understand both quantitative and qualitative research approaches so that they can address and investigate more complex problems.

The five purposes of triangulation, complementarity, initiation, development and expansion were explained and discussed in detail in Chapter 3, followed by an outline of design typologies in Chapter 4. Chapters 5 and 6 discussed the formulation of research questions, data collection instruments and procedures as well as data analysis and making plausible inferences.

It was discussed in Chapters 2 and 6 that the logic for making inferences in MMR is abductive or retroductive. Abductive or retroductive logic makes use of both inductive and deductive logic to produce the best explanation for the understanding of the research phenomenon.

The preliminary chapters of the book provided a rich context for thinking about and writing research proposals for MMR projects. Chapter 7 then elaborated on and discussed different sections of an MMR proposal, thus providing a useful template that graduate students can use to think about and write their thesis proposals with an MMR orientation. Chapter 8 presented a useful framework, FRAMMR (Framework for Analyzing Mixed Methods Research), for reviewing MMR studies. Not only can this framework help researchers review and better understand published MMR studies, it may also be useful for researchers to reflect on their prospective research projects. Using FRAMMR, eight published articles on different topics related to language teaching and learning were reviewed in Chapters 9–12.

The next section presents the major steps in planning and conducting MMR projects.

Major steps in planning and conducting MMR projects

The word 'steps' might be misleading in so far as it may convey a linear approach to research, one step after another. However, the word will be used to highlight major decisions to be made by the researcher in the research process. It goes without saying, though, that the whole research process is recursive. That is, while certain activities need to be completed before other activities can be started, each step in the process may inform and be informed by other steps. Steps can thus be thought of as some of the main decisions researchers need to make during the course of conducting a research process. Six steps will be discussed regarding designing and conducting an MMR study.

Not all research problems might lend themselves to, or even require, an MMR approach for their investigation. There are research issues that could be investigated through purely quantitative or purely qualitative approaches. The first step in designing an MMR study, therefore, is to determine whether such a design is feasible. Depending on how the research problem is conceptualized (Chapter 2) and/or what type of research questions (Chapter 5) are posed, not only can the overall design of the study (quantitative, qualitative or MMR) be determined, but also the appropriate MMR design (Chapter 4) and objective can be identified if MMR is deemed feasible. While thinking about and determining the design of the study is usually one of the initial steps in the research process, the fact is that the initial design might change at any point due to different factors emerging and impinging on the researcher and the project. Reflecting on how and why the initial research design was changed and developed over time during the course of the project can contribute to the overall credibility of the research.

Once an initial MMR design is determined to be feasible, the second step is to rationalize the decision. At this stage, researchers are encouraged to discuss the feasibility of an MMR design in light of the potential worldviews (Chapter 2) informing the use of MMR and the possible outcomes of the research. The argument here would be what outcomes the particular MMR design, as contextualized within an appropriate worldview, will enable the researcher to achieve that could not be achieved using purely quantitative or qualitative approaches. The researcher may also argue for how the use of MMR would help to obtain a more comprehensive understanding of the research problem by drawing on one of the five purposes (Chapter 3) for mixing methods from the two research approaches.

In the third step, and in accordance with the overall purpose of the study and specific research questions, the researcher needs to describe and explain data collection instruments and procedures (Chapter 5). An important question in any research project is whether the data collection instruments and procedures are capable of producing the necessary information to answer the research questions. Accordingly, the researcher must ensure that the instruments and procedures account for the type of information needed to answer the questions. The researcher should, therefore, describe and justify why certain types of instruments and procedures are preferred over others. The decision for using particular data collection instruments and procedures must be justified in light of the research questions posed. Once more, the point should be emphasized that through the research process, new questions might emerge that may require some modifications in the overall design as well as data collection instruments and procedures.

In the fourth step, assuming full or partial data are collected, the researcher needs to make decisions about appropriate data analysis procedures (Chapter 6), although it would be advantageous if researchers could think about data analysis even before collecting data. Several decisions are crucial at this stage. First, when dealing with quantitative data analysis, the researcher must select appropriate parametric or non-parametric statistical tests of significance depending on the type of quantitative data collected. Second, the researcher needs to choose appropriate qualitative data analysis procedures depending on the overall qualitative research approach as well as particular research question(s) to be answered by qualitative data and analysis. Third, the researcher needs to make a decision about the interaction of quantitative and qualitative data analysis so that the MMR question can be answered. One strategy here would be to determine whether the quantitative analysis is to corroborate, elaborate on or inform the qualitative analysis, and vice versa. This strategy may lead the researcher to make a decision as to whether the quantitative and qualitative data are analyzed concurrently (to corroborate findings from one data source with findings from the other), separately (to elaborate on the findings from one data source using findings from the other data source) or sequentially (to inform the analysis of one data source using the findings of the other data source).

Once the data analysis is completed, the fifth step in the process of MMR is to make plausible inferences (Chapter 6). It is common to have three research questions in MMR studies (Chapter 5): a quantitative, a qualitative and an MMR question. Based on the quantitative and qualitative data and analysis, the researcher uses deductive and inductive logic to make appropriate inferences from the data analysis. To answer the MMR question, the researcher will need to mix the deductive and inductive logic and use abductive or retroductive logic to make a meta-inference that could accommodate the MMR question.

Finally, in the sixth step, the researcher writes up a coherent report of the MMR study. The format and the level of detail depend on the type of research report. Where the researcher is preparing a thesis for higher degree research, there is usually plenty of space in different chapters of the thesis to provide full details of the topic under discussion. Detailed explanation of the procedures followed in data collection and analysis will, in particular, enhance the reliability of the whole work. Readers of the research reports should be able to see (not be told) how the research developed from the initial conceptualization to the specific research questions, and then to appropriate data collection and analysis procedures, and finally to drawing plausible inferences or conclusions. In other research reports, such as

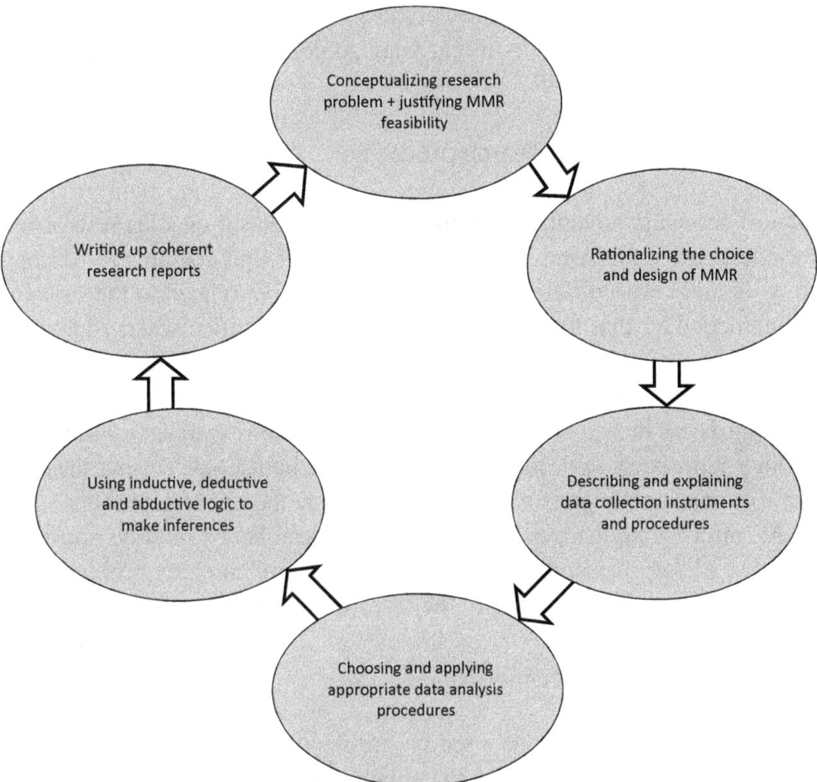

Figure 13.1 Major steps in conducting MMR studies

journal articles, although researchers do not have the luxury of the thesis space, they are still required to provide a concise but adequate and coherent report of their study.

As indicated at the beginning of this section, the six steps discussed are to clarify some of the main decisions and activities MMR researchers need to make. The whole research process should, however, be thought of as a recursive process. Figure 13.1 presents these major steps when planning and conducting MMR studies.

Challenges facing MMR researchers

Notwithstanding the advantages of using MMR in addressing language teaching and learning issues, conducting a sound MMR study poses some difficulties and challenges to researchers. The following are some of the main challenges researchers might want to consider when thinking about and planning to use MMR.

Conceptualization of research problems

One of the main advantages of using MMR is that it enables researchers to investigate more complex problems. However, this requires researchers to be familiar with different theoretical frameworks related to the research phenomenon so that they can draw on multiple theories when addressing different aspects of the phenomenon in one study. For example, researchers may want to investigate both cognitive and social aspects of a teaching and learning issue in one study. This implies that the researcher should have enough familiarity with the extant theories in both fields so that they can draw on relevant theories when conceptualizing the research problem.

As can be imagined, in cases like this, researchers would be aiming at interdisciplinary research in order to address more complex problems and thus gain fuller understanding of the research problem.

Justification of MMR feasibility

As discussed earlier, not all research problems lend themselves to MMR designs. If researchers come to the conclusion that their research problem and questions require mixing methods from different methodological approaches, they need to justify the feasibility of employing MMR. This may pose some challenges, especially to individual researchers, to argue for how the use of MMR could be the best option for addressing the problem posed. Researchers may draw on worldviews, MMR purposes, MMR designs and/ or any other resources they think relevant to justify the feasibility of the MMR approach.

Data collection and analysis procedures

One of the major challenges facing mixed methods researchers is the skills and level of expertise required to collect and analyze appropriate data in MMR studies. Usually researchers are trained for and familiar with one methodological approach, quantitative or qualitative. When it comes to MMR, they need to have developed skills and expertise in both approaches so that they can make best use of them in their MMR project. The challenge would therefore be for the MMR researchers not only to understand

and make themselves familiar with both quantitative and qualitative data collection instruments, but also to know the actual tests of significance and types of qualitative analyses. This may be achieved through formal training and workshops as well as self-directed studies and practices, but also by choosing supportive supervisors who have already developed expertise in these areas. Researchers may thus need to learn about how to design and use both quantitative and qualitative data collection instruments, as discussed in Chapter 5.

The challenge may look more stringent with regard to data analysis. With the computer software programs available (Chapter 6), traditionally researchers may have been trained to use either quantitative or qualitative software programs. When it comes to MMR, researchers may need to develop their analytical skills using both types of programs, although it is always possible to collaborate with other researchers to lessen the load. This is why good teamwork might be a necessary aspect for a successful MMR project. Overall, however, MMR researchers need to improve their understanding of both quantitative and qualitative analytical procedures and software programs to be able to conduct their project more efficiently and to understand the implications of both types of data for drawing meta-inferences.

Making inferences and writing up MMR

Another challenge facing MMR researchers is to make plausible inferences out of their analyses and write up their research. As discussed in Chapter 6, mixed methods researchers are entitled to make more comprehensive inferences in the form of meta-inferences. A meta-inference is basically a more comprehensive conclusion researchers make by mixing results from both quantitative and qualitative findings. The underlying logic for generating meta-inference is abductive or retroductive (Chapter 6), which uses and relies on the interaction between inductive and deductive logics underlying qualitative and quantitative inferences. It is usually not easy to make a meta-inferences given the level of complexity involved in the process as well as the level of experience and expertise required. One helpful strategy in this regard is to rely on the worldview (Chapter 2) that informed the conceptualization of the research problem and/or the purpose (Chapter 3) for which methods from different methodological approaches were mixed.

Writing up a mixed methods report can be different from the conventional report writing for quantitative and qualitative studies. Again, a strategy that may help researchers write a more coherent MMR report is to consider the purpose of mixing methods (Chapter 2; also see rationalizing the choice and design of MMR in Figure 13.1) as well as the research questions. Broadly speaking, MMR studies include a quantitative, a qualitative and a mixed methods question (Chapter 5). Mixed methods researchers may therefore choose to organize their report around these three questions. The conclusion section of the report may also highlight the inferences made from quantitative and qualitative data and analysis and how they were mixed to make the meta-inference(s), all in response to the research questions posed in the study.

When it comes to publishing an MMR study in a journal, researchers may face another challenge: finding an appropriate journal. Although there are now many journals related to language teaching and learning, finding one with reviewers familiar with MMR might be difficult. Available journals have their own methodological and writing styles and more often than not they expect their authors to follow them. It may thus be difficult for MMR researchers to fit in with particular templates usually suggested by journals for writing up findings from recognized methodological approaches. Fortunately, MMR is becoming more and more known to journals and getting more representation (see Chapter 1). Apart from the specialized journals of the field (see 'How to get published in TESOL and applied linguistics serials', TESOL, 2015), where MMR researchers may submit their papers, when the main focus of a paper is on methodological orientation, especially with some innovative methods or approaches, researchers can consider *Journal of Mixed Methods Research* as a potential outlet for their publication.

Fortunately, there are now useful resources on how to publish MMR articles. Readers may want to consult the following when preparing their MMR manuscript for publication.

1. Developing publishable mixed methods manuscripts (Creswell & Tashakkori, 2007).
2. A typology of verbs for scholarly writing (Frels *et al.*, 2010).
3. Publishing mixed methods research (Mertens, 2011).
4. Writing publishable mixed research articles (Leech *et al.*, 2011).
5. Writing mixed methods research reports (Leech, 2012).
6. Publishing a methodological mixed methods research article (Fetters & Freshwater, 2015).

In addition, Heyvaert *et al.* (2013) provided an overview of the available critical appraisal frameworks (CAFs) developed for the evaluation of the methodological quality of MMR articles as well as the criteria presented in these frameworks. The authors as well as the journal reviewers might want to use the guidelines provided in this article and critically appraise the MMR studies for systematic reviews.

Final remarks

Applied linguistics in general, and language teaching and learning in particular, are interdisciplinary in nature. Language teaching and learning may draw on different theoretical backgrounds and research habits to investigate research problems related to the teaching and learning of languages. Like any other field of study in social sciences and in education, the predominant research approach in language teaching and learning has been quantitative. Nevertheless, qualitative approaches are also increasingly used to investigate different issues related to language teaching and learning. As Brannen (1992) reflected, the separation of qualitative and quantitative approaches to research was based on different epistemological assumptions held by researchers in each camp, their belonging to different cultures, and having different biographies that worked against convergence. As indicated in the first chapter, there are now good signs that an MMR approach is being welcomed in applied linguistics and in language teaching and learning.

The potential of MMR will enable researchers to address more complex problems. However, as discussed earlier, this also implies that researchers will face some major challenges in harnessing MMR in their particular areas of interest. To overcome the difficulties and challenges confronting MMR researchers in language teaching and learning, they need to develop their research knowledge and skills. This book and the references at the end of each chapter will hopefully provide a useful resource for readers to expand their knowledge of MMR. Researchers' skills will develop over time, however, and by engaging in actual research projects. There is the hope that a new generation of researchers in our field will use MMR to its full capacity and contribute to the knowledge base. In addition, they can expand on methodological approaches and especially MMR by sharing their experiences with their research community.

References

Brannen, J. (1992). *Mixing methods: Qualitative and quantitative research*. Aldershot: Ashgate Publishing Limited.

Creswell, J.W. & Tashakkori, A. (2007). Editorial: Developing publishable mixed methods manuscripts. *Journal of Mixed Methods Research, 1*(2), 107–111.

Fetters, M.D. & Freshwater, D. (2015). Publishing a methodological mixed methods research article. *Journal of Mixed Methods Research, 9*(3), 203–213.

Frels, R.K., Onwuegbuzie, A.J. & Slate, J.R. (2010). Editorial: A typology of verbs for scholarly writing. *Research in the Schools, 17*(1), xx–xxxi.

Heyvaert, M., Hannes, K., Maes, B. & Onghena, P. (2013). Critical appraisal of mixed methods studies. *Journal of Mixed Methods Research, 7*(4), 302–327.

Leech, N.L. (2012). Writing mixed research reports. *American Behavioral Scientist, 56*(6), 866–881.

Leech, N.L., Onwuegbuzie, A.J. & Combs, J. (2011). Writing publishable mixed research articles: Guidelines for emerging scholars in the health sciences and beyond. *International Journal of Multiple Research Approaches, 5*, 7–24.

Mertens, D.M. (2011). Publishing mixed methods research. *Journal of Mixed Methods Research, 5*(1), 3–6.

TESOL (2015). How to get published in TESOL and applied linguistics serials. TESOL Convention & Exhibit. TESOL 2015 Toronto. Retrieved 1 June 2016 from: www.tesol.org/docs/default-source/books/how-to-get-published-in-applied-linguistics-serials.pdf?sfvrsn=4

CPSIA information can be obtained
at www.ICGtesting.com
Printed in the USA
JSHW010300250822
29664JS00002B/7